CHAMPIONSHIP TECHNIQUE
IN TRACK AND FIELD

COACH DEAN B. CROMWELL

Working on the starting position with Mel Patton, 1947–1948 National Collegiate sprint champion and Olympic champion for the 200-meter dash, the holder of the new world's record for the 100-yard dash of 9.3 seconds.

Championship Technique
in Track and Field

A book for athletes, coaches, and spectators

By
DEAN B. CROMWELL
Head track and field coach
University of Southern California

IN COLLABORATION WITH
AL WESSON

OLYMPIC GAMES EDITION

Whittlesey House
McGRAW-HILL BOOK COMPANY, INC.
NEW YORK · LONDON · TORONTO

PUBLISHED BY WHITTLESEY HOUSE

A division of the McGraw-Hill Book Company, Inc.

PRINTED IN THE UNITED STATES OF AMERICA

PREFACE

Where are the world's track and field records of twenty years ago? Broken, smashed, ruined—devastated so completely that high school boys now frequently turn in far better performances than the old standards. Except for the mark in the hammer throw, which was broken unofficially on at least five occasions in 1939, and the times in a few races at odd distances where there is now little or no competition, there is not an official world's record in the books that goes back beyond 1930.

With our improved techniques and advanced training methods, the records will continue to take a beating. Certain it is that eventually we shall develop athletes who will give us marks that now seem fantastic—the 9-second 100-yard dash, 4-minute mile, 7-foot high jump, 28-foot broad jump, 60-foot shot-put, 16-foot pole vault, and 200-foot discus throw.

The amazing improvement of track and field men has aroused a keen interest in the latest methods used by champions. Although the coach and athlete may be the first to be interested in the subject, the fan also feels that he would like to be on the inside. Although he has never had to read a book to thrill to a foot race or to enjoy watching young men strive to beat each other in jumping, vaulting, or throwing, he can better appreciate the competition if he understands the *why* and *how* of what the athletes are doing.

This book, in which we have attempted to describe the technique of champions, is therefore written not only for the young beginner who wants to learn, the star who desires to improve, or the coach who may wish to check his methods with those of another, but also for the spectator who will have more fun if he knows *why* as well as *who*. In addition to discussing technique, we have traced the progress of each event in record breaking and important championships.

PREFACE

Southern California athletes, most of whom have won national intercollegiate championships, have aided us in illustrating the various events by demonstrating their technique before the camera. We wish to thank them for their assistance.

DEAN B. CROMWELL
AL WESSON

In this Olympic Games Edition I have included a new chapter containing my observations of the 1948 Olympic Games at London, for which I was privileged to serve as head coach of the United States men's track and field team.

DEAN B. CROMWELL

CONTENTS

FOREWORD

By Grantland Rice

Dean Cromwell's place in the lineup of track and field coaches leaves him as one of the top of all time. For forty-one years he has been one of the true masters in the art of instruction and development. "Maker of Champions" is a fitting name for this cheerful, pleasant veteran of track and field wars.

His University of Southern California teams have won nine I.C.A.A.A.A. championships and nine N.C.A.A. titles, an amazing record. Back in the last Olympics held in Berlin, Dean Cromwell's entries stood high among the finest in the world. Dean not only knows his subject but he knows how to handle both boys and men. He has their deepest respect and their highest regard beyond his outstanding ability as an instructor on the field.

Among his top abilities we should mention his moderation in training and at times the slow development of his boys so that they can reach their peak performance at the championship spots.

His patience and his great care through the training program have always been remarkable. Here is certainly a man who loves his profession for, at the age of sixty-nine, he is keener today about his work than he was a quarter of a century ago. He is one of the most optimistic head men I have known in sport and this optimism has undoubtedly been of great importance in creating the winning psychology.

When Al Wesson had to give up a budding track career under Dean Cromwell to work his way through college as a musician, it only increased his ardor as a follower of the cinder-path sport. Later in covering athletic activities at Southern California, he became a special kind of Boswell to the genial Dean, not only recording the Cromwell triumphs but also becoming a student of his system of training champions.

ix

FOREWORD

A wide acquaintance among the nation's leading coaches and athletes has made it possible for him to observe and study their methods also. But Al Wesson's interest in track and field has never stopped with a desire to find out all he could about technique. He has unearthed a fund of history and anecdote about the sport from the time Coroebus of Elis won the feature race of the first Olympian games in 776 B.C. to the latest performances of the record breakers of the 1940's.

As a result of the happy collaboration of Cromwell and Wesson, you will find this book worth while whether you are a mere nonathlete like me seeking entertaining reading or a coach or track man searching for the way to a championship.

x

CHAMPIONSHIP TECHNIQUE IN TRACK AND FIELD

I

INTRODUCTION

Steve Stoner sped around the last turn, heart pounding, feet flying.

The goal in sight, he remembered the close call of his last race and shook his hips to fight off the tendency to tie up that comes in the stretch run. Body leaning well forward, arms swinging freely from his shoulders, knees driving high, and toes flashing over the ground with a light-footed bounce, Steve hit the straight-away, a picture of primeval speed.

Spectators pushed and strained for better vantage points, surging forward almost as one and so gripped by the thrill of the final drive that none thought to utter the customary cry of "Down in front!" Unconsciously, after the manner of true track fans, even in the excitement they were grandstand coaches and critics of form.

"A picture runner!" exclaimed one.

"Look at him pick up those knees!" cried another.

"What leg drive!" ejaculated a third.

"Pour it on, Steve, he's closing in!" yelled one in sudden fear.

"Don't tell him that, he'll start pressing," shouted a companion. "Shake those hips, Steve, relax! Nothing to worry about."

But Steve *was* worried.

Unmindful of the cheering and chattering onlookers, he felt his strength ebb and his form falter. It seemed to him that he could feel the hot breath of his puffing but relentless opponent. Steve's chest ached and despite his effort to relax he felt his muscles tighten. He knew he couldn't hold the pace much longer.

1

Had he rated himself poorly? Should he have held back more in the first part of the race? Or, having paced himself wisely in the early stages, had he given it the gun too soon around the far turn?

Too late to worry about mistakes in strategy now. There at last was the goal not far away. Would the last ounce of reserve get him home? All that was left he called upon for a final burst. But it burned out in a flash as fatigue weighted his arms and deadened his legs.

His opponent—his bitterest rival—was almost up to him now.

Steve's knees locked and went numb. A hot fire scorched his lungs. His aching body cried out to quit. Human flesh and blood could stand no more. Nothing left in Steve now but the will to win . . . Could it carry him through . . . ? Could he make it . . . ?

Well, I guess he did.

If Steve hadn't won, I wouldn't be here writing this. And what is much more to the point, you wouldn't be here reading it. Because, you see, Steve Stoner was our common ancestor—prehistoric man.

His opponent? A saber-toothed tiger or some such cheerful neighbor in Steve's home town.

The goal? His cave.

The prize? Just his life, with perhaps a few remarks tossed in by Mrs. Stoner about his coming home late again and too tired to take her out that night after she'd been slaving all day over a hot ground-sloth stew with dinosaur fritters and mastodon pie.

The spectators? Ah yes, the spectators. Might as well admit they were a treeful of monkeys.

No, in some respects times haven't changed. Before you get in your wisecrack, I'll confess that as far as my personal behavior is concerned the spectator situation is still about the same. After 40 years of track meets, give me a close finish and I'm still a gibbering baboon.

If you stay with me through these pages, you'll find that I can't help but be more the fan than the track coach. Whenever I get incoherent with awe at the performance of some champion, you can always say to yourself that you were warned—you met my type on page one swinging and chattering from the treetops and rooting home Steve Stoner.

Yes, Steve ran his races in those good old pre-gold-medal days. All he ever won for getting there first was his life—and the doubtful honor of fathering the human race. For that we are grateful, although old Steve may sometimes look down upon our bomber factories and poison-gas works and wish that he had come in second.

Steve ran for his life across the plains and over obstacles. Today we use his inherited gifts for our flat and hurdle races. Steve jumped and vaulted streams and hedges and he hurled things at his enemies. Now we use his ability for our field events.

How old are track and field? I'll tell you if you can give me the age of the first man.

How old is your own participation in this ancient sport? Older than your memory. It began when you found out you were strong enough to pick up a rattle or a cereal spoon and throw it; when you learned to move under your own leg power for the first time. It's born in you to want to run and jump and throw things. Born in you also is an urge to excel, a competitive spirit. Put together these inbred characteristics and you have track and field—every man's sport.

The earliest record of the organization of this urge of all mankind is found in the literature and sculpture of ancient Greece telling of the Olympian games. Just when the Olympian games originated there is no way of knowing. In some form they must have been in existence for many years, possibly for centuries, before they were first written into history in 776 B.C. Continuing until A.D. 392, the games lasted for at least 1,168 years. Few man-made institutions are older than that.

Compare this with such upstart sports as football, which can trace its origin back a bare century or so, and, if you are a track man, prepare a withering look for the next all-American halfback who struts your way.

Surely the track and field athlete and fan can take pride in the fact that the Olympian games were originated by a happy race whose art, philosophy, and love of beauty are still the ideal of cultured humanity. History doesn't tell us why the Greeks started their athletic contests, but it tells us about the Greeks themselves.

3

When we learn that they were a people with a sense of humor and a faculty for not taking themselves too seriously, we know that they just had to run and jump and throw things and enjoy themselves.

Now if you don't resemble the ancient Greeks in the possession of a sense of humor and don't have that human urge to have fun, stay away from sports. Especially from track and field, the most fun of all.

In our sport there is a place for everyone. Your build or your inclinations in your early teens often determine the event or events in which you are most likely to excel. If you are fourteen years of age and weigh 200 pounds, naturally you are going to be a weight thrower. If you are sixteen, slender, and split to the ears, it looks like the hurdles or the high jump. The hurdles if you have some speed in your long legs or the high jump if you lack speed but have spring and bounce. If you have always caught the other fellows easily in your boyhood games of tag, you are probably a sprinter. If it took you a turn around the block to run them down, then it's the distances for you. If you enjoy the bars and trapezes at your playground, your gymnastic ability suits you for the pole vault. If your right arm has a whip that enables you to throw stones farther than your playmates, you will probably make good at the javelin.

No matter what his size or build, every boy finds something in his play that he can do a little bit better than most of the other fellows. Whatever it is, he can find an event in track and field with which to match it. By training, application, and enthusiasm he can become an excellent competitor, perhaps a champion.

Naturally heredity and to some extent inherited racial characteristics may affect the young candidate's choice of an event. It isn't likely that the offspring of a long line of piano movers will have the pliable, springy muscles suitable for sprinting. Or that a boy whose ancestors were all short will come up with the lanky build that fits high jumping.

Charley Paddock, who broke nearly every sprint record in existence back in the early 1920's, is a good example of the gifts of heredity. Charley had tremendous leg power and yet was so light-footed that one could scarcely find the mark left by his spikes on the track. He got his power from his father, a strong man who had done some quarter-mile running in his day. Although Charley's mother was small and slender and one who would certainly never be picked out of a crowd as the parent of a great athlete, her delicate touch and grace no doubt contributed much to her son's lightness of foot.

Charley Parsons, Jr., also a sprinter at the University of Southern California, was still another outstanding example of the forces of heredity. When he swung into full stride, he was the exact picture of Charles Parsons, Sr., in action. Charley, Jr., had never seen his father sprint, but when he went out for the same events in which his dad had excelled 25 years before, he showed the same type of leg drive and body lean and swung naturally into the same arm action I had seen Charley, Sr., use on many occasions.

To be a track and field performer it isn't necessary for you to have had athletic parents, but it should be borne in mind that your ancestors very often hand down characteristics that will be of benefit.

The international competition of the Olympic games in recent years has shown how racial history and racial physical characteristics contribute to track and field ability. In the past few games we have seen supremacy demonstrated by the Negroes in the sprints and jumps, by the Japanese in the hop, step, and jump and broad jump, by the Finns in the long distances, by the British in the middle distances, and by the central Europeans in the weight events.

Eddie Tolan and Ralph Metcalfe, American Negroes, ran first and second in the 100- and 200-meter dashes in the 1932 Olympic games in Los Angeles. Jesse Owens, another American Negro, was the outstanding performer of the 1936 games in Berlin with his victories in both sprints and the broad jump.

In previous games, the Negroes had proved supreme in broad jumping with the victories of DeHart Hubbard in 1924 and Ed Gordon in 1932. Former record holders in this event include Hubbard and the colored jumper from Haiti, Silvio Cator, who was runner-up to Edward Hamm in the 1928 Olympics.

In the 1936 Olympics Archie Williams, another colored star, won the 400-meter dash. Cornelius Johnson, also an American Negro, was the high-jump winner, and Dave Albritton, another

5

colored athlete with whom Johnson shares the world's record, was runner-up.

John Woodruff won the 800-meter run to add to the laurels of the colored athletes. Runs of any great length, however, are not ordinarily events in which the Negro excels, although Phil Edwards, representing Canada, has turned in exceptionally fine performances in Olympic competition, and other colored runners have shown that it is possible for them to develop championship ability here, too.

To account for the superiority of the Negro in the sprints and jumps, the theory was advanced that he has a longer leg tendon than the white athlete and consequently can generate greater speed and spring. This notion did not hold up in actual investigation and no one has yet been able to back up any theory in the matter with positive proof.

Since theories are inexpensive and anyone is allowed to have them, I'll offer the opinion that the Negro excels in the events he does because he is closer to the primitive than the white man. It was not so long ago that his ability to sprint and jump was a life-and-death matter to him in the jungle. His muscles are pliable, and his easy-going disposition is a valuable aid to the mental and physical relaxation that a runner and jumper must have.

Because of the short stature and comparatively small size of most of their people, the Japanese have had difficulty competing on even terms in championship competition in many track and field events. However, they are extremely well muscled from the hips down, and this has helped them excel in the jumps. Why they have such sturdy legs I cannot say, but the fact that they are a race of pedestrians and not motorists possibly has something to do with it. Also the Japanese rest position is a squat that after 5 minutes would be painful for one of another race. Years and years of squatting in this position may have built the iron leg tendons that the Japanese use so well in the jumps.

Back in 1924 Mikio Oda threatened to put the Japanese on the athletic map in the hop, step, and jump when he placed sixth in the Olympic games in Paris. Four years later he had come along so well in this event that he won it in the games in Amsterdam.

6

Another outstanding Japanese jumping star was Chuhei Nambu, who was fourth in the 1928 games and moved up to first in 1932. At one time Nambu held the world's record in both the hop, step, and jump and the broad jump. After winning the hop, step, and jump in the 1932 Olympics, he placed third in the broad jump.

In the 1936 games Naoto Tajima repeated Nambu's feat of winning the hop, step, and jump and placing third in the broad jump. Tajima set a world's record in his victory in Berlin. The 1936 runner-up was Masoa Harada, to make this a thoroughly Japanese-dominated event. The Olympic performances of both Nambu and Tajima prove that the Japanese, although invincible in the hop, step, and jump, where leg strength and bounce count most, are not able to match the Negroes in the broad jump where speed is the most important factor.

Placing men fifth and sixth in the Olympic marathon in 1932, the Japanese showed a threat in this race which requires endurance with leg strength. In the next games in Berlin, the Nipponese had developed so well in the cross-country race that Kitei Son was the winner with a new Olympic record.

Japanese track and field ability is not limited to the jumps and overland distances, however, as Shuhei Nishida proved by placing second in the pole vault in 1932 and 1936, with his team mate, Sueo Oye, right behind him in the Berlin games. The Japanese also showed development in the high jump when Kimio Yata took a fifth in Berlin.

Taking up American training methods, the athletes from the land of the rising sun were making great progress in track and field until the attention of the Japanese youth was taken from sports and centered on warfare.

Paavo Nurmi's exploits in record breaking and in winning championships over the span of three Olympics gave the Finns world-wide fame as distance stars. Finnish superiority in the long runs, however, was shown 8 years before Nurmi's first Olympic victory when Hans Kolehmainen won both the 5,000- and 10,000-meter races in Stockholm in 1912.

Nurmi first flashed into world track prominence with his Olympic 10,000-meter victory in 1920. Four years later he won both the 1,500- and 5,000-meter races and in 1928 returned to the

10,000-meter distance to win a fourth Olympic championship. He was still in top running form and ready for more championship efforts in 1932 when he was declared ineligible by the International Athletic Federation.

The victories of Willie Ritola in the 10,000-meter run in 1924 and in the 5,000-meter race in 1928 added to Finnish fame in the distances; but Ritola, Nurmi, and Kolehmainen are only three men from a long list of distance champions developed by this sturdy people. Finns have won every 5,000-meter race in the Olympics except for the victory of J. Guillemont of France in 1920. They have won all the 10,000-meter titles except for the victory of Janusz Kusocinski of Poland in 1932. They gave the Olympic games the winners of the marathon in 1912 and 1920 and the 1,500-meter champions in 1924 and 1928. They have won all the 3,000-meter steeplechases except for the first one in 1920, which was taken by P. Hodge of Great Britain.

Greatest of the Finnish distance runners in recent years has been Taisto Maki, who started running in 1932 at the age of twenty-one and who began breaking world's records in 1938 when he cracked the mark for 10,000 meters that had been set by Ilmari Salminen of Finland. The following year during a 3-week period he smashed three more records. First to go beneath his flying feet were the marks of Lauri Lehtinen, another Finn, for the 3-mile and 5,000-meter distances. These are distances not often run in the United States, and Maki's accomplishments drew only passing interest until he dropped down to 2 miles and lowered to 8:53.2 the world's record of 8:56 set by Miklos Szabo of Hungary in 1937. Later in the season Maki lowered his own 10,000-meter mark and, while en route to this record, also cracked Salminen's 6-mile time.

Running long distances takes courage as well as physical ability. Tired, aching muscles and burning lungs cry out for the relief of rest that is so near if the runner will only quit or slow down. But champion long-distance men have the will that relentlessly drives them on, the determination that draws from their bodies the maximum in muscular power and nervous energy.

Great javelin throwers as well as superb runners have also been turned out by the Finns, although they have had keen rivalry in this event from the Swedes. Although the Finnish throwers

8

have done most of the world's record breaking, the Swedish have the edge in Olympic championships with four to three. In the 1936 Olympics the spear-throwing championship was taken from the Finns and Swedes for the first time in eight games when Gerhard Stoeck of Germany won it.

Seek the background of Finnish superiority in the long races and you will probably find it in the fact that Finland is a country of great stretches of forests and that the hardy people of this land for many hundreds of years had only their legs for locomotion in covering long distances. They kept up the development of their sturdy underpinnings in wintertime by traveling on skis and snowshoes. Nurmi is said to have been employed 5 miles from his home and to have made the trip each way daily by the old Finnish custom of running. By marking off distances en route from his house to his place of employment and by carrying a stop watch, he became a marvelous judge of pace.

Finns used the spear in fishing and hunting, and it is only natural that they should become excellent javelin throwers as well as long-distance runners. They were also wood choppers, as were the Swedes, and the shoulder and back strength developed in swinging axes contributed to the javelin-throwing ability of both races.

I don't mean to go the evolutionists one better by conveying the impression that I believe a race of spear-throwing and wood-chopping people will necessarily produce javelin-throwing offspring. But many generations of men who have been engaged in occupations that produce powerful back and arm muscles are likely to produce young in whom back and arm strength can be readily developed—more readily developed, at least, than in the offspring of a race of desk sitters.

Great Britain's strength in international track competition has been shown principally in the middle distances. Britain has furnished the only athletes who could upon occasion break up the American domination of the Olympic 400-meter flat and hurdle races. The British have shared the championships in the 800-meter run with the United States and have won more 1,500-meter titles than any other nationality.

Seeking an explanation for this, we find that mental more than physical racial characteristics have played an important part in

9

the British success. Middle-distance running, as the name suggests, requires neither the natural speed of the sprinter nor the inherent staying power of the long-distance men. Because no natural physical qualifications are needed other than a sound body, it is a branch of running in which practically everyone starts from scratch. Consequently, those who excel do so not because of physical reasons but because they are equipped with greater determination and doggedness than their opponents.

The Englishman has shown these qualities in his political theory, and the same characteristics that have built the British Empire make John Bull's sons hard to beat in events that put a premium on strong-willed determination.

In the 1928 Olympic games I recall that Lord Burghley was not awed when the times and records of more favored runners in the 400-meter hurdles were told to him. The Englishman said simply, "No matter how fast they have run, I am determined to win." Trained principally for the 110-meter high hurdles, Lord Burghley had not attempted to build up the stamina required for the 400-meter event. But he was bent on being a winner in the games, and this bulldog determination brought him through to a championship in the longer, more grueling hurdle race, even though he was not prepared for the distance.

A. G. Hill, who won Olympic championships in both the 800- and the 1,500-meter runs in the 1920 Olympics, and Douglas Lowe, who won the 800-meter run in 1924 and came back to win it again in 1928, are other outstanding examples of English runners who displayed no great physical qualifications but showed a will to win that could not be denied.

In the 1932 Olympics, Tom Hampson was the most awkward looking runner in the 800-meter race in its early stages, but this gangling English schoolteacher fought his way past runners of superior build and stride to win in Olympic record time that far exceeded any of his past performances. When he was able to talk at the end of his race, he gasped, "I am completely run out."

In middle-distance races of such importance as those in the Olympic games, the test of the champion is this self-disciplining ability to run himself out. If he could have run another step past the tape, he knows he didn't give everything to the race that he could.

10

Racially, the American, although somewhat of a conglomeration, is admittedly closer to the British than to any other people. Consequently we find him excelling in the same events as the Englishman and closely paralleling the latter in athletic ability. The American goes on farther and reaches greater success in all phases of track and field because he has become a bit more sports-minded than his brothers from across the sea and has made greater advances in training and technique.

Germany came up with three individual champions in the 1936 games in Berlin and showed the prowess of the central European people in events depending mainly on feats of strength. Hans Woellke won the shot-put and Karl Hein was first in the hammer throw. The javelin throw was won by Gerhard Stoeck to mark the first time this event had been taken from Finland and Sweden. Ordinarily unable to furnish serious competition in the middle distances because of the muscle-bound state of most of its athletes, Germany won real prominence for the first time here during the summer of 1939 when Rudolf Harbig, a twenty-five-year-old Dresden athlete, broke the world's records at 400 and 800 meters.

In modern times it is my guess that the Europeans' fondness for mass gymnastics is no help to their track and field development. Gymnastics practiced as seriously as they work at it may result in big muscles, but the coordination so necessary to successful participation in athletics does not always follow. I have seen excellent running prospects of European nations obviously muscle-bound and spoiled for their events because of an over-indulgence in physical-culture work.

Muscle is important in physical development but it is not the whole thing. There are coordination, stamina, relaxation, and mental attitude to think of, too.

The United States has been an easy victor in the track and field division of every one of the modern Olympic games because we combine a love of these sports with a willingness to study them and develop scientific techniques. As a race it cannot be said that we are better fitted for certain track and field events than other peoples. We are not specialists as are the Finns in the long distances, the Japanese in the jumps, or the Germans in the weights. The only event in modern Olympic history that America

11

has won every time the games have been held is the pole vault. And this is an event in which championship heights depend entirely on developing proper techniques.

American athletes have won nearly all the Olympic high-hurdles championships. Here again is an event in which proper training and technique are of the greatest importance. In the short races, hurdles, and field events, where knowledge of the right way to do things can often defeat superior strength, the Americans have won the majority of international championships.

From the 1,500-meter distances on up, however, the United States has never produced an Olympic winner. We might have been on our way to at least one long-distance victory in 1940 had not the games been called off because of the war, for we have shown remarkable distance-running improvement in recent years. The excellent performances of Gregory Rice, Charles Fenske, Walter Mehl, Louis Zamperini, Archie San Romani, Don Lash, Blaine Rideout, Gene Venzke, and others indicated that had the games been held America would have been ready to compete on equal terms with the world's best. Despite the comparatively poor record of American distance men in international rivalry through the games of 1936, our boys have still demonstrated a decided all-round track and field superiority and have won three of the six decathlon championships that have been staged in Olympic competition.

On the track, Americans now officially hold all world's records up to 1,000 meters, although two of these will be lost with the recognition of Harbig's marks. They also hold all hurdle records and relay running marks. In the field Americans hold five of the eight world's marks as now officially written into the record books. In the decathlon, the ten-event program made up of both track and field events, the world's record is held by an American.

Fortunately Americans have a sense of humor and can hold these honors without conceit or a bigoted claim of racial superiority. They took to track and field naturally to express their love of play and because of the American virtue of wanting to excel individually. Unless some catastrophe changes our national outlook on life, Americans will continue to enjoy themselves by running and jumping and throwing things in track and field and by watching others do it.

12

INTRODUCTION

In seeking to excel, we have developed certain techniques of our own, but we have also found value in many foreign methods. Personally I have always felt that the reason for the Finnish skill in javelin throwing and distance running could not be traced entirely to racial background. Perhaps they know a little bit more about the technique of hurling a spear or striding over great distances than we do. Perhaps the Japanese have a little something in their hop, step, and jump that we would do well to copy. Maybe something the German champion does in tossing the shot or discus could be combined with what we know about it to help us add more distance to our throws.

With this in mind, along with the thought that the greatest teacher of all is the natural form given to athletes by Mother Nature, I have spent my years of coaching in watching athletes in action and in learning from them. Frequently I have been able to pass on what I learned from one athlete to another. In this way I have fooled a few people into thinking I'm a coach.

Charley Paddock taught me far more about sprinting than I ever taught him, probably because his running form appeared to be so unorthodox that many critics just shut their eyes and said, "A man simply can't run that way." In studying the manner in which Charley naturally ran, I found that it wasn't really so unorthodox and I learned that athletes can run a lot of different ways and still be right.

A few things that Paddock taught me I tried to pass on to Charley Borah, and Borah had some things to show that I used along with the Paddock lessons on Frank Wykoff.

Fred Kelly, Southern California's first Olympic champion in 1912, showed me plenty about the high hurdles that I was later able to pass on to Leighton Dye, Phil Cope, and Roy Staley. And, of course, as these boys developed, I tried to learn from them, too.

Bud Houser's shot and discus form has been a model for many other men who followed him in this event at Southern California. Houser's ability came principally from his amazing speed across the ring and his terrific finishing snap.

Kenny Carpenter, a head taller than Houser, couldn't master Houser's style, however, and Kenny and I experimented with modifications picked up from European discus throwers. He found them more suitable to his build and was the only man to defeat the Germans in the throwing events in the 1936 Olympics in Berlin.

In the pole vault the greatest little stylist I ever saw was Lee Barnes. Although I was supposed to be his coach, we worked together in such a way for a world's record that I always felt that Barnes was my teacher. I used much of the Barnes technique on Bill Graber, who succeeded Lee as the record holder. In working with Bill I learned things that I combined with the Barnes form and passed on to Earle Meadows and Bill Sefton, the present coholders of the official world's mark.

So it goes in every event in track and field. The greatest teacher a coach has is the athlete, because the athlete's first teacher is Mother Nature. A coach must first study his athlete. Only when he has made a thorough job of that may he apply knowledge gained from past experience. Then he may introduce the refinements of technique that will augment the athlete's natural form and bring improvement.

So, being still a faithful and humble student of the track and field star, I'd like to pass on a few tips that he has shown me, event by event. If you are a coach, I hope that what I have to say may help you to discover and develop new abilities in your athletes. If you are an athlete or aspire to be one, I hope that some of my suggestions will help you to be more skillful and will enable you to give greater performances with less effort.

And if you are a fan, descended like myself from the bleacher crowd that cheered Steve Stoner in the good old days, I hope that you can add still more to your understanding and appreciation of the sport of track and field.

II

TRAINING

If training means turning down food you like for a restricted diet, going to bed early when others are still up enjoying themselves, and rigidly denying yourself all the little pleasantries and luxuries of life, then there is no such thing as training in track and field.

There is only one reason why we run, jump, vault, hurdle, or throw and that is to have fun. Any system of training that takes the joy out of the sport is a lot of nonsense. To be able to give his best performance in competition, an athlete must feel on top of the world physically and mentally. So-called "training" aims to get him up to this point. It won't do it if it cramps and upsets his normal existence by regulating his life with a lot of silly rules.

The key word in what we miscall training for track is moderation. One can eat too much, sleep too much, study too much, play too much, or exercise too much. The track and field man's life off the athletic field is simply the normal life that is led by anyone interested in keeping in good health and spirits.

Diet is the least of the worries of the track and field candidate, especially for the young man in high school or junior high who wishes to embark on a cinder-path career. Most boys at this age live at home and for a long time have been getting good home-cooked meals. If the young man has grown well and strong enough to want to go out for athletics, it is a good bet that he has been raised on the proper kind of food or he wouldn't be well and strong. Therefore, there is no reason for him to change his way of living and he should go right on eating the food upon which he has been raised with nary a worry about vitamins or calories.

Eating habits are often a matter of geography and the whim of nature in products of the soil or the sea. The Finns may live principally on fish, the Japanese on rice, the Mexicans on tortillas, the Hawaiians on poi, and the South African natives on bananas,

15

but all these races produce sturdy men and none can say that only the dietary habits of his country are correct.

Diet habits vary a great deal in our own country. In Iowa, corn is likely to be an old stand-by at dinner time. In Boston it may be beans. Oregonians will eat more apples than the people of California or Florida, who will go for oranges. Residents along the seacoast may have fresh fish nearly every day of the year, and in a cattle land, like Wyoming, the food staple may be beef.

It is recognized as common sense that one should not try to make a meal of desserts and for this reason the athlete in training is moderate in his consumption of them. However, the growing boy has a natural craving for sweets and candy, and they are good for him if he eats them immediately after meals.

Eating between meals is not good because it upsets regular habits. However, doctors often tell us that we would be just as well off, better perhaps, if we would eat five or six light meals a day instead of three heavier ones. Any habits that have been formed with regard to the number and kind of meals and the time they are taken should be adhered to when the young man goes into training for athletics.

Indigestible food naturally should be avoided. Rich spices and seasoning on foods or frying them in grease usually makes them hard to digest, and when the gastric juices have to make a long and sometimes violent attack on such stuff the athlete loses that top-of-the-world feeling that he should have.

Since tea and coffee are slight stimulants and have little or no food value, they are not necessary for a growing boy or young man. However, the English athlete who has had tea since he was a small lad will probably find his condition interfered with rather than aided if he stops drinking it. By the same reasoning, the Frenchman or Italian who has had light wines at mealtime for years can go right on drinking them when in training; the same beverages for others not accustomed to them might be decidedly detrimental.

Pastries and pies that are heavy and soggy and likely to throw the gastric machinery into considerable turmoil are unfriendly toward the good health of anyone, athlete or not, and are to be avoided.

The athlete's wary attitude toward piecrust reminds me of an

16

incident with one of our new sprint candidates a few years ago. The budding champ had heard me say that all he needed to do in the matter of diet was to go right on eating moderately and regularly the food to which he was accustomed.

One Sunday afternoon early in the track season I received a long-distance telephone call at home in Los Angeles. It was our new candidate whom we shall call "Joe."

"Say, coach," he said, "I'm home for the week end and mother just brought in some pie for dessert. You didn't say anything about that. What'll I do?"

"Don't worry, Joe, you'll probably live through it," I replied. "Incidentally, where are you phoning from?"

"I'm home in El Centro," said Joe. "Now how about this pie?"

El Centro—wow! Two hundred and twenty-five miles from Los Angeles. Toll charges at that distance are no joke.

"Eat the inside and admire the crust," I said hastily, and hung up to stop the mounting phone bill.

That happy thought has made our athletes models of diplomacy in skipping over food that might not be kind to their digestion and general condition. Whenever they are dining out, they are all well trained to eat what is good for them and admire what is not.

At the time of strenuous competition, one's digestive system should not still be wrestling with the remains of a meal. To be sure that the stomach is empty, we change the meal hours on the day of a track meet. If a man is used to having breakfast early, he eats at the regular time and then has a very light lunch late in the morning. If he is used to eating a light breakfast and a hearty lunch, he combines the two in a moderate midmorning repast. He also combines the two meals if he is used to a heavy breakfast and a light lunch.

For the light lunch that the athlete eats about 3½ or 4 hours before competition, many coaches favor crisp toast with honey and tea. To this easily digested meal may be added a little light custard if the athlete craves a bit of dessert. After the meet the competitor can pitch into the good big meal of the day.

Sometimes the beefy weight man thinks that this starvation diet won't give him enough strength to toss his shot and discus, and it is usually all right to keep the delicate 200-pounder from worrying about his health by adding a chop or small steak to his pre-meet meal.

When the athlete travels away from home, I have always found it best for him to arrive at the scene of the meet on the day of competition. An overnight train trip should be taken the night before the meet and not two nights before, as is the general college custom. The athlete may lose sleep on the train, but if he knows how to relax he will rest and store up energy anyway.

Many coaches and athletes seem to think that it is necessary to take an overnight trip two nights before competition in order to rest up after the train ride and become accustomed to new conditions. When this is done, the athlete has to sleep in a hotel the night before the meet and this is not much better than the train. He misses two nights from his own bed and regular daily habits instead of one.

On long trips it is still a good idea to plan to arrive on the day of competition. The important thing in the case of a long journey is to have the athlete in good condition when he begins it. This top form can be kept during a train trip and no attempt should be made to hold workouts or strenuous exercise periods en route in order to try to gain any additional conditioning.

With the comfort that is provided in modern transportation, long trips are no handicap to good performances if they are wisely supervised. They can be detrimental if the athlete either tries to continue his workouts en route or does not know how to relax.

Long trips are also definitely bad if the athlete arrives at his destination too soon. This is directly contrary to the system used by most coaches and athletes, but my experience in traveling with teams for many years confirms this belief.

For example, in 1939 the Southern California track team in taking in the I.C.A.A.A.A. championships made one of the fastest trips across the continent ever taken by a group of athletes. In order to keep the absences from class as low as possible, the boys left Los Angeles by train on Tuesday night and arrived in New York City on Friday morning just in time to take part in the I.C.A.A.A.A. qualifying round at Randall's Island.

The next morning we went out to see the World's Fair and to take part in a Southern California Day celebration; in the after-

18

noon we returned to Randall's Island for the finals. After this rush, all the boys did was win the intercollegiate championships with a record high score of 71½ points, and while so doing win or tie eight of the individual championships and establish or equal five meet records.

After the meet we went back for a last look at the Fair, took a train at midnight, and arrived home on Tuesday morning. Here was a 6,000-mile trip across the continent and back, two days of competition in a championship track meet with the athletes performing right at their peak, only four days of school missed, and not a boy feeling any the worse for all the hurry.

To illustrate what too long a trip will do, the Southern California team of 1933 offers a horrible example. The squad was as good as the 1939 team and started its trip by winning the I.C.A.A.A.A. championships at Harvard University. We did not have to return to the campus that year as our spring semester had finished, and we had three weeks to kill before the National Collegiate Athletic Association championships at Chicago.

We traveled in a special Pullman car that was routed through Canada, giving us several days of vacation at the Thousand Islands, and then arrived in Chicago ten days before the N.C.A.A. meet. We had excellent quarters in one of the best hotels along the lake shore and enjoyed splendid facilities for training at Stagg Field at the University of Chicago.

But despite the fact that everything seemed in our favor, I could see the boys getting flatter in their condition each day. Physically they were all right, but, what with homesickness and boredom and the departure over a long period from their usual way of life, they went stale mentally. When the N.C.A.A. championships were staged at Soldier Field, the performances of the Trojans in practically every event were far below par and, although we had been favored to win after our I.C.A.A.A.A. victory, we finished second.

This is another argument along the line that training is simply normal, everyday life. Trips are only a handicap to performances when they interrupt for too long a period the normal living habits.

When taking a trip that requires two or more days, the team should have at least one limbering-up session of about 10 minutes in track suits. Just to put on uniforms and trot around the grass near the depot, or on the station platform if there is nothing else, seems to help the general pep of the squad as well as keep the boys loose and limber.

On long trips, athletes should get out and walk whenever possible to get the circulation going in their legs. Little other exercise is necessary, although sometimes a bar can be placed between two upper berths to let the boys do pull-ups in the aisles.

Meals should be planned and ordered by the coach, or by the team physician if he accompanies the athletes on trips. Railroad menus have a habit of furnishing three big meals a day and inexperienced or hungry athletes if left to their own devices may overdo the groceries and lose their fine edge by putting on weight.

Sleep is important to the athlete and regular habits in this regard should be formed. Some boys require more sleep than others, but between eight and nine hours is the average for athletes. Sleep that is lost by staying up unusually late cannot be adequately made up by lying in bed late the next day.

No great amount of equipment is necessary for the athletic field outside of a good track along with rings for the throwers and runways and pits for the jumpers. It will help if a set of parallel bars and a horizontal bar are provided and perhaps also a suspended pole or rope. These articles of apparatus can usually be erected out of the way where they may be used for limbering-up exercises by the candidates for practically every event.

If the broad jumpers cannot use the high-jump or pole-vault pit for their form work, a special pit of shavings should be provided for them. This does not need to be a long pit, like that usually required for the broad jump, since it will not be used for distance leaping.

Starting blocks should be provided for practice sessions so that the track will not be continually torn up by starting holes. The part of the field allotted to the weight men should have room for two shot and two discus rings. The spikes of the weight men tear up rings quickly and two are needed so that they can be alternated and kept in repair.

Most athletic fields are located close to a gymnasium where the track and field candidate can find all the exercise apparatus he will need, such as wrist developers, Indian clubs, dumbbells, rings, rope, parallel and horizontal bars, long horse and side horse, punching bag, and mats. Gym apparatus should be used in moderation as suggested in the chapters on the various events.

The track and field man should always remember that his aim is not to become a mass of muscle, like the advertisements in the physical culture magazines, but to develop sinews that have elasticity, limberness, and the ability to relax and then explode into action. Athletes of today are no more powerful physically than the athletes of twenty years ago, but they are making far better marks because they have learned how to train their muscles for special duties.

No elaborate system of exercise is necessary if one will just remember that the aim is to develop muscular coordination rather than just muscle. A country lad far from a gymnasium can develop himself just as easily as the boy who has the advantage of all the elaborate apparatus ever made.

The two basic exercises that everyone should take are walking and chinning the bar. Walking develops the body from the waist down and pull-ups develop it from the waist up. These most fundamental and simple of all exercises give the athlete a good physical background. From that point on, he goes in for any type of exercise that stretches the muscles and tendons and makes them pliable and relaxed. To these he adds the course of training on the track and field that has been suggested for each event to develop proper technique.

To safeguard the health of their athletes, most colleges have a medical staff working in cooperation with the coaches. Those in charge of track and field in high schools often have to act as coach and trainer, too. Since track is not a rough-and-tumble contact sport like football, most ailments are of a minor nature and the coach usually knows what to do about them. The combined coach-trainer, however, should always keep in mind his own limitations and should see that proper medical attention is provided in any cases that have the slightest chance to prove serious.

Before a candidate is permitted to take up any form of athletics, he should be given a thorough general physical examination. The examination given by universities today includes a check on the condition of the joints and muscles and a search for

21

heart weakness, including an investigation of its size and its ability to return to normal after exercise. The examination also looks for diseases of the lungs, infections, body deformities, and numerous other conditions that would make athletic participation inadvisable.

Because schools keep close tab on the health of their students, few boys are found not to be fit for athletics. Another reason, of course, why it is rare for a candidate not to pass the physical examination is that a boy who is ailing does not feel like going out for sports.

After the candidate has passed his physical examination and is ready to go out for the track squad, he is warned by the team physician, as well as by the coach, to build up his muscles gradually and to increase his endurance and wind before he attempts any strenuous competition.

In track and field the most common ailment is a pulled muscle, which can be avoided by careful preparation and a thorough warm-up before any strain is undertaken either in practice or competition. One reason why we are strong for stretching exercises is that it is almost impossible to injure a muscle or tendon that has been stretched out and made loose and supple.

Along with pulled muscles another common type of injury to the boy in track and field athletics is a spike wound. Jumpers and vaulters sometimes make bad landings and spike themselves. Runners occasionally get into jams and are stepped on by opponents or caught by their flying feet. Spike wounds that are mere scratches may be treated with antiseptics, but tetanus antitoxin treatments should be provided for punctures.

Sprains occasionally occur among track and field men and these may be of many degrees. Some are slight, and the athlete can go right on training and competing if the injury is given the proper protective support. Other sprains are so severe that the athlete may be forced out for a month or more.

Athletes occasionally suffer from what we call "shin splints." This involves an irritation of the attachment of the muscle to the bone and is usually due to too much activity before the muscle is properly built up or warmed up. Here again the preventive is the slow, gradual development and training of the muscles before strain is put on them.

22

Besides a proper warm-up before competition or a heavy workout, the athlete should be careful to keep warm for a time afterwards. After a hard race the runner should stay on his feet and cool off slowly as he walks around. This will prevent catching cold and will also gradually relax muscles that have a tendency to tighten when tired.

To compensate for excessive sweating during a long, hard race on a hot day, distance men are often provided with enteric salt capsules which are swallowed 2 or 3 hours before the race with a small amount of water. A certain amount of salt is needed in the blood stream to avoid upset metabolism, and cramps or a general unpleasant feeling after a long race can be avoided by taking this preparation.

Boils and skin infections will never bother athletes if their track suits and training quarters are kept clean. College athletes are usually given a clean set of training clothing each day. If fresh sweat suits are not provided, those that have been used are hung each night in well-ventilated lockers so that they will be thoroughly dry for the next day's workout.

Some field-event men, particularly the weight throwers, wear fairly heavy socks, but runners and jumpers do not like the type of heavy sweat socks used by football and basketball players. In practice, runners usually wear lightweight wool socks or skin socks that cover only the feet.

In competition many track men favor "pushers." These are made of the thinnest chamois skin obtainable and cover just the toes and the bottom of the feet to prevent blisters. The track man is a thoroughly streamlined youth from head to foot, and to carry as little weight as possible most of them wear no socks at all in competition.

During his varsity high-jumping career at Southern California, Johnny Wilson wore a shoe only on his take-off foot, believing that removing the weight of the other shoe aided him in getting altitude even though it meant the difference of only a few ounces. Many other high jumpers took up Wilson's idea and started a one-shoe jumping fad on the Pacific Coast.

Among the equipment of a training quarters or athletic department medical office should be rubbing tables and heat lamps. Heat is excellent for the treatment of sprains and to relax muscle

23

tension. Massage is the lazy man's way of getting exercise, but it is good for athletes who may have sore, tired, or tight muscles.

Other equipment should include a medical cabinet with material for the treatment of infections, colds, etc., and such general training quarters necessities as bandages and tape. The most important item of training-quarters equipment for the coach who is also the trainer is a telephone. When anything looks serious, he should be in the position to summon proper medical attention immediately.

In the university organization of the athletic medical staff, trainers often work under the doctors' supervision in massaging, taping, and taking care of minor wounds. Advanced medical students or former athletes who have had experience with athletic ills and who have worked around training quarters under proper supervision are usually employed for this type of work.

Track athletes are a particularly temperamental brand of biped. Some can be seriously ill or suffering a severe muscle injury and will never report the matter. Others may complain of symptoms by the carload and actually never have anything more deadly than a hangnail. To handle the wide variety of personalities as well as injuries and illnesses that a team may have, the man whose job it is to take care of an athletic squad must have human understanding and tact along with his knowledge of bones, muscles, and general physical condition.

No one who has watched children running their heads off in tag games around a schoolyard can argue with conviction that running can be injurious to a highly trained full-grown athlete. Running is a natural activity for the human race and when one is fit for the event he competes in, it is a healthful form of exercise.

To protect his good health, when the athlete has finished his competitive days, he should taper off slowly in his exercise to give the heart muscle and other muscles a chance to take care of the body normally in a more sedentary life. When one has been in strenuous competition for a long time, he should remember the number of years that have been devoted to building up to this activity, and he should slow down just as he built up. Track athletes in particular who have competed in the more strenuous races from the quarter mile on up should never stop all exercise

24

at once but should take a year or more to taper off to a nonathletic existence.

Alarmists used to make much of what they called the "athletic heart," although medical research has quieted nearly all the old fears and superstitions. If there is such a thing as an athletic heart, it is a strong heart.

The heart is a muscle and as the distance runner develops his leg muscles he also builds a stronger heart muscle. When he tapers off after his competitive days and allows his legs to become accustomed to a more inactive life, his heart muscle also adjusts itself to quieter conditions.

Besides being properly trained physically for competition, an athlete must be trained right mentally. Every coach has his own way of figuring out the psychological angles and nearly everyone can give examples of how his boys went out and defeated better athletes on occasion because they were fired up mentally.

It has been my theory during more than three decades of coaching that boys will react better to praise than to anything else. My standard greeting to a University of Southern California track man for years has been "Hi, champ!" In doing this, I am not kidding anyone. Everyone on the team knows that I call everyone else "Champ." But each one knows that I believe in him. It helps him to develop a belief in himself and he puts out to the point where frequently he does become a champion.

A few coaches believe that best results can be obtained for their athletes if they are hard-boiled with them. They seem to believe that if they accuse their boys of being yellow or no good they will develop a fighting I'll-show-you spirit that will bring out inspired performances. This type of firing-up may work in a few cases, but I really think that the athlete will come through best when he is sent into competition with a pat on the back and the coach's sincere belief in him.

The right word at the right time will work wonders. Track men on the average are more high strung than athletes in other forms of sport and more than any other type of competitor they must be keyed right.

Many times boys feel tired, tense, or discouraged and do not realize their own capabilities. During the 1940 season I remember that Southern California won the Pacific Coast Conference

25

championships by scoring points with the most tired-out motley collection of misfit mile-relay runners that I have ever assembled in a big meet.

We went into the last event, which was the relay, five points ahead of Stanford. The Indians were cinch winners in the relay, having set a new world's record early in the season, and to win the meet we had to finish at least fifth in the event, the scoring being on a 5-4-3-2-1 basis.

As the entry lists in the conference championships were limited and we had only one quarter-miler of any speed, we had not entered any relay men in the meet, gambling on winning the championship before the event came around. But now we had to scrape up some kind of foursome to try for the winning point. Five other teams were entered—Stanford, California, U.C.L.A., Washington, and Montana. Washington had won the Pacific Coast Conference northern division relay at 3:17.3 and Montana had run the event in about the same time. We knew we had to beat one of these two; the other three teams were much too fast.

Looking over the Trojan athletes available, I could see that this was our only possible combination: Louis Zamperini, miler; Art Laret, low hurdler; Art Reading, half-miler, and Howard Upton, quarter-miler. They were not only men from the wrong events, except for Upton, but they were all either tired or off form.

Zamperini had run himself out to beat his Stanford rival, Paul Moore, in the mile in the fast time of 4:11.6. When he had tried to double up later in the half mile, he was so tired and tied up he had to drop out after running one lap. Laret had just run fifth in the low hurdles, the event preceding the relay, and was still winded. Reading and Upton had run fifth in the 880 and 440, respectively, and seemed to be suffering from the effects of the final semester examinations which were being held during that week. Both were sure after their poor showing in their events that their condition was terrible.

It took some high-class oratory to nurse this crew along when they came up to the stands where I was sitting just before the race. Each of them seemed to doubt his ability at that point to walk a quarter mile.

"Louie," I said to Zamperini, "a nice little lap around the

26

track will get that tension out of your legs and send you home feeling like a million dollars. Just follow the boys around and take it easy. Don't run hard unless you feel like it at the finish."

"Laret," I said to our puffing low hurdler, "you finished that race looking as fresh as a daisy. Anybody who can step over the sticks like you will find striding this flat race just a breeze."

"Reading, the way you sprinted up from nowhere to score a point in that half mile shows you are full of speed today," I told our disappointed 880 man. "Put the same kick at the end of your relay lap and you'll start Howard out where he can pick somebody off."

"And Upton," I said to our disconsolate quarter-miler, "You're the best 440 man in this meet. It wasn't your fault you got elbowed and pocketed in the quarter mile. Now go out and show 'em how a champ can run without interference."

Zamperini responded with a better quarter mile than he can run when fresh. He finished last but his 51-second lap kept us in the race. Laret breezed around and found some hidden pep somewhere and also turned in a 51-second lap, which was about his peak when not tired.

The rest of the field, however, had gone far ahead and Reading was 20 yards back of the nearest man when he entered the far turn of the third lap. Suddenly he came to life with a finishing kick and when he reached Upton he was only 8 yards behind. Upton quickly pulled up within striking distance and I knew we were in. When he poured it on down the home stretch he passed not one man but two, giving our team fourth place and a two-point margin in the meet.

Checking on the lap times I had caught, I found that Reading, who a few minutes before had felt that he was a sad excuse for a broken-down half-miler, had set his all-time record by running his quarter in 48 seconds, and Upton, who had also been the picture of discouragement, had turned his lap in 47 flat.

The collection of misfits had run a 3:17 relay. This may not be marvelous time but it was phenomenal for that foursome and no world's-record-breaking performance ever made me feel any happier.

And what about the poor tired lads who had been sent into the race when they were weary and downhearted? They were out

27

there on the track jumping up and down and pounding each other on the back and forgetting even to be winded. None of them had known what he was capable of until he had done it.

Every coach in track and field can recall similar experiences with his boys. Sometimes when they think they feel their worst, a psychological stimulus will suddenly fire them to come through with their best performance. Every man in athletics sooner or later comes to realize that winning requires equal parts of inspiration and perspiration.

Boys go out for athletics to have fun. It is human nature to have the most fun in sports when we win and that's why we train and do without a few little things like piecrust and tobacco, which as far as we know have never yet improved the health of anyone. But it is so easy to do this that we don't need to call it training at all. It is just living a normal, moderate, regular life. It is also the secret of how to live to be a hundred.

III

THE SPRINTS

A coach cannot put speed in a boy's legs, wind in his lungs, or courage in his heart. But there are a few important things that a coach can do.

He can correct a runner's faulty habits and give him technique that will help him improve his natural speed. He can put him through a course of exercises and training on the field that will help him reach top physical condition and so plan his development as to have him at his peak when his best races are needed.

The coach can also be an important psychological aid by building self-confidence in the boy and by making him mentally right for his best efforts against any competition.

It is necessary for the young man who wishes to be a good track and field performer to understand right from the start that the burden of effort is on him. All the master-mind coaches rolled into one cannot make a champion out of a candidate unless that person supplies the fundamentals—a sound body and a determination to train faithfully and fear no competitor.

There are many things to learn about sprinting form that will increase natural speed, but the star sprinter is born and not made and no one without natural fleetness of foot can ever become a champion. The champion, however, does not get there without technique and it is the combination of natural speed and the knowledge of correct form that produces outstanding sprint runners.

No matter how much a runner strains to put forth his greatest effort, it is not possible for him to maintain his maximum speed very long. Although we look upon all races up to a quarter mile as sprints, we know that even in the 100-yard dash no runner is traveling at his utmost speed from start to finish. Proper technique, therefore, is needed by the sprinter if he is to develop his greatest speed over a given distance.

Natural speed may be found in almost every classification of build. Sprinting champions of the past have been tall, slender, short, and heavy.

Charley Paddock was fairly short and stocky, weighing 160 pounds when in best running condition and being 5 feet 8 inches in height. Charley's first bid for sprinting fame came during the Inter-Allied Games immediately after the First World War. When he left for the meet in Paris, he weighed 174 pounds. When he returned, he was down to 145. But even when he was up around 170, he had plenty of speed because he had the husky frame to carry it.

Loren Murchison and Jackson Scholz, two of Paddock's greatest rivals during his sprinting reign, were small and slender. Eddie Tolan, double winner in the 1932 Olympics, was quite short, and Percy Williams, two-time victor in the 1928 Olympics, was also considerably smaller than average, weighing about 130 pounds.

Frank Wykoff and Jesse Owens, coholders of the world's 100-yard dash record, were medium-sized athletes, the former weighing 152 when in condition and the latter 156. Both were 5 feet 10 inches in height.

The evidence seems to point to the fact that boys who are comparatively short but have fairly long legs are most likely to have natural speed. However, Ralph Metcalfe, who was national champion three straight years at 100 meters and five consecutive years at 200 meters, was 6 feet in height and weighed more than 180 pounds, and Perrin Walker, who won the national 100-meter championship in 1937 was 6 feet 4 inches in height and weighed just a shade under 200 pounds.

Bernie Wefers, a three-time national champion in the 100-yard dash in the late 1890's, was a tall man and became one of the holders of the world's record at $9\frac{4}{5}$ seconds. A few years after the Wefers regime a very small star came along in Arthur Duffey and this man, whose build was so radically different from Wefers, was the first to run 100 yards in $9\frac{3}{5}$ seconds.

Archie Hahn, who won considerable fame for his sprinting feats soon after the turn of the century and was national 100-yard champion in 1903, was also a small athlete, but in 1904 he was succeeded by a big man in Lawson Robertson. A great sprinter in his college days, Mr. Robertson is now better known as the coach of the University of Pennsylvania and the American Olympic track and field teams. Robertson was succeeded as national champion in 1905 by another big man, Charley Parsons of Southern California, also a six-footer and a powerful flier.

Physique does not seem to be so essential in the making of a sprint champion as temperament. The start and pickup are so important that exceptionally quick reactions are necessary. Practically all good sprinters, consequently, are of the nervous, high-strung type, able to react instantly to the starter's gun.

The feat of cracking 10 seconds in the 100-yard dash, which is becoming common even for prep runners in this modern era of speed, was rarely accomplished in the early days of national track competition.

The first I.C.A.A.A.A. champion on record, H. W. Stevens of Williams, ran the event in 11 seconds flat. The first national champion, F. C. Saportas of the New York Athletic Club, covered the distance in 10½ seconds. The first I.C.A.A.A.A. championship and the first national open championship both took place in 1876.

In 1888 the amateur best-on-record time was credited to F. Westing of the Manhattan Athletic Club, who won the N.A.A.A.A. 100-yard dash that year in 10 seconds flat. However, W. C. Milmer of the Short Hills, N. J., Athletic Club had won the national meet in the unofficial time of 10 seconds back in 1878.

John Owen of the Detroit Athletic Club came along in 1890 to be the first man to beat even time. His mark of 9⅘ seconds was tied during the next few years by Bernard J. Wefers of Georgetown, J. H. Maybury, J. H. Rush, William A. Shick, Jr., of Harvard, C. Blair, W. D. Eaton, and Charles L. Parsons. Owen came out of Detroit to startle the easterners, hitherto supreme in sprint ranks, by winning the A.A.U. championship in 1889 and 1890. It took a lot of running for Owen to convince the Atlantic Coast dashers that he was their master, but he finally established his supremacy beyond any doubt when he ran the century in 9⅘ seconds at Analostan Island, Washington, D. C.

Other excellent sprinters who came along about that time were Luther H. Carey of the Manhattan Athletic Club, Harry Jewett

31

of the Detroit Athletic Club, C. W. Stage of the Chicago Athletic Association, and Tommy Lee of the New York Athletic Club, all of whom followed Owen as national 100-yard champions.

In college ranks the outstanding sprinter was Charley Sherrill of Yale, who many claim was the originator of the crouching start in sprint running. The impression has lasted, however, that the great Blue runner favored the stand-up start, or what was known as the "jab" start at that time. Sherrill was I.C.A.A.A.A. 100-yard-dash champion for four years, 1887 to 1890, and 220 champion for three years, but he was never able to get down to even time in the intercollegiate championships.

Luther Cary of Princeton was the first runner to negotiate the century in 10 seconds in the I.C.A.A.A.A. games. He hit this time in 1891 and in the same championship meet he ran the 220 in 21⅘ seconds for a new world's record. Previously the best furlong mark had been held by Wendell Baker of Harvard, who was credited with records of 22 flat in the 220 and 47¾ seconds in the 440 in 1886.

With good sprinters growing more and more numerous, it remained for Bernie Wefers to become the outstanding man of a fast field by three times equaling Owen's 100-yard-dash record of 9⅘ seconds and also establishing a new mark of 21⅕ seconds in the 220. His record century races were in 1895, 1896, and 1897; in 1896 he established the furlong mark in winning the event in the I.C.A.A.A.A. championships. Wefers was universally hailed as the king of sprinters and well he deserved the title. He stood 6 feet 1 inch in height and weighed 175 pounds when in top running condition. He looked as well as acted the role of the perfect sprinting machine. Probably his greatest accomplishment took place in the international games between the New York Athletic Club and the London Athletic Club at Travers Island, N. Y., where he won both sprints from the fleet Charley Bradley of England in 9⅘ seconds and 21⅕ seconds. In 1896 he set a 300-yard record of 30.6 seconds that lasted for a great many years.

Two other splendid sprinters of this time were Walter Tewksbury and Alvin C. Kraenzlein, both of Pennsylvania and both intercollegiate champions. Kraenzlein was one of the greatest all-round stars in the history of track and field, at one time holding the world's records for the high and low hurdles and the broad jump.

The sprint reign of Wefers, Kraenzlein, and Tewksbury held full sway until the season of 1899. Then from out of New England came a two-legged comet in Arthur Duffey. The flier from Boston England High School stood a scant 5 feet 7 inches in height and weighed 138 pounds in top condition. The first races to bring him into prominence were over the 40- and 50-yard distances. His schoolboy time of 4⅗ seconds for 40 yards was particularly outstanding.

It was at Worcester Academy that Duffey really came into his own. Representing Worcester in the Harvard Interscholastics, he became the first prep athlete to run 100 yards in 10 flat. While still a prep-school boy, Duffey faced a terrific test when he competed against the veteran Wefers, Kraenzlein, Tewksbury, Maxey Long, and Harry Stevens, the Canadian champion, in the national A.A.U. championships in 1899. Although pitted against the best in the land, Duffey reeled off his trial heat in 9⅘ seconds and then came through in the finals to defeat Kraenzlein and Wefers handily.

Following his triumphs in the national championships, the Boston lad entered Georgetown University and became one of the greatest of college sprinters. He won the I.C.A.A.A.A. championships three years in a row, in 1901, 1902, and 1903, and undoubtedly would have taken four titles but for the fact that the freshman rule barring first-year men from competition had just been passed.

In the 1902 I.C.A.A.A.A. championships Duffey faced what was probably the fastest intercollegiate field ever assembled up to this time. Among his stellar opponents were John A. Westney of Pennsylvania, F. R. Moulton of Yale, and Earl Cadogan of California. Despite the speed of this field, Duffey was an easy winner and the clockers were amazed to read on their watches the sensational story that he had run the fastest century ever recorded up to this time. Three of the timers caught Duffey at 9⅗ and one clocked him at 9⅖ seconds. This record time of 9⅗ seconds was not to be bettered for nearly three decades, until Frank Wykoff of Southern California ran the distance in 9.4 seconds in 1930.

33

For several years the Boston speedster met all kinds of competition at home and abroad and won many championships. Besides taking the I.C.A.A.A.A. 100 three years in succession, he won the British Amateur Athletic Association championships four years in a row, from 1900 to 1903.

Some of his marks that were the fastest on record in his day were the following: 35 yards, 4 seconds, made in Baltimore in 1903; 40 yards, 4⅗ seconds; 50 yards, 5 seconds flat, made at Washington, D. C., in 1901; 60 yards, 6⅕ seconds, made on loose dirt with rubber-soled shoes; 75 yards, 7⅖ seconds, made on grass in Auckland, N. Z., in 1905; 100 yards, 9⅗ seconds, I.C.A.A.A.A. championships in New York in 1902; and 120 yards, 11⅖ seconds, established on turf in Stowbridge, England. Duffey ran on so many odd courses during his travels that he wound up his career with a variety of unofficial records. At Abergavenny, Wales, he ran a 100-yard dash slightly downhill in 9⅕ seconds. At Barrow in Furness, England, he made the same time with a favorable wind. At Leeds, England, he became the first man to run the 100 in 9⅘ seconds on grass.

Shick of Harvard followed Duffey as I.C.A.A.A.A. 100-yard-dash champion and also won the 220 in 1904 and 1905. Shick in 1902, Blair in 1903, Eaton in 1904, and Parsons in 1905 all were caught in 9⅘ seconds in the century, and in 1906 Dan J. Kelly of Oregon hit the 9⅗-second figure.

In the same year Kelly tied Wefers' 10-year-old 220-yard-dash record of 21⅕ seconds. Kelly was a great broad jumper but in subsequent races he did not show outstanding speed and he does not have the long list of championship triumphs that will be found to the credit of other record-breaking sprinters.

The furlong mark proved an easier one to equal than the century time. R. C. Craig of Michigan tied the mark of 21⅕ seconds in 1910 in winning the I.C.A.A.A.A. 220, and the following year he repeated his victory in the same time.

In 1912 and 1913 another schoolboy sensation came along in Howard P. Drew of Springfield, Mass. High School, who won the national A.A.U. century from the college and club stars. The following year he hit his peak and tied the world's record of 9⅗ seconds in the 100 and also joined the ranks of sprinters who had run the 220 in the record time of 21⅕ seconds. Drew later continued his sprint triumphs at the University of Southern California.

During the First World War one of the youngest Americans to win a commission was Charles W. Paddock of Pasadena, Calif. At Pasadena High School he had won a number of century races in 10 seconds flat and one or two in 9⅘ seconds, but he was unknown outside his own part of the country until he went to the Inter-Allied Games in Paris, France, immediately at the close of the war.

On the way across the Atlantic some of the nationally known sprint stars of the American team while talking of their races asked young Lieutenant Paddock what his best time was for the 100. Charley said it was 9⅘ seconds. In those days 10 seconds flat was still considered championship time and when the stars were incredulous and spoofed about high school timing, Charley apologetically added, "Well, it was a slow nine-four."

"Slow Nine-Four" became Paddock's nickname on the boat. But like the audience that laughed when the young man in the advertisement sat down at the piano, they stopped their doubting and kidding when Charley defeated all comers, American and European champions alike, in the 100- and 200-meter dashes in the Inter-Allied meet. These were Paddock's first notable triumphs and they were to be followed by many more. During his varsity career at the University of Southern California, he won so many championships, tied the 100-yard dash record so often, and set so many new marks that he became universally hailed as the "World's Fastest Human."

In fact, when veteran track followers think back to Paddock's many achievements they are inclined to believe that, if anyone in the history of the sport is entitled to the all-time title of "Fastest Human," it is Paddock. In his prime he was unbeatable and practically every important sprint mark from 100 yards to 300 meters belonged to him.

Paddock won the Olympic 100-meter championship at 10⅘ seconds in 1920. In 1921 during a dual meet between Southern California and the University of California at Berkeley, he tied the world's record of 9⅗ seconds in the 100-yard dash and established a new world's 220 mark at 20⅘ seconds. He equaled the century record four times officially in 1921, one of the occasions being in his winning of the national A.A.U. championship. In 1924 while running for the Los Angeles Athletic Club, Charley again equaled this mark. In the 220 he was national champion in 1920, 1921, and 1924. He tied his world's 220 mark in winning his third championship in 1924.

Paddock also set the 100-meter record at 10⅖ seconds in 1921. His 220 figure of 20⅘ seconds eventually also became the world's 200-meter record since this distance is 218.725 yards. The 100-meter distance is 109.362 yards.

World's marks at the standard sprint races were not enough for the Pasadena speedster and during his career he made the fastest time on record at many odd distances. Many unofficial world's records, which were given official recognition as noteworthy performances or American records, fell beneath Charley's flying feet, among his marks being the following: 90 yards, 8⅘ seconds; 110 yards, 10⅕ seconds; 125 yards, 12 seconds; 130 yards, 12⅖ seconds; 150 yards, 14⅕ seconds; 200 yards, 19 seconds; 300 yards, 30⅕ seconds; and 300 meters, 33⅕ seconds. Sometimes Paddock collected records in wholesale lots. His marks at 90, 110, 130, 150, and 200 yards were all made on June 18, 1921, in Pasadena.

During his running career, Paddock had plenty of fast company. Among the speedsters of his day were Morris Kirksey of Stanford, Loren Murchison and Jackson V. Scholz of the New York Athletic Club, and Robert McAllister of New York City.

Charley Borah succeeded him as sprint champion at the University of Southern California. In 1926, when Borah was running as a Trojan freshman and Paddock was still going strongly as a member of the Los Angeles Athletic Club team, these men ran what was the fastest 100-yard race on record up to that time. In a finish so close that no more than an inch separated the runners, Paddock was the winner in 9.5 seconds. At that time, tenth-seconds were not given official recognition by the gentlemen who grant world's records and Paddock thus lost his chance of becoming the sole holder of the century record after having tied the old mark so often.

Paddock lost his 220-yard and 200-meter dash records in 1926 to Roland A. Locke of the University of Nebraska, who ran the furlong in 20.6 seconds. Locke, a powerfully built sprinter, won the N.C.A.A. 220 championship that year in 20.9 seconds. Meanwhile, the 100-yard-dash record had been tied in 1922 by Cyril H. Coaffee of Canada. In 1927 Chester Bowman of the Newark Athletic Club also earned a place in the record books as coholder of the 9⅗-second mark by his victory in this time in the national A.A.U. championships.

A year or two later the first of the great Negro sprinters of the 1920's and 1930's came along in Eddie Tolan of the University of Michigan. National champion in the century in 1929, Tolan while on a tour of Europe with an American team twice tied Paddock's 100-meter record of 10.4 seconds, running this time first in Stockholm and later in Copenhagen.

With so many great sprinters having come and gone since Duffey, who had run 100 yards in 9⅗ seconds back in 1902, followers of track and field were beginning to think that perhaps the limit of human speed had been reached. Dan Kelly, Howard Drew, Charley Paddock, Cyril Coaffee, Chet Bowman—all had equaled the mark, and many others had come within ⅕ second of it. To the majority of veteran track followers it seemed that the record had been shaved down to the point where it was not humanly possible to beat it.

Frank Wykoff, a University of Southern California sophomore from Glendale, Calif., gave the track and field world the answer in 1930 when on May 10 on the Occidental College track he became the first runner to speed the 100-yard distance officially in 9.4 seconds. A month later in the N.C.A.A. championships in Chicago, he ran the 100 in the same time again to prove that his record-breaking race was no fluke. During the preceding year George Simpson of Ohio State had been timed in 9.4 seconds in winning the N.C.A.A. century but his record was not considered because he had used starting blocks.

Wykoff again proved that championship speed is fundamentally a gift of nature, for he had flashed into prominence in the track and field world by winning the national 100-meter championship in the summer of 1928 just after his graduation from high school.

The sprinting hero of the 1928 Olympic games was Percy Williams, a diminutive Canadian youth who won both dashes. Two years later he cracked Charley Paddock's 100-meter record by $\frac{1}{10}$ second, running the distance in 10.3 seconds in Toronto. Two years afterward, in 1932, Tolan tied this record in winning the Olympic 100-meter dash in Los Angeles.

Ralph Metcalfe, the powerhouse Negro flier from Marquette University, tied the 100-meter record in 1933 in Budapest and on the same day also tied the 200-meter record of 20.6 seconds held by Roland Locke. Metcalfe, who won more national sprint championships than any other runner in history—three at 100 meters and five at 200 meters between 1932 and 1936—tied the 10.3-second mark twice in Japan in 1934. In the same year this record was also equaled by Eulace Peacock, the Negro star from Temple, and Christian D. Berger of Holland.

After the great records of Tolan and Metcalfe, the track and field world had grown to expect phenomenal things from Negro sprinters, and fans therefore were well prepared for the exploits of Jesse Owens. Running in the N.C.A.A. championships at Ann Arbor, Mich., in 1935 as an Ohio State sophomore, Owens first tied Wykoff's 100-yard dash record of 9.4 seconds and then smashed by $\frac{3}{10}$ second the world's mark of Locke in the 220. He ran the furlong in 20.3 seconds, the mark that stands in the record books today for both 220 yards and 200 meters. As if this sprint work was not enough, on the same day he also broke the world's records in the broad jump and the 220-yard low hurdles.

The smooth-running flier added another world's record to his collection in the N.C.A.A. championships of 1936 when he broke the 100-meter dash mark with a time of 10.2 seconds. Later that summer he was the outstanding star of the Olympics in Berlin when he won the 100- and 200-meter sprints and the broad jump and also ran on the record-breaking 400-meter relay team with Wykoff, Metcalfe, and Foy Draper.

In the national A.A.U. championships of 1939 Clyde Jeffrey of Stanford won the 100-meter dash in 10.2 seconds but officials did not apply for the record as the wind gauge showed a blow beyond the allowable limit. Jeffrey, who had been a schoolboy sensation at Riverside, Calif., started the swing of sprinting supremacy back to the white race. Early in the 1940 season in the Long Beach, Calif., relays he was timed in 9.4 seconds for the 100-yard dash, equaling the record of Wykoff and Owens. But later in the season he was defeated in the N.C.A.A. 100 by Norwood Ewell, Penn State's Negro speedster. It remained for Hal Davis, a youngster from the little California town of Morgan Hill, to put the white man on top in the sprints.

Davis, running for Salinas, Calif., Junior College, showed that he was on his way to being the top sprinter of the year early in June when he ran 100 meters in 10.3 seconds and 200 meters in 20.5 seconds in the Compton Invitational meet, defeating Jeffrey in the latter race. Later he proved beyond all doubt that he was the leading sprinter of the 1940 season when in the senior national championships of that year in Fresno he won the 100-meter dash in 10.3 seconds and the 200-meter sprint in 20.4 seconds.

Ewell, who was I.C.A.A.A.A. champion in both sprints and the broad jump and N.C.A.A. champion in both dashes, was runner-up to Davis in the two A.A.U. races. He and Mozel Ellerbe of Tuskegee Institute were powerful runners with particularly fine early speed and were worthy successors to Owens as the fastest Negro sprinters in the country.

In the national junior A.A.U. championships of 1940 the swing of sprinting supremacy back to the white race was further indicated by the victories of Eddie Morris of Huntington Beach, Calif., High School in both sprints. Morris turned his victories in brilliant time for a prep runner, winning the 100 meters in 10.4 seconds and the 200 meters in 20.6 seconds.

To get in shape for speed running, the sprint candidate must train his entire body as does a boxer. Training should start during the semester before competition. In this period the candidate need give little thought to speed. He should be merely laying a physical foundation. Gymnasium work on the apparatus and setting-up exercises are splendid for this building-up process.

Once or twice a week it is wise for a sprint candidate to take to the track for jogging. One should swing into this type of work very gradually, for legs must be taught and no sprinter should attempt to get into condition too fast. Long-distance work is out entirely and sprinters should never jog more than two laps at a time. Training over long distances in attempting to build up stamina is likely to give the legs a jolting that will spoil the bounce that is the essential part of sprinting form.

It is well to bear in mind right from the start that overwork must be avoided in training for any form of track and field athletics. There are two ways of looking at the problem of how much work an athlete should have in training, and coaches often take widely separated viewpoints on this subject. Some believe that hard work and plenty of it is necessary to bring athletic success; others advocate comparatively light training.

Track seasons are long and it is difficult to keep an athlete from going stale after several months of training. The viewpoints on the amount of training that athletes should have vary because coaches have different ideas on the causes of staleness in their competitors.

Those who favor fairly light practice do so because they believe that overwork is likely to cause physical and mental staleness just when the athlete should be at his peak. They agree that hard work may be a stamina and muscle builder but they contend that it eventually causes physical weariness and an exhaustion of nervous energy. This takes the edge off the athlete's ambition and leaves him in a depressed state that makes it impossible for him to produce his best efforts.

The advocates of heavy training believe that staleness is not a physical condition but a mental state that is likely to affect anyone no matter how he has practiced. They contend that long, hard work is necessary if one is to develop a fighting spirit as well as the foundation for grueling competition.

Their creed is simple. If one is to become a runner, he must run, and run a lot. If he is to be a jumper, he must jump, and jump often. If he wants to be a vaulter, the principal thing to do is vault, and keep at it. Some coaches of this school of thought have turned out champion athletes and can point to them as proof that their contention is right.

For my part, however, I go for moderation, and if it should come to the question of having an athlete enter a meet either undertrained or overtrained I would prefer to have him in the former condition.

Athletes who are not overworked may not seem to have the muscular power of those who have trained hard and strenuously, but they make up for this in the added fire and nervous energy that fill them when lined up for competition. I like to have an athlete raring to go when he enters a meet, not tired from a too rigorous program in preparing for it.

40

The training, of course, should always be suited to the athlete. Some men can stand hard work and others will fade under it. I advocate undertraining rather than overtraining because I like a fine mental edge rather than a mass of muscle. There is another factor—you can't hurt a boy by undertraining him. You don't get pulled muscles, strains, and sprains in practice among boys who are not constantly being driven to put forth their mightiest efforts.

Before the sprint candidate starts any speed work he should have a good sound physical foundation built up through several months of preseason work. This training before speed work is attempted is no period of drudgery but is a gradual building up of a solid physical background. Games such as tennis, handball, badminton, and volleyball that stress alertness and quick starting without too much strenuous exertion are good conditioners. Walking, of course, is not only good but absolutely essential, and the not-less-than-two-miles-a-day rule should be religiously followed. Jogging soon leads to wind sprints and a few of these two or three times a week during the fall will have the legs ready for speed work in the spring.

As soon as one is in shape to run short distances fast without strain or fatigue he should study his natural form. The terms usually given to the two most common classifications of sprinters are "floaters" and "drivers." Floaters are comparatively rare among American sprinters. The name describes their style well. They sail along easily and pull rather than dig in.

Charley Borah, a national A.A.U. and I.C.A.A.A.A. champion in both the 100 and 220, was the best example of floater I ever had at Southern California. Probably Borah was the best example of this type of runner America has had in several decades because practically all our champions have been drivers.

Morris Kirksey of Stanford, who gave Charley Paddock his greatest competition during Charley's college running career and who was runner-up to the Southern Californian in the 1920 Olympic games 100-meter dash, was another great floater. An interesting thing about Kirksey was that, although he had a powerful physique, he lost his running form and with it his speed when he attempted to drive. He was at his best and a truly great sprinter when he relaxed and ran in his natural smooth flowing

41

style. Kirksey was so smooth that it seemed as though he could have carried a glass of water balanced on his head over the 100-yard route without spilling a drop.

Among United States champions who were drivers have been Charley Paddock, Eddie Tolan, Ralph Metcalfe, Eulace Peacock, Perrin Walker, Ben Johnson, Clyde Jeffrey, and Harold Davis.

Occasionally the two types are combined in one runner. Jesse Owens was an example who could combine floating and driving. He had great leg speed and at the same time possessed so much kick that he was a record-breaking broad jumper and low hurdler as well as sprinter. Frank Wykoff was about two-thirds driver and one-third floater. He had an easy stride through the middle of his race but ran like a driver in his opening pickup and in his final dash to the tape.

Percy Williams of Canada was probably the greatest example of a floater that has been seen in international competition. The new, soft track at Amsterdam in the 1928 Olympics was made to order for him. While he was floating over it in his light-footed stride, the American runners were having a terrible time with their footing. Lacking firmness, the track would not hold their pounding spikes and Williams had little trouble flying away from the Americans in both sprints.

Track meets are not often held in the rain or on wet tracks but if you want to pick a likely winner in the sprints under such conditions find out if the field of runners contains a floater. If there is one, he is your man, for you'll find that a floater is a natural "mudder."

Leg speed is the principal asset of floaters. Usually their stride is not long but they have a rapid leg movement that makes them appear to be sailing over the ground and scarcely touching it.

A driving movement of the legs at the ground is the principal feature of the driver, or puller, type of runner. Naturally he must have good leg speed too, but the rebounding of his legs from the ground is the motion that chiefly characterizes his running. Since we insist on hard firm tracks for our sprinters in America, the driving type of runner has the advantage under our conditions.

The development of spring is of the greatest importance in sprinting. "Bounce" in running can be used as a synonymous

42

term. Practically all born sprinters have this bounce to an exaggerated degree. Made sprinters will not get far unless they can cultivate it. A coach who knows how to develop and utilize bounce in his runners is of vital importance to a sprinter. Many a born sprinter has been wasted for lack of a coach who could work with him day after day on this extremely important fundamental of speed running.

It may help you to a better understanding of the leg action of a sprinter if you compare the striking of his foot on the ground to the bouncing of a rubber ball. The action of the rebound in the rubber ball is too fast to see. You see the ball go down and come back up, but you are not conscious of any momentary rest of the ball on the ground at the moment of rebound.

If you tried to follow the movement of the feet of a sprinter you would find the same result. In long-distance running or even in the striding that takes place in the quarter mile your eye can follow the contact of the athlete's feet with the ground. You cannot trace this movement in the sprinter, however, unless your eye is extremely quick and you have trained yourself to do it, for the feet hit and bounce up with the immediate split-second reaction of a rubber ball.

Because this rebound action occurs so quickly, many people do not realize what is taking place and for this reason they overlook one of the most important items in sprinting.

The use of high knee action is necessary to get this bounce. Sprinters must work constantly on bringing their legs well up in front and then driving them straight down. In the sprinter's stride the knee is picked up high, the leg shoots out ahead, the foot is driven down hard against the ground, and immediately it rebounds and is up again.

The higher the knee is lifted the harder the ball of the foot can be driven against the ground to get the rebound. Beginning sprinters should practice for hours to get this high knee action. A good exercise is to stand on one foot and bring the opposite knee up as close to the chest as possible. Then the leg should be snapped out.

The bicycle pedaling exercise is another good one for sprinters. In doing this, the athlete lies on the ground on his back. Then while balancing himself on his back and neck with the arms holding up his hips, he goes through knee and stride motions in the air.

When the runner raises his thigh in starting his stride, he finds that it is natural for his foot to swing easily in a circular motion. Great force is put into the downward drive of the leg. At this point it should be taken into consideration that unless the body is being carried at the proper angle, the rebounding force would be sent upward and would be of no use to the runner's forward progress.

The carrying of the body in a lean in such a way as to get full benefit of the bounce forward instead of upward is called the "sprinting angle." This angle varies with individuals but is usually about 20 degrees from the erect position.

Sprinters always strive to use their greatest leg speed but soon find a limit they cannot exceed. But when they cannot move their legs any faster, there is always one way they can develop more speed. This is by increasing the spring, or bounce, of the stride. In his constant war on fractions of a second, the sprinter can wage a winning battle by constantly developing greater ability to rebound from the track.

Although his exercises and running in training will do much for his bounce, the sprinter should never overlook the importance of proper walking in creating spring. One who makes a habit of walking with a springy step will also improve his chances for athletic success by developing loose hips and ankles. Also the walker who strides with a bounce will not find himself in later life among the large portion of our population that suffers from foot trouble. The springy walk strengthens foot muscles and keeps in place the small bones that have a tendency to slip.

Start, stride, and finish are the usual divisions of the 100-yard dash when we take it apart to examine its mechanics. The start includes about the first 35 yards of the race since it also takes in the pickup to maximum running speed. Stride refers to full running speed. The finish includes that part of the race in which the "gather" occurs for the final drive at the tape.

The standing start has long since given way to the crouch, which has proved the most efficient method not only for springing the athlete from his marks but also for putting him at the correct body angle for his pickup to full speed.

44

Charley Paddock, who once held nearly every world's record from 100 yards to 300 meters, working at his favorite conditioning exercise—bicycle pedaling.

Undoubtedly the competitors in the early days of sprinting experimented considerably with various kinds of starts. Since our modern crouch start is an outgrowth of much trial-and-error work by many runners, track historians do not all agree on the question of just who invented this method. Many of them seem to think that the credit should go to Tommy Lee of the New York Athletic Club who was national A.A.U. champion in the 100- and 220-yard dashes in 1894.

Starting holes should be dug carefully to give the feet firm support for the opening spring. The back of the first hole should be about a foot behind the starting line. The back of this first hole is dug out at a slant to accomodate the angle of the foot when it is at rest in it.

The location of the second hole is determined by kneeling. The knee of the rear leg should be even with the toe of the front foot or possibly a little behind it. When the second hole is dug, the back of it should be nearly perpendicular so that it will support comfortably the ball of the rear foot.

The holes should be about $2\frac{1}{2}$ or 3 inches deep. By experimentation the athlete will soon find the proper depth and the most comfortable slant of the first hole for his particular crouch. One of the principal things to be watched is the firmness of the backs of the holes, for the ground must not give way when sudden pressure is applied. Often the ground around the starting holes is loose and uncertain because many athletes have dug it up for previous races, and a runner should give himself plenty of time before his event is called to prepare his start.

When the starter announces, "On your mark!" the athlete places his forward foot, usually his left, in the first hole. When that one is comfortably set, he kneels and places his rear foot firmly up against the back of the second hole.

It is well to move the feet a little and to exert some pressure to make sure that the footing is firm. Too much squirming in the holes, however, will not only tear them down and leave them uncertain for the start but will also create a nervous tension and lack of self-confidence in the athlete.

With the feet well set in the holes, the runner places his fingers up to the starting line. The fingers should be well spread out in a tripod position. It is not wise to try to balance on the tips of the

46

fingers as some runners do because firm support for the body must be given by the hands. Since the runner will want his arms to swing clear of his trunk when he starts, he should place his hands far enough apart so that they are at a point just outside his hips.

The starter's signal "Get set" brings the knee of the rear leg about 3 inches off the ground and with this motion the body moves forward. The main point here is to have the athlete's back parallel with the ground. Since the runner cannot see how his back is lining up with the ground, he needs a coach or an experienced runner to give him advice on this point early in his start taking.

Great care in getting the proper balance should be taken at this point. A common fault is to raise the buttocks too high. If this is done, the start sends the runner into a diving motion at the ground and he will lose ground as he struggles to recover his balance during his early pickup. If the angle is the other way and the buttocks are too low, the runner is likely to drag his rear leg in coming from his marks and also will probably straighten up to his running position before he has gathered full speed.

When the athlete has made sure that the line of his back is correct, he should try to have his weight evenly divided between the forward leg and the arms. The body should be moved forward in a natural position that will bring the shoulders above a point just beyond the starting line.

In order to avoid tenseness the runner should focus his eyes on a point 7 or 8 yards out in front. Attempting to look down the track at the finish line will cause the muscles in the neck to tighten and this strain may spread to other muscles that must stay relaxed.

If a false start is made, the starter usually gives the command "Stand up" to the rest of the runners. This enables them to ease the tension and prepare to get in perfect balance for another start. The runner when on his marks should concentrate on nothing but his own start. If he allows himself to watch others out of the corner of his eye, he may catch some nervous motion or false start that may cause him to jump the gun.

When a false start takes place, the runner should get off his marks and move around a little, making sure he is well relaxed before resuming his position at the starting line.

47

Runners and their coaches often need to experiment together for some time before they can be sure of the exact distance that the starting holes should be apart. Some runners must have their holes considerably farther apart than others in order to feel properly balanced.

Hard driving runners seem to require a greater distance between starting holes than floaters. Charley Paddock, a sprinter of terrific drive, found comfort and balance in holes somewhat farther apart than most runners. Frank Wykoff, who was something of a driver himself in the early stages of a race, had holes 20 inches apart, which is about average. Charley Borah, a floater who did not seem to be driving hard even in the pickup of the first 35 yards, dug his holes several inches closer together.

You cannot take these comparisons to mean that you can increase your opening drive by digging your starting holes a greater distance apart, however. After a certain point is reached, your legs will be spread so that they will lose power instead of gain it.

It seems to be natural for a right-handed person to take his starting stance with his left foot forward but if a runner feels more comfortable and better balanced with the right foot advanced, he certainly need not follow the majority.

When the athlete comes up to the "Get set" position, he should take a deep breath. He holds his breath and does not exhale until he is well down the track and his exertions call for more air.

When the starting gun goes off, the runner pushes his feet hard against both starting holes and springs from his marks. The greater part of the effort is put into the front foot, but the rear foot starts the pushing movement first by a split second.

Arm action starts at the same moment. If the rear foot is the right foot, the left arm is thrust forward as the back leg swings up from the starting hole. At the same time the right arm swings back. Thus the rhythm of the arm swing with the leg stride starts for the entire race with the sounding of the gun, the left arm swinging forward with the right leg and the right arm swinging with the left leg.

The first steps after leaving the holes are important but again individual peculiarities must be taken into consideration. Instead

48

of going by hard and fast rules, the coach and athlete must be sure first of all that the runner's opening strides are natural.

Considerable emphasis has been given for years by experts in sprinting on the necessity of short strides when the runner pulls out of his starting holes. So much has been said on this point that many athletes now overdo the chopping of their opening steps.

The best way to hit upon the most natural first steps away from the starting line is to concentrate on the proper body angle and let the strides take care of themselves. If the body is slanted well forward, the angle will necessitate the taking of moderate strides that will be neither too long nor too short. If the body is carried in too much of an upright position, the strides will naturally be too long at first.

Those who make a study of stride lengths have found that there can be much variation not only in the steps of different athletes but frequently also in different starts taken by the same athlete. Because Frank Wykoff was the fastest American runner I have ever seen in the first 35 yards, I measured his opening steps from time to time in an attempt to determine if they had a standard length when he made his best starts.

In a typical fast start, I found that his right foot finished the first stride 3 feet 6 inches beyond his front starting hole. His second stride picked up 4 feet 3 inches. This distance was increased a foot in his third stride. His fourth stride added 3 more inches, for a length of 5 feet 6 inches. His strides continued their gradual increase in length until they reached approximately 7 feet 6 inches, which is unusually long, at his full running speed.

Just for comparison but not to prove anything except perhaps my old argument that every runner has his own way of doing things, let us take the first few strides of Mickey Anderson and Barney Willis, leading Southern California sprinters of the 1940 season. Anderson was national junior 100-meter champion in 1939 in 10.5 seconds and Willis was credited with a 100-yard mark of 9.6 seconds.

In a tryout race with Willis, Anderson's first stride, measured from the front starting hole, was 3 feet 7 inches. His second was 3 feet 2 inches, his third 4 feet even, his fourth the same, his fifth 4 feet 8 inches and his sixth 4 feet 9 inches.

Willis's first stride was 4 feet 5 inches, his second 3 feet 5 inches,

49

a foot short of his first step since he had overreached in leaving his holes. His third stride was 4 feet 3 inches, his fourth 4 feet 6 inches, his fifth 5 feet 4 inches, and his sixth 5 feet 2 inches.

At full running speed, Anderson's stride was 7 feet 2 inches and Willis's was 7 feet 1 inch.

If the first four strides for Wykoff, Anderson, and Willis are totaled separately, we find this result: Wykoff traveled 18 feet 6 inches; Willis, 16 feet 7 inches; and Anderson, 14 feet 9 inches.

An interesting question arises: Was the leg speed of the three boys the same, so that Wykoff would have been leading at the end of four strides, with Willis about 2 feet back, and Anderson nearly 4 feet back of the leader?

It so happens that the leg speed of these three sprinters was about the same. Because Wykoff could combine a long pickup stride with leg speed, he had an amazing burst of speed. Although he was nearly a decade ahead of Willis at Southern California, I am sure that in their best races Wykoff would have been 2 feet ahead of Willis at the end of four strides. And Willis, it should be added, was an exceptionally fast starter. In the race in which the strides of Anderson and Willis were compared, the latter actually was 2 feet ahead at four steps from the starting holes.

A question in this case that naturally faces the coach is this: Should Anderson arbitrarily be made to lengthen his opening strides? And the answer, of course, is, remember the importance of leg speed. Lengthen the stride as much as you can without sacrificing leg speed. If the movement of the legs is slowed down, what good has been done by increasing the length of the steps?

Many things have to be considered, and in the case of Anderson and Willis an important item was the respective builds of the runners. Both were 5 feet 10 inches in height, but Anderson, a star triple-threat back in football, was a sturdily built young man of 172 pounds, and Willis was a streamlined youth of 152 pounds.

Anderson was forced to take shorter steps to get his bulk rolling but once he reached full speed he had greater power. In the particular race in which the measurements were made, Anderson trailed 3 feet at 35 yards but finished the century 2 feet in front of Willis in 9.7 seconds. Anderson's last stride, incidentally, was a normal one of 7 feet 2 inches. In an attempt to catch him, Willis made a lunge that lengthened his stride to 7 feet 6 inches.

Yoshioka, who was Japan's leading sprinter in the 1932 Olympics, ran the fastest first 30 yards I have ever seen. Hardly more than 5 feet in height, he was naturally quite short-legged. Although I did not have the opportunity to measure his opening strides, I observed his spike marks on the track and could see that his steps were much shorter than those taken by any Americans. His greatest asset in sprinting was an amazing leg speed which began right from the starting gun. He took such short steps, however, that when the Americans reached full running speed their longer strides more than made up for his leg speed and they soon caught and passed him.

The first thing for the runner to remember when he springs from his starting holes is to lean well forward. If he does this, he will find it necessary to bring his legs up high to keep from falling. Thus the high knee action that is stressed in sprinting is begun at once. It not only keeps the runner's bounce but also facilitates his quick development of speed. Then when he reaches full stride, he finds that he has gradually raised his body to the proper and natural sprinting angle.

In taking the first step the runner should not raise his foot more than 6 inches off the ground. There must be no lost motion. Fractions of a second consumed in the opening step or two can mean the loss of a race.

The starter in the dashes has the difficult job of seeing that a group of high-strung athletes get off evenly. A reasonable length of time is needed between the "Get set" command and the starting gun to give all the runners a chance to reach proper balance. The pause should never be less than 2 seconds; if it is too long, it will cause tenseness among the runners and someone will invariably break.

Incompetent starters sometimes give a quick shot after the set command and often this not only causes uneven starting but results in athletes becoming jittery in future starts under the same official. An experienced starter will have little trouble with his runners once they know that he will not fool them with a quick gun.

Because starters vary so much in their handling of runners on the marks, wise athletes are ready to go the instant they are brought to the set position, but they hold steady and never try to beat the gun and risk a penalty for a false start.

51

In order to prepare his runners for whatever kind of starting they may run into, coaches should drill them in both quick guns and slow guns and should immediately discourage any tendency that may be revealed on the part of an athlete to try to jump the gun. Attempting to sneak an edge on the field is not only unsportsmanlike but is sure to boomerang on the offender when he gets into important competition under experienced, hard-boiled starters.

In high school competition, anticipation of the gun often is due to nervousness and inexperience more than any desire on the part of the runner to be unfair. It is because of this erratic starting and difference in timing that a 10-flat college sprinter can nearly always trim a 9.8-second high school sensation.

In the second main consideration of sprinting—full stride, or running speed—the athlete must concentrate on his bounce and on the high knee action that creates it.

When Charley Paddock, who developed his tremendous drive through exceptionally high knee action, broke the world's record for the 220-yard dash in 1921, his knees came up so high that at one point he kicked himself in the chin. I have Charley's own statement for this, but I would not advise others to try to knock themselves out in an endeavor to set a record. However, Charley gave me demonstrations of high knee action that I will never forget. When Paddock was at the height of his career, some coaches criticized his form as freakish and unorthodox, but to me the rhythmic power in his leg and arm action was a thing of beauty.

Some of the greatest thrills I have had in my thirty-three years of coaching and cheering track and field have come from watching Paddock's terrific leg action when swinging into a 220 and Wykoff's amazing pickup in the first 35 yards of the 100. When I witness things like these in track, I am like a lover of the arts who makes a show of himself over a painting. It fires an enthusiasm that keeps me young.

In full stride the sprinter must bring his knees up high in front and thrust them down violently to get the rebound that creates his forward drive. In hitting the track the foot makes both a quick pull and a push. If it were not for this, spikes would be unnecessary, for a runner could probably rebound better in tennis shoes than in track footgear. The striking of the toes on the ground brings a quick pull and as the foot bounces up it leaves the ground with a push.

Runners should check occasionally on the direction in which their toes point. Pointing of the toes in or out or twisting them when they strike the ground causes a loss of power. Toeing out is a common fault of beginners but it can be easily corrected by accentuating a pigeon-toed stride for a time in training.

Another common fault is wobbling. Those who cannot go from the starting holes to the tape along the straight and narrow should practice straddling a line marked on the ground as they run.

Since speed can be developed only while the runner is well up on his toes, the heels of a sprinter should never touch the ground. A flat-footed sprinter is the greatest atrocity track and field can produce.

One of the many points in favor of an exaggerated high knee action in sprinting is that it prevents a wasteful kick-up of the feet in the rear. Paddock's extremely high knee style left him with so little back kick that critics of form used to say, "He looks as if he is running sitting down."

In his struggle to subdue fractions of a second, the sprinter can afford no waste motion of any kind. The coach should watch his runner in action from all angles to try to detect any small violations of correct form that may cause the difference of a yard or two in a 100-yard race. Waste motion can be brought about by running bowlegged or knock-kneed. Flipping the feet out to the side is a common bad habit.

Power can be lost by running with the feet too far apart. Putting one foot directly in front of the other is just as bad and causes wobbling and an overdone hip swing.

The arms should be bent slightly at the elbow as the runner swings them along. Proper arm swing keeps the body in perfect balance and enables the runner to head in a straight line at the tape. The swinging of the arms also is important in driving the runner forward.

In considering the movement of his arms during a race, the athlete should remember that the important thing is really his shoulder swing. If his shoulders swing right, his arms will be carried properly. Athletes occasionally do some fancy twists and loops with their arms in the belief that they are helping their running. They are only wasting energy and probably also upsetting their body balance, for the arms should merely follow the natural shoulder swing.

Although it would be difficult for a runner to watch the action of his shoulders, he can see the result of his shoulder swing in the movement of his arms. An overly exaggerated shoulder swing will force the arms to swing across the chest; this should be avoided, although many European runners apparently are taught by their coaches to follow this style. When the shoulders swing correctly, they bring the hands up about shoulder high in the swing to the front. The swing to the rear should bring the elbows behind the body a few inches, just far enough so that the hands do not go behind the hips.

Although it is advisable to try to swing the arms straight forward, no harm is done if there is a slight movement of them across the chest. The natural easy shoulder swing of some runners will cause this slight cross-chest motion although most beginners will be better off if they try to avoid it.

Tension that is fatal to good running form can be developed by improper carriage of the shoulders and arms. Hunching of the shoulders and clenching of the fists can cause a tightening to spread to other muscles of the runner and make him tie up. Running corks were once considered part of a sprinter's equipment but these are now known to be harmful rather than helpful. Hands should be carried open with the fingers assuming a natural relaxed slightly bent position. Wykoff overcame an urge to clench his fists by pointing his thumbs up. Although his fingers closed in his hands this thumb position kept him from clenching his fists.

Like the old ideas regarding the carrying of cork grips, the belief that a sprinter should go as far as possible on his first breath is also a thing of the past. Some sprinters used to try to make the entire 100 yards of the short sprint on one breath. It is no great trick for one to hold his breath 10 seconds even when undergoing great exertion, but we have found that there is no point in not taking the breaths naturally as the body requires them.

A great many sprinters still hold their breath until about the 75-yard mark and then take another that carries them to the finish. One of the theories advanced in favor of this system is that it enables the runner to concentrate better on his race and to keep his body in better balance than it would be if his chest were heaving up and down in heavy breathing.

The human body, however, knows when it requires more oxygen and it will respond better when it is allowed to function naturally. After filling his lungs at the "Get set" command, the sprinter is steady and alert for the starting gun. Once off his marks, he can forget his breathing and let nature take care of it for him.

He will usually find that the extreme exertion he puts forth in his opening strides will make him ready for a breath at between 30 and 40 yards. In another 30 or 40 yards he will usually be ready for another breath which will likely carry him to the tape although there is nothing wrong in breathing again if comfort demands it before the finish of the race.

Since breathing often bothers beginning runners, they should develop regular habits in this regard. Runners who seem to be in good condition but fade near the finish are often found to have poor breathing habits. It is not well to be exhaling in the last drive at the tape as a filled pair of lungs at this point aids in the lift that one needs here.

The finish is the third element of the sprint race that takes special attention in a detailed study of the dashes. Since it is impossible for a sprinter to turn 100 yards at his utmost speed even though he may be trying his hardest every inch of the way, he must concentrate on a final "gather," during which he really is forcing himself to his maximum. This gather takes place about 25 yards from the finish. It is a concentration of effort, but it must not be a muscular exertion that will bring tenseness. Trying too hard without keeping the proper form in mind will only defeat the runner's purpose.

Body angle, high knee action, bounce, running on a perfectly straight line, easy shoulder and arm swing, relaxation—these are the things the runner must be thinking of in his final burst for the tape.

He must concentrate particularly on them in the closing yards because it is at this point that he will be fighting fatigue. He will finish poorly if he lets his head tilt backwards, causing a tightening of the muscles in his neck and trunk and the resulting loss of the correct body angle, or if he lets fatigue take away his high knee action and bounce.

Nature through tired muscles will be trying to force him to vary from what he knows is correct form, and it is at this point that he calls upon his knowledge of technique and his determination to defeat his natural urges.

Most short-sprint races are won or lost in the last 20 yards and the champion is the man who can gather all his resources and use them properly at this point. Running straight through the tape as though it were not there is usually the best way to hold the correct form and finish at the greatest possible speed, but with training a slight increase in the forward lean of the body can be made of assistance.

Judges decide the places at the finish of a race not by the position of the feet or even by who hits the tape first but by the bodies that have crossed the line. Naturally the farther one can thrust his body ahead of his feet, the better off he is at the finish line.

Leaps at the tape may give the athlete the sensation of flying through the air but as a rule they decrease his speed rather than increase it. The only man I have ever seen with a spectacular leaping finish who really benefited by it was Paddock. Charley unleashed his pent-up running energy to the point where he literally exploded at the tape in his flying leap which would gain as much as a foot over contestants. He had this leap perfectly timed, starting it from 7 to 8 feet from the finish line and hitting the tape as he was midway in it. Had he hit the tape at the finish of his leap, he would have lost momentum and the jump would have had no advantage.

Beside leaning forward and increasing the body angle, a sprinter can sometimes gain a few inches by turning a shoulder into the tape but this can have no advantage unless perfectly timed.

Throwing up the arms to hit the tape with the chest is harmful to good running form and a fast finish even though one sees pictures of leading athletes doing it all the time. Perhaps the pose makes a good picture or maybe the winning runner is afraid of getting tangled up in the tape, but as a part of the race itself the finish with the arms in the air is only a time-waster. It not

FOOTBALL COACHES WILL APPROVE

Like the charging lineman in football, sprinter Charley Parsons, Jr., keeps his hips low in starting.
Note how close the right foot stays to the ground to save time in the opening stride.

BODY ANGLE IS IMPORTANT

In full stride Parsons keeps a fairly acute lean to generate his drive forward and not upward. In 1905 Charles Parsons, Sr., won the national A.A.U. 100-yard dash. The running form of Charles, Jr., was an exact copy.

infrequently happens that the runner who thinks the race is won and strikes the pictorial pose at the finish is nosed out by a fast finisher who ignores the tape and speeds through it in correct running form.

Trying to sneak a look at opponents in a sprint race is an unforgivable sin. Turning the head wastes time and takes the runner's mind off his own form. This rule should be applied to all running races. Only a few champions who are certain of their ability should be permitted the luxury of exceptions.

Sprinters should run through the tape, not at it. If their goal is a point several yards beyond the finish line, they will be sure not to lessen speed too soon and will not be nipped by an opponent who should have been defeated.

After keeping his top speed until he has gone well through the tape, the runner should slacken his pace gradually. Muscle injuries and ankle sprains can result from trying to make quick stops in spiked shoes.

Not all 100-yard dash men have relatively the same ability in the 220 although most sprinters double up in these dashes. Some runners use up most of their speed in 100 yards and are unable to build up to the furlong.

On the other hand, others may not be able to develop enough early speed to do well in the 100 but really start to fly when they get midway through the 220. The two races are quite different and no coach should expect his sprinters to perform equally well in both although it occasionally happens.

In some cases a 100-yard dash man is unable to do himself justice in the 220 no matter how hard he tries. Such a runner should be allowed to specialize in the shorter race and should not be tired out by being forced to run a distance to which he is not suited. Occasionally also an excellent 220 man is just a dead loss in the 100.

We have seen that even in the century it is impossible to run the full distance wide open and in the furlong we find that much of the race must be run at a speed we call "coasting." This does not mean loafing, however. Coasting is simply the process of breezing along at full sprinting stride without straining to give the maximum effort at each step.

As in the 100-yard dash, every ounce of energy should be put

57

into the start, pickup, and first 25 or 30 yards of the full running stride. After this part of the race, which has carried the sprinter some 60 or 65 yards, the runner is traveling at such a rate that his momentum will carry him along at a coasting stride, the speed of which is only slightly less than his top sprinting pace. During this stage of the race the stride is a little longer than that used in the 100 and the shoulder swing is also greater.

After this coasting period, which may last until the finish is from 50 to 70 yards away, the runner should gather himself for his final drive at the tape. This should be made just as it is in the 100.

Although the sprinter in the century has no time to do much thinking about the rest of the men in the race, in the 220 the runner can sometimes use a bit of head work. Without turning his head, out of the corner of his eye he may be able to spot his opponents and observe whether or not they are running themselves out or saving something for their final gather.

In planning his race as he runs it, he may find it the best strategy to continue to coast even though he may be slightly behind, for if he finds his opposition running itself out he may rely on his final drive at the tape to bring victory. I do not advise runners to base their hopes for 220 victories on the superiority of their intellect, however. If they will learn how to run their best 220 in advance, knowing when to ease off from the opening burst of speed to the coast and when to go from that to the final gather, they are more likely to win than if they depend on outsmarting the opposition.

If the furlong race is held on a curve, runners should cut corners as much as possible by keeping to the extreme left side of the lane. Two hundred and twenty-yard straightaways are found on nearly all tracks in this country, but because the straight 220 stretch is still rare in Europe, the Olympic games 200-meter dash is still run on a curve.

In working with sprinters I never let the 100-yard dash man go the full distance in training. However, I am perfectly willing for the furlong runner to turn in one or more 220's every day. He can go out and run several, one right after the other, as long as he is building up and not tearing down.

In running such training races, the object is not to see how

58

fast the athlete can sprint them but to build up form, speed, and stamina.

The reason for this difference in policy is that in the 100 there is a point of extreme speed which is not necessary in the 220 except in actual competition. The effort is there in the furlong but it is delivered at the end of the race rather than down the entire stretch.

Training races of from 200 to 300 yards are good for all track athletes in building up speed and strength. Candidates for the distance races need to work considerably at these routes to improve their speed. Most field event men also find such training distances helpful in developing their stamina.

One of the many reasons why coaching is a particularly fascinating business is because it calls on a man's Philo Vance instincts. In his quest for perfection in his athletes the coach must be continually investigating and analyzing. This he must do mostly by observation. Some experimentation is necessary but if this goes very far the athlete on whom the changes are being tried is likely to become confused and to lose confidence both in the coach and in himself.

Whether his sprinter is a beginner or already a star performer, the coach should try to determine early in the season the principal problems connected with his running. Perhaps a few examples of what was done with sprinters we have had at Southern California may illustrate this point.

Charley Paddock's weak point when he started his varsity running career was the first part of his race. Most track fans who saw him run thought he was slow off his marks, but this was not the case at all. Extremely high-strung, intelligent, and alert, Charley was as quick as any sprinter I have ever seen in reacting to the sound of the gun.

Once off his marks, however, he lacked early speed and it was on this matter of pickup that we worked together day after day. To develop his pickup, I had Charley do a tremendous amount of short sprinting. While he was doing this work at from 35 to 50 yards, he was given the objective of lengthening his stride, particularly the opening steps away from his holes. To check his stride we would first smooth off two adjacent lanes. He would take a start and short sprint in one lane and would then go back and deliberately try to lengthen his stride while starting out in the adjoining lane. Then we could go back over the two lanes, beginning at his start, and compare the length of his strides by observing his spike marks.

Charley accentuated the angle of his body while reaching out for longer strides and this aided him in developing a fast pickup. His principal fault in his early sprinting was that, although he responded quickly to the gun, he had a tendency to jump up in the air and come down with his legs pounding the ground with amazing rapidity but also with extremely short strides. It looked to me at first as though in Charley's mechanism his clutch was slipping.

Cutting down his body angle and making him reach out for longer strides eventually gave him as much early speed as any of his leading competitors. We found that his improved stride gave him a gain of about 2 yards during the first half of the 100-yard dash. When he added his natural running speed and terrific finishing kick to this during the early 1920's, he became the greatest record smasher in the history of sprinting.

When fans found that Charley was no longer behind men like Morris Kirksey and Jackson Scholz and Loren Murchison at 50 yards, they flattered me by giving me credit for helping him get off his marks faster. Actually he needed no improvement here. What he did develop was a faster pickup in the opening 35 yards, but it took long, hard work for him to do it.

In the case of Charley Borah we had a sprinter who was as outstanding in floating as Paddock was in driving. Borah took wings when the gun went off and had no trouble with his pickup. He was as smooth as silk all the way but could be picked off at the finish by a great driving runner. He would get worse instead of better when he attempted a final gather himself.

Like Kirksey, Borah could have balanced a glass of water on his head down the 100-yard dash without spilling a drop. In an attempt to improve his finish, however, I deliberately set about trying to take away some of this smoothness.

The object in Borah's case was to develop more kick in his legs and this was done by having him accentuate the high knee action and also put more vigor into his hip, shoulder, and arm swing. A longer stride while this was going on was also needed,

60

and we used the plan of smoothing off two lanes in order to compare the length of his steps.

This campaign of training did not interfere with Borah's leg speed. To this natural asset it added greater power, increasing the length of each step to the point where in a 100-yard race he saved an entire stride, which was 7 feet.

Frank Wykoff had remarkable natural acceleration at the start of his race. Coming out of his holes he used the longest stride of any sprinter we have had at Southern California. The big problem in his case was to get his finish as strong as his first 60 yards, which reminded veteran track followers of the flying first 60 of Arthur Duffey. At first Wykoff had no gather, but we developed it as soon as possible and once he had it he had no fear of any competitor in the final drive at the tape.

Frank made perfect starts and led the field all the way on the two occasions when he was caught in the 100 in the world's record of 9.4 seconds during the 1930 season, but for a time a few skeptics still refused to believe that he could match his gather with that of any of the outstanding driving runners of his day.

In 1931 he proved his finishing ability as well as his starting qualities so often that even the most dubious finally became convinced. In winning the I.C.A.A.A.A. 100-yard dash in Philadelphia he was behind Eddie Tolan, one of the most terrific finishers in the history of sprinting, at the 80-yard mark. At this point he summoned a gather that brought him to the front in spite of Tolan's closing drive. He also won the N.C.A.A. championship again this season and made it a grand slam for 1931 by taking the national A.A.U. century title.

Wykoff's race in the latter meet was the fastest 100-yard dash I have ever seen, Olympic games and world's record performances notwithstanding. Wykoff was off to one of his customary quick pickups, coasted slightly to the lead for a time, and then called upon a finishing burst that put him so far ahead of a great field of sprinters that I knew he had turned in sensational time. Well behind him in order were Emmett Toppino of Loyola of New Orleans, Eddie Tolan of Michigan, and Cy Leland, running for the Olympic Club of San Francisco. Unplaced was another great star in Ralph Metcalfe.

When I checked with the clockers I found that four of the official and alternate timers—there were about eight of them on this race—had caught Wykoff at 9.3 seconds, which had beaten his world's mark. Other watches had 9.4 and 9.5. Timers sometimes won't believe their own watches and they finally settled on 9.5 seconds, which was the highest figure caught by anyone, as the official mark for his race.

In helping Wykoff develop his finish, I found a problem somewhat different from the one that faced us in Charley Borah's case. Borah needed leg drive. Wykoff already had it. We could use longer steps on the part of Borah but it was inadvisable to experiment too much with Wykoff's stride because he was already using a good one. Wykoff's hip and shoulder swing also was vigorous and there was little improvement possible there. He was already a splendid runner when he came out of high school in 1928, and being ever an ardent foe of overcoaching I had no desire to make much change in his natural style.

But there were two ways in which I found that Wykoff could be helped in his last 20 yards. One concerned his breathing and the other was purely psychological. Although his breathing was easy and natural, which is a good thing, it frequently varied. A regular dependable breathing habit was needed in his case and we found that if he took a breath at the 80-yard mark it helped him to a lift in the final dash for the finish line.

Frank also needed a mental boost for his gather. Although my booming baritone might not get me anywhere at the Metropolitan Opera House, I found it had a stimulating effect on Frank. Above the roar of the crowd, he needed a man in authority to roar a command at the time and place for his final kick.

It was no trick at all to see that Wykoff was reminded of his breath and got his psychological jolt because both things could be done at the same time. Just before the 100 started I would find a seat low in the stands, next to the rail if possible, at the 75-yard mark. When the race got under way and my boy flashed by, I would yell "Frank!" at the top of my lungs. There wasn't time for anything else, but it was all that Frank seemed to need. It reminded him of the breath he must take and at the same time gave him a mental kick in the pants that sent him home like a scared rabbit.

62

You never can tell from an athlete's build how he develops his speed. On a freshman team at Southern California one year we had two sprinters, Jim Abbott, who was 6 feet 4 inches in height, and Foy Draper, who was 5 feet 5 inches tall. Believe it or not, Draper had the longer stride of the two. Abbott got along on leg speed, Draper on a lengthy leg reach.

Draper was able to take a long stride because he had the best hip action of any sprinter we have ever had at Southern California. He had a natural hip swing that required nothing from a coach but to be let alone. In fact, I never even mentioned hips to him. There would have been no point in making him self-conscious of a sprinting asset he didn't even need to think about because it was a gift from nature.

What Draper did need was more leg speed, the sprinting aid that little men usually come with naturally instead of long stride. To develop this, we called for many short dashes day after day. With these short sprints had to be long practice in relaxation, since so much effort was being put in speeding up the movement of his legs.

Draper was very faithful in his training. At the first sign of tenseness he would shake loose from it. Frequently at the height of a race he could be seen running with his arms dangling like those of a puppet and his head flopping from side to side as though he had no muscles in his neck.

Concentration on relaxation enabled him to finish his races with terrific drive. Although he took much longer to get in shape than most sprinters, the effort was worth while, for among his accomplishments were championships in junior national, Pacific Coast Conference, and I.C.A.A.A.A. competition and a place on the American 400-meter relay team that set a world's record of 39.8 seconds in winning at the 1936 games.

Many other examples could be cited to show how each sprinter presents a particular problem or a series of problems. Ordinarily the needs are easily apparent. Occasionally, though, the situation is not so simple and a worried coach finds he needs the deductive reasoning of a Sherlock Holmes.

The main thing from the coaching standpoint is to study the boy and his natural running gifts. Then sit down and do a bit of thinking. Don't experiment blindly and upset the athlete.

And now for a final brief summary on sprint training.

General conditioning to build a sturdy but not muscle-bound body comes first. Walking and exercises should be a part of the conditioning program not only during the preliminary period but throughout the season of competition.

The exercises that feature stretching, bouncing, and lifting the knees and the bicycle pedaling motion while lying on the back are those most helpful to the sprinter. Strong stomach muscles are needed and raising the legs while lying on the back will help build them up.

For a general conditioner of the torso, nothing is any simpler or more effective than daily pull-ups on a horizontal bar and push-ups from the floor.

Starts should never be practiced early in the training program and never during cold weather. Fast running should not be tried until plenty of preliminary time has been given to walking, jogging, and wind sprints.

Jogging should not be overdone but wind sprints are always good. They consist of walking, jogging, running, and working up to a short sprint, then slowing down to a walk and repeating the operation.

By giving the fastest men handicaps to make up in practice, the best runners will not develop habits of loafing and everyone will try harder.

Training programs during the competitive season should be carefully worked out by the coach on the basis of what the athlete needs; no cut and dried schedule should be attempted. If the athlete is going to compete on Saturday afternoon, he should rest and stay off his feet as much as possible all day Friday and Saturday morning. On all other days he should go through his stretching and general conditioning exercises as well as whatever has been planned for him on the track.

A typical training schedule during the week would include jogging and a few wind sprints on Monday; from six to ten starts and from one to three 220-yard dashes at a breezing rather than sprinting pace on Tuesday; more starts with the candidate sprinting from 30 to 50 yards and winding up his heaviest day of training with a series of wind sprints or a 300-yard dash on Wednesday; short sprints up to 50 yards on Thursday; and rest on Friday.

It is the coach's job to determine the condition of his athlete, to get him in shape, and to keep him there. Hard training may be indicated for a time but once at his peak, the athlete should not be overworked.

When the athlete goes to his marks, the coach should have prepared him so that he has splendid general physical condition, a theoretical and practical knowledge of form and technique, a store of nervous energy, and a combination of determination and self-confidence.

The sprinter here is in full stride, driving off his right toe. Note the body angle with the heel, hips, shoulder, and back of the head in a straight line. The thigh is lifted to develop a long stride and also to be in position to come down hard for the next forward drive.

The runner has just bounced, or sprung, from the tip of his toe. As his left thigh is raised, his foreleg swings forward and reaches out. The shoulders are loose, swinging easily to balance the hips. The left foot is coming down at an angle that will cause it to land on the toe.

The left leg lands without any "locking" of the knee. To eliminate waste motion and delay, there is practically no kick-up of the back leg. Despite the change in the position of the legs since the first picture, the body angle from hips to head remains the same.

The toe strikes the ground with a relaxed ankle, cushioning the landing and putting the foot in position for the rebound or forward spring. This picture and the two that follow demonstrate the development of bounce and leg drive. The shoulders, arms, and hands are always relaxed.

The runner's body is bounding forward through the springing action of the foot. As the right hip comes forward for the next stride, there is a moderate shoulder swing for balance. Observe how swiftly the right leg has been carried forward since the previous picture.

The forward drive off the left leg is completed as it straightens out with explosive force. The shoulders and hips have now reached their greatest point of swing. The right foreleg is completely relaxed as it swings out to lengthen the stride. For a fraction of a second in the midst of each stride the runner's feet leave the ground.

The right foot is coming down fast for the next spring forward. Because little time should be wasted sailing through the air, overstriding must be avoided. The runner is reaching out for a stride of slightly more than 7 feet, but he is also endeavoring to reach his maximum in leg speed.

Again the runner is ready to hit the ground for the next forward spring without locking the knee. His excellent relaxation is apparent even in his face and neck muscles. The sprinter pictured in this series is Mickey Anderson, national junior 100-meter champion at 10.5 seconds in 1939.

IV

THE QUARTER MILE

As far back as the gay nineties, Maxie Long of Columbia showed the track and field world that the quarter mile was a sprint and not a run, but no one believed him. Long won the national 440-yard championship three times in a row, in 1898, 1899, and 1900, but, unfortunately for the development of later quarter-milers for many years, no one considered it significant that in 1899 he was also 220-yard champion and that in 1900 he was national titleholder at 100 yards.

The idea that the quarter mile was sort of an orphan distance race persisted until the Olympic games of 1924 when track followers were given the eye opener that caused them to look at the event in a new light.

It all came about because of the religious scruples of a sprinter on Great Britain's team. Eric Liddell, great little Scotch athlete, was the reason. Entered in the 100-meter dash in the Paris Olympics, he discovered that the trials were to be run on Sunday. A conscientious young man studying for the ministry, Liddell withdrew from the race because he did not wish to run on the Sabbath. In order to have some part in the Olympics as a member of Great Britain's team, he entered the 400-meter run instead.

Knowing nothing of the accepted strategy of the time in racing over the metric quarter-mile course, Liddell treated it as though it were just a long sprint. He gave it everything he had in the opening drive, "floated" through the middle part, and then "gunned it" again in the final stages. Liddell's performance of winning in the Olympic record time of 47.6 seconds was a revelation, especially in the light of earlier incidents.

One of them, of course, was Long's sensational 440 mark of 47 seconds flat on a race-track straightaway in 1900. And the other was the fact that J. E. (Ted) Meredith of the University of Pennsylvania had also tried to show track experts that the

68

quarter mile was essentially a sprint when he had run his 47.4-second official world's record race in 1916.

Probably because Long and Meredith were considered by the average track athlete to be superrunners, their times were so awe-inspiring that 440 men of the day didn't stop to consider that it might be possible to match their marks by running almost wide open from the starting gun.

When Liddell showed them how comparatively simple it was to run the distance in time heretofore considered phenomenal, runners and coaches finally became convinced that a quarter-miler could sprint most of his distance. Henceforth in championship competition there proved to be little chance for the men who tried to stride through the race at a semidistance pace.

In considering Meredith's record, it also began to occur to them that the versatile record-smasher had been a sprinter of no mean ability as well as a middle-distance star. Like Long, he had shown them how to run the race, but no one had believed it.

As in sprinting, athletes do not have to be of any particular type to become successful at the 440-yard distance. Liddell and Bill Carr, the 1932 Olympic champion who won the 400-meter title in the present Olympic record time of 46.2 seconds, were small men. Ben Eastman, who set the present 440-yard record of 46.4 seconds was tall. Archie Williams, winner of the 400-meter dash in the 1936 Olympics and holder of the present official 400-meter record of 46.1 seconds was of medium height. Erwin Miller, national champion in 1939, was the power type of runner with bulging leg muscles. Ray Malott, national champion in 1937 and 1938, and Grover Klemmer, 1940 champ, were slender and willowy.

Harold Smallwood, national champion in 1936, and John Woodruff, a half-miler with a number of 440 championships to his credit, were both big men, 6 feet 2 inches in height and around 180 pounds in weight. On the other hand, Vic Williams, national champion in 1930 and 1931, and Ivan Fuqua, holder of the same title in 1933 and 1934, were 150-pounders.

Most of the outstanding quarter-milers of recent years got their start as sprinters and their first fast marks were made in the 220-yard dash. Bill Carr, Archie Williams, and Ray Malott all were sprinters in their high school days. At the peak of their 440 fame they could still successfully double in the 220 and defeat most of the leading dash men at this distance.

Although we now classify the 440 as a dash instead of a run, an athlete to be a topnotcher here must have great stamina. Most half-milers, therefore, can drop down to the quarter mile and turn in good performances. Many of the 440 champions of the past have been what we would classify as the half-miler type of runner.

Ben Eastman, former world's record holder in the 880-yard run, was the half-miler type who made outstanding time in the 440. However, like other quarter-milers of this type who are not primarily sprinters, he had to develop sprinting speed before attaining excellence in the quarter. In the race in which he set the quarter-mile mark of 46.4 seconds, he was unofficially timed at 21.3 seconds for the first 220.

But even though Eastman became a record holder in the 440 and was the outstanding example of the half-miler type running the quarter mile, he could not match in competition the pace of Bill Carr, the outstanding sprinting type, in the 440. Three times straight in the season of 1932—in the I.C.A.A.A.A. championships, the national championships, and the Olympic games— Carr, the natural sprinter, won by a yard from Eastman, who was primarily a half-miler.

John Woodruff, 1936 Olympic champion in the 800-meter run, dropped down to the quarter mile on numerous occasions to turn in exceptional performances and many track followers predicted that he would eventually break Eastman's record at this distance. But even though he had exceptional speed and won three straight I.C.A.A.A.A. championships at 47 seconds flat, he was never able to live up to such expectations, for he was primarily the half-miler type.

Although fast 880 men are usually also good quarter-milers, we find that as a general rule, the 440 distance is dominated by those who excel first of all as sprinters. The principle demonstrated by Eric Liddell in the 1924 games and reaffirmed by the Olympic victories of Bill Carr and Archie Williams in 1932 and 1936 seems destined to hold true from now on. Runners who do not possess outstanding natural speed at the outset of their

70

track careers should not be discouraged from the quarter mile, however.

The blazing speed of a Frank Wykoff or a Jesse Owens is not necessary for 440 running and most aspirants can be taught to develop sufficient speed for a good quarter mile.

National champions Vic Williams, Harold Smallwood, and Erwin Miller were far from being speed burners in their early track careers; Ben Eastman likewise showed little aptitude for sprinting when he started running. Yet all of them developed speed to the point where they could cover the first 220 of their races with the dash of a sprinter.

Glancing back over the records of old 440 champions we find that quarter-milers have developed a lot of speed since H. W. Stevens of Williams won the first I.C.A.A.A.A. race at this distance in 1876 in 56 seconds. In national championship competition, the first title race went to Edward Merritt of the New York Athletic Club in 54½ seconds.

Early in the days of the national championship meets L. E. Myers of the Manhattan Athletic Club dominated the event by winning it six years in a row, from 1879 to 1884. Myers was one of those versatile stars who could take on all comers at any distance up to a half mile. In addition to his quarter-mile victories, he was also national champion at 100 yards in 1880 and 1881, at 220 yards in 1879, 1880, and 1881, and 880 yards in 1879 and 1880.

Myers was the first man to break 50 seconds in the national meet, running the event in 49.4 seconds in 1881. No other athlete was able to get below 50 seconds in national championship competition until T. E. Burke of the Boston Athletic Association hit 49.6, 48.8, and 49 flat in his three straight victories in the meets of 1895, 1896, 1897.

For a long time the best quarter-mile mark on record was held by Wendell Baker of Harvard. He was I.C.A.A.A.A. champion in 54.4 seconds in 1885; the following year he was credited with the time of 47¾ seconds.

This mark stood until Maxie Long's race of 47 seconds in 1900. Three times national champion and Olympic 400-meter winner in 49.4 seconds in the 1900 games in Paris, he was given a chance to see how fast he could go under unusual but highly favorable conditions. A 440-yard course was measured on a race-track straightaway at Guttenberg, N. J., and on October 4 he went the route wide open in 47 seconds flat. Timers stationed at intervals en route came up with marks showing that Long attempted to sprint all the way in his record try. At 350 yards he was caught in 36.4 seconds and at 400 yards his time was 42.2 seconds. Although there are no official world's records at these freak distances, Long's marks for them are still in the record books under "noteworthy performances."

Championship time in national open and national intercollegiate meets remained around 50 seconds until Meredith came along with his fast race. An exception was in the case of C. D. Reidpath of Syracuse, who won the I.C.A.A.A.A. title in 50 seconds flat in 1910 and then cut his mark to 48 seconds in the 1912 meet. In 1912 he also added an Olympic victory to his collection of honors by winning the 400-meter dash in the then Olympic record time of 48.2 seconds. Meredith was timed in 47 flat for a quarter mile in the national championships of 1915 but the mark was not allowed because of a wind. He was so outstanding in the event, however, that he was destined eventually to get a mark entitled to recognition, and in the I.C.A.A.A.A. championships of 1916 he sped the 440-yard distance in 47.4 seconds. On the same day he won the I.C.A.A.A.A. 880-yard run in the meet record time of 1:53.

Because Long's 47 flat time had not been made under the usual conditions, it was not taken too seriously by the International Amateur Athletic Federation when it was organized in 1913, and soon after Meredith ran his 47.4-second race, this mark was recognized by the federation as the official world's record. It also lasted as the world's 400-meter record until 1928 when long-legged Emerson (Bud) Spencer of Stanford ran the metric quarter mile in 47 seconds.

For 15 years after Meredith's record race, his time was scarcely threatened. Then two record-making runners came along in Ben Eastman of Stanford and Vic Williams of Southern California. These boys were shortly followed by Bill Carr of Pennsylvania, two outstanding Negro stars in James LuValle of the University of California at Los Angeles and Archie Williams of the University of California at Berkeley, and many other boys capable of 47-second time, among them Ivan Fuqua of the University of

Indiana, Glen Hardin of Louisiana State University, Edward O'Brien of Syracuse, Ray Malott of Stanford, Harold Smallwood and Erwin Miller of Southern California, and the powerful John Woodruff of Pittsburgh.

Quarter-mile competition in 1931 was featured by the record-equaling races of Eastman and Williams. For the first time in 15 years, the 440-yard dash was run in 47.4 seconds when Eastman defeated Williams in a Stanford-Southern California meet in Los Angeles. Two weeks later the boys met again in the I.C.A.A.A.A. championships in Philadelphia and this time Williams was the victor in 47.4, making the western runners joint holders of the world's record with Meredith.

The next year national quarter-mile competition sizzled with the races between Eastman and Carr. In a record try at Palo Alto, Eastman cut the 440-yard world's mark to 46.4, but Carr became the world's record holder for 400 meters when he defeated Eastman in 46.2 seconds in the Olympic Games in Los Angeles. Carr lost this record to Archie Williams in 1936 when the latter turned the 400-meter distance in 46.1 seconds in a heat in the National Collegiate Athletic Association championships. Williams went on to win the Olympic games that year in 46.5 seconds, leaving the 46.2-second Olympic record still in possession of Carr.

In eleven Olympic championships through the 1936 games, American 400-meter men had been beaten only three times. Yankee supremacy at this distance had been unchallenged since Liddell's Olympic victory in 1924, but in the summer of 1939 Rudolf Harbig, a twenty-five-year-old athlete of Dresden, Germany, brought Europe to the fore with a series of sensational races at both the 400- and 800-meter distances.

After breaking the 800-meter world's record in a German-Italian meet at Milan in July, a month later he ran the 400 meters in 46 seconds flat in the Frankfort Jubilee Festival meet at Frankfort on the Main. As Harbig had previously broken the world's 800-meter record with the sensational time of 1:46.6, he seems to refute our assertion that quarter-milers must be primarily sprinters. An investigation of his record, however, shows that the foundation for his middle-distance ability came from his sprinting speed.

Lee Orr of Washington State College, who was the leading

quarter-miler of the 1940 season, built the foundation for his 440 success upon an earlier sprinting career. Orr, a driving type of runner, who won the Princeton Invitational quarter mile at 46.8 seconds and the Pacific Coast Conference 440 at 46.9 seconds and who was also N.C.A.A. champion, had placed fifth for Canada in the 1936 Olympic games 200-meter dash.

Other outstanding quarter-milers of the 1940 season were Grover Klemmer, a University of California freshman who won the national senior A.A.U. 400-meter dash in 47 seconds flat, and Cliff Bourland, a University of Southern California freshman who was national junior A.A.U. 400-meter champion in 47.4 seconds.

Sprinting ability and physical condition, the latter being necessary to sustain one's speed over a long distance, are still the two main essentials, although it should be noted that quarter-mile sprinting is of a different type from that in the short dashes. In the 100 and 220 the runners put forth a violent explosive effort in attempting to attain their utmost speed during as much of the race as possible. In the quarter mile the sprinting pace is more even and rhythmic. The runner seeks to maintain his speed without putting forth his maximum amount of exertion.

The two general classifications of 440 men—the half-miler and the sprinter types—were mentioned early in this discussion of running the quarter mile because it is wise to determine at the start of conditioning the class into which the candidate fits. Each type runs the race differently. Therefore each type must prepare a little differently during his training period.

Experienced runners always cover the first 220 yards faster than the second furlong. If you will time a 50-second quarter-miler of the sprinter type, you will find that he usually runs the first half of his race in close to 24.5 seconds and the second half in 25.5. If the runner is the half-miler type, his first furlong will usually be run 2 seconds faster than the second 220, and his furlong times will be approximately 24 and 26 seconds.

A good general rule is to train the half-miler type to run the opening 220 yards 2 seconds faster than the second furlong and to coach the sprinter type to cover his first 220 only 1 second faster than his last one.

Perhaps you might think that the sprinting type should

74

endeavor to get out in front and stay there and that it should be the half-miler type that should lay back. It is the other way because the sprinter after starting fast can drop down to "coasting" or "floating" at a good rate of speed while his opponent is working hard to hold the pace. Thus when it comes time to turn on the heat in the final 50 yards of the race, he has conserved his energy enough to make his superior sprinting ability really count.

The half-miler type must count on his stride more than speed. Since he cannot keep up if the race turns into a sprinting match at the finish, he needs to kill off his opposition early in the running or build up a lead that the sprinters cannot catch up with at the finish.

Because the quarter-mile race is really a sprint, it should be run in lanes just as the 400-meter race is handled in the Olympics. Unfortunately, however, lanes are rarely used in this event. This means trouble for runners who do not use good headwork and lay a foundation in training for the proper kind of race.

Most of our 440 races today are run either around a quarter-mile oval or are started on a 220-yard straightaway. In either case, the first part of the race means a battle for the pole, the distance-saving inside lane around the curve. The race is so short that much depends upon the runner's position when he hits the first turn. He doesn't necessarily need to be in the lead but he should be taking the short way around close to the inside lane and should be free of interference.

Runners who allow themselves to get into a box or pocket on the turns will usually find those who have escaped interference piling up such a lead that they can never overcome it when once they do find racing room.

Since the quarter-mile dash is over so quickly that there is little time to make up for mental or physical mistakes, runners must not only plan their campaigns ahead but must be constantly on the alert after the race has started. Trouble can usually be escaped by early speed and this is one of the principal advantages that runners of the sprinter type have in this race.

Fouls are more frequent in the quarter mile than in any other race since there is so much jamming on the turns as the runners seek favorable positions. Officials seem to expect this crowding and fouls are rarely called, particularly when the fields are large.

Consequently the runners themselves must be continually on the alert to prevent being knocked off stride by bumping or accidental fouls.

For this reason, smart 440 runners when in danger of being run over usually carry their elbows spread out far enough to protect themselves from being jostled by competitors. This is often necessary, particularly in the opening break for the pole when runners in outside lanes may be overanxious and crowd more than the rules allow in seeking to work over to inside positions. Deliberate elbowing of opponents is unfair and shows a lack of sportsmanship, but it is perfectly justifiable for runners to keep their elbows high enough to protect themselves when in danger of jamming.

Regardless of what type of runner a 440 man may be, to make good time he needs a strong initial burst of speed. This first hard drive should be maintained for at least 35 yards, just as it is in running the 220.

Despite the fact that it may appear that heavy exertion might tire the athlete right at the beginning of a hard race, it will be found that this opening burst of speed takes little out of the runner. Nervous energy stored up for the start will carry him through the first drive with little if any loss of physical strength.

The quarter-mile candidate should train much of his time with the sprinters. He must realize, though, that the speed he needs is not of exactly the same type as that employed in the 100- and 220-yard dashes.

Because the 440 man's speed is not of the explosive, quick-burning type, it follows that the quarter-miler can stand much more arduous training than the sprinter. The sprinter can lose his edge if he tries too much to develop endurance. The quarter-miler needs to combine endurance with speed and should have some of the training of distance men as well as his sprint work.

First of all, the quarter-miler can stand much more preliminary jogging than the sprinter. Although it is unwise to allow 100-yard dash men to jog more than a half mile at any one time, part of the training for a quarter-miler calls for him to jog as far as a mile and occasionally 2 miles.

In developing his running form, the quarter-miler follows the training methods of the sprinter, taking his regular body-building

76

exercises and running many short sprints. When he begins to round into shape, his running form should resemble that of other sprinters except that his stride should be longer and his arms should be carried with a greater swing.

The quarter-miler should rarely run the full distance in practice. His best training distance is the 220. Running many furlongs will help develop endurance without sacrificing speed. A good procedure for the quarter-miler in training is to run a fairly fast 220, then walk back to the starting line and run another at the same speed as the first. Doing this frequently will be as beneficial as running the full 440 distance without stopping and will not sap the athlete's strength.

To the frequent question as to how an athlete should run the quarter mile, I have to answer that there is no one and only right way to do it. The method must be suited to the type of athlete. If he is a sprinter, he will get best results after a fast pickup, a period of "floating," and then a final kick in the last 50 to 100 yards. If he is in danger of being outsprinted by his opponents, his most effective means of seeking victory may be to attempt a uniform pace throughout or to run the opening 220 to 300 yards at such a pace that his rivals can never catch him.

The ideal manner to run the race in championship time is to cover the first furlong at very close to top speed, then stride through the next 100 to 120 yards at a slower pace, and finally to pull up to top speed over the last 100. The slowing-down process at the end of the first 220 is necessary to give the runner a chance to recuperate from the fatigue of the first burst of speed.

Often to the fan this slowing down isn't perceptible because the runner's momentum from his opening 220 seemingly carries him along at the same pace. But it is a vital part of the runner's racing strategy, for he must have a brief period in which to summon all his vitality for the hardest test of the race—the final 100 yards.

Known as the "man-killer" of track and field because of the tremendous energy it consumes in a short space of time, the quarter mile demands perfect condition on the part of those who would run it in fast time. The 440 candidate, therefore, needs to start his training many months before actual competition. Failure to lay the proper physical groundwork for this event can put a severe strain on an athlete's constitution and can take all the pleasure out of running it.

Despite its "man-killing" aspects, the quarter mile is real fun for the boy who is in proper shape. The athlete who has a sound background in training can apparently run himself completely out in a 440 dash and yet recuperate so rapidly and thoroughly that he can come back an hour or so later and make even faster time in a quarter-mile lap in the mile relay.

Important in all track and field events in preliminary as well as regular season training, body-building exercises are doubly necessary for the 440 men.

Let us say that a young man has decided that when track season comes around in the spring he wants to run the quarter mile. To get himself into proper physical condition for the hard competition he will undergo, he should start his exercising and preliminary track work in the fall.

A most important set of exercises for him are those that emphasize the stretching of leg and hip muscles and the strengthening of abdominal muscles. The exercises for this are simple. From either a standing or sitting position, bend forward as far as possible at the waist and then return. Lying on the back, raise the legs to a perpendicular position and then lower them slowly. This type of exercise should be done daily and often. The building up of the abdominal muscles cannot be overemphasized, for these muscles have a great deal to do with lifting up the thighs in running.

Another splendid exercise is the one used a great deal by hurdlers to stretch the leg and back muscles. Sit on the ground with the right leg straight forward and with the left thigh at right angles to it. The left knee is flexed with the toe pointing straight back. This is the leg position of a high hurdler when clearing the barrier. While the legs are in this position, reach over with the left arm and stretch straight out, touching the right toe. The same exercise can then be done using the opposite foot and arm.

Quarter-milers can also get much valuable leg stretching on the parallel bars. Sitting on the parallels, which spread his legs apart, he can loosen his hips and crotch by twisting and turning exercises

High kicking as practiced so religiously by high jumpers will also loosen the legs and hips. Raising up on the toes and stretching will help strengthen the feet.

The ankles in particular should be well exercised. A good way to do this is to stand on the heels on the edge of a stairway, chair, or table with most of the foot protruding. First point the toes down and then slowly bring them up as high as possible.

As a general body-building exercise the good old ordinary pull-ups on the horizontal bar should be practiced every day. This "chinning the bar" should be done with the backs of the hands toward the face.

Long walks, taken with a springy step that raises the walker up on his toes with every stride, are very important. Every quarter-miler should walk at least 2 miles a day; many splendid runners make a practice of walking from 6 to 8 miles. Walking when properly done not only builds up the legs but does much to give a runner the proper hip swing and sense of relaxation.

Exercising is so important that it could well be undertaken every day in the year, except of course on days of competition and only lightly, if at all, on the days before competition.

Along with his regular exercises in the fall, the 440 man should go out on the track with his spiked shoes twice a week. If he cannot train out of doors because of bad weather, he should still practice on spikes on an indoor track.

On one day he should jog three or four laps. On another day he should go through a routine of walk, jog, and run, walk, jog, and run. He should be very careful to start his track work easily and work into a faster pace at a very gradual rate.

When the candidate's legs begin to get into shape from this light track work, he is ready to swing into wind sprints. He should walk, jog, run, and sprint 20 yards at full speed, slowing down to a walk and then repeating. At first, two or three wind sprints a day are sufficient. When a runner begins to round into good condition, he can cover a mile in this manner, running a series of eight wind sprints by taking two to each lap around the track.

Wind sprints are the dash man's best early season developer. The quarter-miler not only uses them to develop his speed like

79

The quarter-miler hits the ground with his ankle well relaxed, the heel almost touching the ground as the jar of the landing is cushioned. The runner here could get along with less kick-up of his back leg. The body lean from hips to shoulder is similar to that of the sprinter.

The runner rocks up on the ball of his left foot which springs him forward for his next stride. He is starting a quick lift of his right thigh with the foreleg swinging out easily from the knee. No strain is shown on his face and the relaxation is also apparent in his neck and shoulders.

The left leg straightens out with a snap as the runner gets his drive off his left toe. The rebound of the left leg is aided by the lift of the right thigh. The angle of forward lean varies with runners and this athlete moves with a somewhat erect torso after the Finnish style.

As the runner reaches out for a good stride, he completes a smooth swing of his right hip. The stride length of a quarter-miler is about the same as that of a sprinter, usually varying between 6 feet 6 inches and 7 feet 3 inches. The stride of this runner is 7 feet.

Although the position of the right toe looks as though it will cause a flat-footed landing, the bend of the knee and the body angle will bring the runner down on the ball of his foot. His loose shoulders help the body rotation, which in turn assists in the hip swing.

The bend in the knee as well as the relaxed foot helps take off the shock of hitting the ground. Although there is more back kick than necessary, no harm is done if the leg is well relaxed. Many great runners, among them John Woodruff, show this much kick-up, although it is not recommended.

The bend in the right knee continues and the leg will not be straightened until it is in position for the forward drive. Because of the fatiguing distance of his event, the 440 man cannot get the sprinter's extreme rebound from the ball of the foot throughout all of his race.

Good knee lift is shown in the reach for the stride. Lacking some of the extreme spring off his toes that the sprinter strives for, the quarter-miler develops a good hip swing and high knee action to lengthen his stride. The runner here is Howard Upton, who has run the 440 in 47 seconds.

the sprint runner but also runs more of them in succession than the dasher in order to build up his endurance.

We have noted throughout this discussion of quarter-milers that there are two types, the sprinter and the half-miler. It is important to take into consideration what type you are dealing with when midseason training is reached. The sprinter type cannot stand so much work as the half-miler type. Like the regular dash man, if given too much he will lose some of his speed and fine edge. The other type can stand longer training races and needs them since his hopes for victory depend mainly on fast pace and stamina.

In suggesting a training schedule, the warning is appended that methods must be suited to the athlete's type and also to his constitution. Therefore, there can be no definite program that one can arbitrarily say should be given for all quarter-milers. However, average requirements for midseason training after condition has been reached involve a schedule much like this: Monday, stamina work of a ¾-mile run or a mile run, or three or four laps of wind sprints; Tuesday, several 220's at three-quarters speed, the number of furlongs varying from two to four according to the runner's condition, and starts with the sprinters; Wednesday, the hardest training race of the week, either a 330 or 660, and more starts; Thursday, light work, short sprints of from 30 to 50 yards and more practice on starts if needed; Friday, rest for Saturday competition.

Exercises should be taken daily before the running part of the program, and training sessions that do not include distance work should be topped off by an easy lap around the track.

V

THE HALF MILE

With the present tendency to turn the half mile into a sprint or semisprint, speed is a major essential for 880 men just as it is for quarter-milers.

A half-miler running in the old-fashioned way of jogging a lap and a half and then sprinting wouldn't finish within a full midiron shot of the runners in the modern-day 880. The pace is fast from start to finish and the athlete who can't turn in a speedy 220 will find himself in the embarrassing position of getting run over by the competitors in the next race.

Although Ted Meredith held the world's 880-yard record for ten years—from 1916 to 1926—the mark has been lowered frequently in recent seasons as half-milers of increasing sprinting ability have aimed at championship time. Meredith was the first runner of considerable sprinting ability to attack the 880 record. One of the greatest middle-distance stars of all time, he could turn in outstanding performances at any race from 220 yards to a mile.

Even though many seconds have been knocked off the 880 mark of 1:52.2 that he set in 1916, I am sure that, if he were running under the improved training methods and fired by the faster competition of the present day, he could hold his own with any of our current champions.

Going back into the past of 880 running, we find that in 1885 L. E. Myers ran the fastest half mile on record at that time when he turned the distance in 1:55.4. This is the same versatile athlete from the Manhattan Athletic Club of New York City who was mentioned in the preceding chapter as having held the national quarter-mile championship for six years as well as numerous national titles in the sprints. His record stood for ten years.

During this time there seem to have been few half miles run at better than 2 minutes until C. H. Kilpatrick of the New York

Athletic Club came along in 1894. National champion in 1894, 1895, and 1896, in times ranging from 1:55.8 to 1:57.6, Kilpatrick cracked the mark in the season of 1895 with a race of 1:53.4. Again there followed almost a decade during which there were few fast marks in the half mile.

The next athlete to run the distance in creditable time was J. D. Lightbody. In 1904 he lowered the Olympic 800-meter record to 1:56. Primarily a miler, he doubled up in the 1904 Olympics to take the 1,500-meter championship, and he repeated his victory at the latter distance in the 1906 Olympics.

Succeeding Lightbody as national half-mile champion in 1906 came Mel W. Sheppard of the Irish-American Athletic Club of New York, who enjoyed a long and glorious reign in the middle distances. Sheppard won both the 800-meter and 1,500-meter championships in the 1908 Olympics, sending the record in the former distance down to 1:52.8. Although he won five national titles at 880 yards, taking them in 1906, 1907, 1908, 1911, and 1912, Sheppard never enjoyed the distinction of holding the world's half-mile record.

Fourteen years after Kilpatrick set his 880 record, it was broken in 1909 by E. Lunghi, who was credited with a mark of 1:52.8, in a race in Canada.

When Meredith entered the 880 field, sprinting as the basis of fast half-mile running was given its introduction. The fast University of Pennsylvania boy went out in the 1912 Olympics to lower Sheppard's world and Olympic mark in the 800-meter run to 1:51.9. Then for a time his greatest accomplishments were in the 440, in which he was national champion in 1914 and 1915. In 1916 he reached his peak and the speed work from his quarter-miling sent him to a new world's half-mile mark of 1:52.2. He set this record in May of 1916. To show that his speed made him the king of middle-distance runners of his day, he established a world's quarter-mile record of 47.4 seconds in October of the same year. For 10 years no one could combine the speed and endurance that had been possessed by Meredith to threaten seriously his half-mile record.

Half-milers in general were running much faster than they had during the preceding decade, among the leading American stars during this period being Earl Eby and Alan Helffrich, who won

84

various national and intercollegiate championships; but it remained for a European, Dr. Otto Peltzer, to be the first to crack Meredith's mark. Peltzer lowered the record to 1:51.6 and it stood there for several years although it was frequently closely approached by numerous athletes, among them Lloyd Hahn, Phil Edwards, Ed Genung, Charles Hornbostel, and Glenn Cunningham.

Ben Eastman of Stanford, who could start his half mile with a terrifically fast 220, cracked the mark with a 1:50.9 race in 1932, and two years later he made the official record book with a half-mile race in 1:49.8.

When this record was set it seemed to be destined to last a long time. Eastman, however, had demonstrated again that the race was no longer a distance event but a semisprint, and just three years later, in 1937, Elroy Robinson of Fresno State College cut the record down to 1:49.6. Robinson's 880 mark also went into the books as a record for 800 meters, which is 5.1 yards less than a half mile.

Light-footed Sydney Wooderson of England soon cut deeply into Robinson's 800-meter figure with a race of 1:48.4 in 1938, and the following year husky Rudolf Harbig of Germany was credited with the sensational time of 1:46.6 in a German-Italian meet in Milan, Italy. The difference in time between running 800 meters and 880 yards is usually figured at from $6/10$ to $8/10$ second. Harbig's half-mile time, had he run 5.1 yards farther to stretch his 800 meters into 880 yards, can therefore be approximated at from 1:47.2 to 1:47.4.

Close followers of track and field for some time had been saying that the 880- and 800-meters marks were far too slow in comparison with other world's records; after Harbig's amazing performance they could well have risen in a body and said, "I told you so."

Harbig had just the background one would expect of a record-breaking middle-distance runner. His first serious track work at the age of nineteen was cross-country running. Not liking this particularly and finding that he had considerable natural speed, he dropped down to the middle distances and then to the sprints. Thus with a foundation of cross-country work to build endurance and several years of sprinting to develop speed, at the age of

85

twenty-five, when middle-distance and distance runners are in their prime, he was ready for his sensational 800-meter time.

One can call Harbig a sprinter without fear of exaggeration as he had run 100 meters in 10.6 seconds and 200 meters in 21.5 seconds unofficially, and during the summer of 1939 he turned 400 meters in the record-breaking time of 46 seconds flat. Put that speed together with the stamina of a cross-country runner and the result was bound to be a record-smashing middle-distance performance.

Harbig has not been the only European to show unusual half-mile speed in recent years. It was the terrific competition of Mario Lanzi, an Italian coached by the veteran Boyd Comstock, that had much to do with Harbig's record feat in the Milan meet. Lanzi set the pace in the German-Italian race, running the first 200 meters at almost a sprint in 24 seconds and the first 600 meters in the excellent time of 1:20. He needed only a final 27-second 200 meters to finish in what would have been the world's record time of 1:47, but Harbig, following closely on the early pace, came through with a killing sprint to pass the Italian star and win in the unheard-of time of 1:46.6.

The principal reason why the half-mile record has never been lowered to where it should be is that the race has usually been neglected by our best athletes in the past. There have been few 880-yard specialists. Quarter-milers, like Meredith, have run up to it. Milers, like Lightbody and Sheppard, have run down to it. Eastman came along with a beautiful combination of sprinting speed and endurance and lowered the mark considerably. It is likely that he could have cut much more time off the mark had he not turned most of his attention to the quarter mile at the height of his running career, to the neglect of the half.

Robinson was one of the few 880 specialists that we have had and he showed what it is possible to do when a runner concentrates on this race. Even though he never seemed to have the speed or natural ability at this distance that Eastman had, he broke the latter's record with a 1:49.6 mark. Robinson, of course, had developed his speed to the point where he could run a fast 440, but he was essentially more of a pace runner than the sprinting type.

Since Robinson and Harbig made their respective record times at 880 yards and 800 meters, the two-lap race has been clipped off consistently at a much faster pace than it had been run in the past. During the 1940 season outstanding marks were recorded by at least a half-dozen runners.

Continuing in competition after leaving the University of Pittsburgh, John Woodruff turned in world's indoor marks of 1:47 for 800 meters and 1:47.7 for 880 yards in the Dartmouth Invitational Games. Later in the Compton Invitational meet, which is staged outdoors, he ran 800 meters in 1:48.6. Had he been running the 880-yard distance that night, he would have knocked Robinson's half-mile record down to about 1:49.3.

Ed Burrowes of Princeton, who was 1940 I.C.A.A.A.A. 880 champion, matched Eastman's former record time of 1:49.8 in winning the Princeton Invitational half mile. Campbell Kane of the University of Indiana; Charles Beetham, former Ohio State runner; James Kehoe of Washington, D. C.; Paul Moore of Stanford; and Jim Lightbody of Harvard were other outstanding performers of the 1940 season.

To make the best time, the 880 should be run like the 440, with the first half of the race being negotiated about 2 seconds faster than the second half. Thus a high school boy who aims at a 1:58 half mile should run the first lap in 58 seconds and the second lap in 60.

The timing of the first lap is extremely important. Therefore, one of the first things that a half-miler must learn is pace. Regardless of what the other competitors in the race are doing, he must know within a few tenths of a second the time of his first lap. Otherwise he might find himself badly fooled by an opponent who has been put in the race deliberately to mislead him by either drawing him into too fast a pace or holding him back to one that is too slow.

Because of the importance of pace in the half mile, the race is one in which teamwork is often employed. Pace setters are frequently used either to kill off the opposition or to set the proper rate of speed for a team mate. When used judiciously by a coach, a pace setter can be very valuable because the opposition can never know whether he has been sent out to set the right pace or a wrong one.

Often a coach has a runner who has yet to learn judgment of

pace but who can be depended upon for a good race if he covers the first 440 or 660 at the proper rate. If the coach has another runner on his team who knows pace, the latter can be sent out to "carry" the other athlete along at the right speed.

On the other hand, if the opposing runner or runners can be fooled into going too fast or too slow for their own good, a pace setter can sometimes be used to draw them out or hold them back and thus aid a team mate to victory.

In order not to be fooled, it is therefore imperative for a half-miler to know exactly how fast he is traveling. Then he will always be sure to turn in his best race. Also a pacemaker won't have to be wasted by his coach to show him the way and a pace setter of the opposing team will never be able to upset him.

Like the quarter-miler, the 880 man should run many short dashes to build up his speed. The 220 is a splendid distance for him in training. He can also stand to run many quarter miles in practice at the half-mile pace. This is a variation from the 440 man's training program as the latter rarely runs this distance during the week.

When the 880 candidate has trained himself to the point where he can turn out a fairly fast 440, the first quarter mile of his half-mile race can be run at a good clip without fatigue. For instance, the high school boy with his goal of a 1.58 half mile was mentioned. If he can develop himself to the point where he can run a quarter mile in 51 or 52 seconds, he will find it no trouble at all to breeze through the first lap of his 880 in the necessary 58 seconds.

As in the quarter mile, there can be a greater variation than the 2 seconds between the first and second halves of the race, depending on the type of runner. The boy who is not the sprinter type and cannot count on a fast finish naturally must set a faster pace, aiming to kill off the sprint of his rivals or to leave them so far behind in the early stages that they cannot catch him. The sprinter type can follow a conservative pace, knowing that he will have the speed to outrace his rivals at the finish.

Half-milers, like distance men, should finish well run out. They should so time their race that when they finish they know they have given every ounce of speed and energy they have to it. This business of running oneself out can make an ordeal of half-miling if the athlete is not in shape. In good condition, however, he can give everything to the race and despite his exhaustion at the finish make a quick recovery.

Naturally one has to force himself to the running-out process and for that reason the temperament of the athlete has much to do with successful middle-distance work.

It was pointed out in the opening chapter that past winners of the Olympic 800-meter race have all been either British or American runners. Racially they apparently have been strongly equipped with the bulldog tenacity that runners need for this grueling race. They have the determination to stay with a fast pace and the strength of will to call on tired muscles for the final finishing sprint that brought victory.

The course of training to run the half mile is similar to that used for 440 men except that a little more distance work is given. Preliminary work should start in the fall, just as it should for any track and field event. The same set of exercises that the quarter-miler uses should be on the program for the half-miler. These are the exercises that stress stretching and loosening of the leg muscles and the hips and crotch.

The bugaboo of running the half mile is the tendency to "tieup" in the home stretch. To prevent this, exercises that create loose, pliable, relaxed muscles are stressed. Exercises that tend to create heavy rather than pliable muscles should be avoided. Weight-lifting exercises are definitely harmful to track men.

There should not be too much work on the gymnasium apparatus, such as parallel bars, rings, and horizontal bar. These are good developers for the upper torso but when a runner is too heavily muscled from his waist up it is likely to increase his tendency to tie up when tired.

A good preseason sport for half-milers to take part in is basketball since the continual running in this game builds stamina. Tennis is also a satisfactory preliminary sport. Football is detrimental to distance running because the blocking involved overdevelops the shoulders and back. It also tends to create the heaviness in the legs that is common among weight lifters.

Although swimmers have to stress relaxation like track men, the muscular development brought about by much aquatic work is not good for runners. The overarm stroke will create shoulder and arm muscles that will tie up at the end of a distance race. Runners also need much more exercise in building abdominal muscles than swimming gives them.

The half-miler should never finish a race or a practice run with tired arms and shoulders. Pull-ups—chinning the bar—constitute a good daily exercise to give the proper muscular strength in this region.

For the abdominal muscles, simple bending exercises are good. The ground-stretching exercise of the hurdlers described in a previous chapter and the high kicking of the high jumpers are valuable in creating pliable muscles and loose joints.

Long walks and considerable jogging in the fall are necessary for the creation of the endurance needed by a half-miler. While the 440 man rarely jogs more than a mile in training, the half-miler can frequently jog 2 miles when his legs begin to get into shape.

Like the 440 man, the half-mile candidate should don his spikes and train on the track twice a week in the fall. One workout should be devoted to jogging from a mile to 2 miles. On alternate days he can go through the quarter-miler's routine of walk, jog, and run, walk, jog, and run. Later as his legs grow stronger and his wind gets better, he can swing into wind sprints, working up to a mile with two wind sprints to each 440-yard lap.

The old idea of preparing for the 880 was that the best training distance was 2 miles. Running this distance is all right, but it used to be overdone, with a resultant neglect of speed work. In present training methods the half-mile candidate is ready for his wind sprints and speed work just as soon as exercises, walking, and jogging have prepared his legs for it.

The 880 aspirant should remember from the first that his aim is to develop speed with relaxation. Without speed he can't keep up; without relaxation he can't last.

His wind sprints, 220's, starts, and short dashes during the training season with the sprinters will develop his speed. His exercises, long walks with a springy step, and easy jogging will give him relaxation.

During his training the half-mile candidate should strive to develop a long, easy stride. The 880 man does not attempt to achieve the accentuated high knee lift of the sprinter or to run all of his race on his toes with a pronounced bounce, as this would be much too tiring. He develops his long ground-covering stride by using an easy hip swing. While the hip-swing type of stride cannot produce the speed of the sprinter's bounce, it is much less tiring and enables the runner to keep his legs well relaxed as they swing forward in long strides.

At the start of his race to pick up speed and in the finishing sprint, the half-miler runs up on his toes. But when he settles down to the long striding of the middle part of his race, he allows his heels to touch the ground. There is no pounding when the heels touch, however. The ankle must be very flexible and the weight of the body swings quickly over to the ball of the foot, from which the drive for the next stride is developed.

The 880 man strives for relaxation in his arms and uses an easy rhythmic swing. He should forget his arms if he can and let them follow the natural roll of the shoulders. If his arms tire during a race, he either needs more pull-ups and similar exercises to make them stronger or else he has been guilty of straining and should concentrate more on relaxation.

If the race is run with proper relaxation, the half-miler will find that his sprinting muscles are ready to respond in the closing drive for the tape. To some extent he will be calling upon a different set of muscles when he uses the higher knee and arm action in his finish. For this reason, coaches continually preach relaxation to their half-milers. Relaxation for the first lap and a half is the secret of saving up the sprinting muscles for the all-important final homestretch run.

In addition to working on his arm and leg action, the half-miler needs to watch his body angle closely. The body should be carried well forward at all times. This is easy to do early in the race when the runner is fresh, but when he is tired he has a tendency to straighten up or even to throw his head back. This is about the worst possible thing he can do. Many a runner who has lost his body angle in the last 10 or 20 yards of the race has found himself "coming in on the back of his neck" and practically marking time while his opponents are sprinting by him.

All good half-milers in the past have run with decided body leans. Eastman and Woodruff ran with a sharp body angle.

91

Robinson was more erect with his torso but was very good from the hips down, always driving forward.

In spite of all attempts to learn relaxation, athletes frequently do tie up at the end of this grueling race and we might as well consider what can be done about it when this disaster occurs.

When the tying-up process hits the victim, he is faced with the necessity of using a different set of muscles as far as possible, as well as of trying to work the tenseness out of already tired muscles. The tied-up athlete comes in with face muscles taut, neck sinews sticking out, head thrown back, and arms, shoulders, and legs pink with strain.

One little thing can help him first of all, and that is to relax the face muscles. This will relieve the cords in his neck and help to correct the faulty head position. Then he should drop his arms and shoulders, letting his hands go limp and perhaps even shaking them. This will relieve the tension in the upper part of his body.

To get new muscles into action, he should use a strongly accentuated hip swing. Along with this there should be a shoulder throw, which is also an aid to the stride.

Frequently after a few strides with arms dangling and hips swinging the legs, the runner finds that the momentary rest has been just enough to help him recover. He can then raise his arms to their normal position, lift his knees and swing into sprinting form for the finish of his race.

Sometimes the heavily muscled type of runner who just can't help tying up at the end of a hard race can make up for his lack of sprint by using a greatly exaggerated hip swing at the finish and by coming in with a longer stride rather than with greater leg speed, as in sprinting.

Several seasons ago I had an unusual type of middle-distance runner at Southern California in Estel Johnson, a husky athlete who looked much more like a wrestler than a foot racer. He just couldn't help having big muscles all around, and near the end of a fast half mile they would tighten up and practically strangle him with his own strength.

But Estel learned to stop trying to lift his legs when he tied up and would throw them out with a terrific hip swing. It gave him the appearance of running all over the track, but at the same time it increased his stride and consequently his speed, enabling him to defeat runners who could come in with the proper sprinting form. He ran the 880 in 1:53.5 which, considering his type of physique and the continual battle with his own heavy muscles, was amazing time.

Although there is no definite type of athlete best suited for the half mile, the best performers are usually men of better than medium height for whom it is easy to develop a long stride.

If the athlete can combine more than average strength without heaviness, like Woodruff, he has a still further advantage. Height and long legs are not necessities, however. Ted Meredith was less than medium in height and had a fairly stocky build.

Considering national champions of the past decade, we find that Phil Edwards was slender and fairly tall. Ed Genung was of medium height and slender. Glenn Cunningham was less than medium in height, light in the legs, and barrel-chested. Ben Eastman was tall and slender and in street clothes was the last person one would suspect of being a star athlete. Elroy Robinson was of medium height and stocky. Charles Beetham was slender and of slightly more than medium height. John Woodruff was tall and powerfully built. Howard Borck was fairly tall and well muscled. Rudolf Harbig possessed a stocky build much like that of sprinter Charley Paddock.

In general the half mile is a race that demands qualities of temperament rather than physique. It takes hard training to get into condition for it, determination to run it, and brains to plan the best possible race and to meet emergencies during it.

Because a good 880 man must have both speed and endurance, we find that most of them can fill in when necessary at any event from a 220-yard sprint to the mile run. Few good 880 men find their day's work done after their regular race in a dual meet, for most of them have speed enough to run a good quarter mile lap in the mile relay.

The value of proper temperament in the half-mile distance was prominently demonstrated in the 1932 Olympic Games. Tom Hampson of the British team was far from being the best looking prospect in the 800-meter race, but he combined a background of sound, faithful conditioning with excellent judgment of pace.

Although not a natural athlete, this angular, stoop-shouldered

The importance of a flexible ankle in running the middle distances is shown in this series of pictures. The right foreleg is at a sharp forward angle as the runner starts to come up on the ball of his foot. The body is well balanced with a lean that will cause the leg drive to be all forward.

A very flexible foot is shown here. It is too tiring in the half mile for the runner to try to get the explosive bounce of the sprint stride, but strong foot muscles and tendons nevertheless aid the development of a powerful stride. The 880 man must be loose in his hips, rotating them in an easy hip swing.

The runner is in full stride here. Although he is reaching out, he is not getting so long a stride as if he were sprinting up on his toes. This particular athlete swings his arms fairly high, like the Finns, and has an individual peculiarity of carrying them well away from his body. A good drive has just been made off the right foot.

The shoulders are rotating smoothly and keeping the body in balance as well as aiding the swing of the hips. The position of the arms is no matter of great concern, as they may be carried high or low, close to the body or away from it, as long as the shoulders are right. As in the faster strides of shorter distances, the lead leg reaches out for the next step without locking at the knee.

The runner comes down for an almost flat-footed landing, but the heel barely touches the ground. Except for the opening spurt and the finishing sprint, the half-miler finds it too fatiguing to run high up on his toes like a sprinter, and his stride becomes a cross between that of a sprinter and that of a long-distance man.

The heel is touching lightly in the landing and the flexible foot is momentarily relaxed before the next drive. A good head position is shown. It should be held up well for ease in breathing but must never be tense. The shoulders are starting a swing that will aid the next stride.

The right hip is coming up fast for the stride and a good thigh lift has been started. Most half-milers find it too tiring to carry their arms as high as this runner but he found the position natural for his accentuated shoulder roll.

The runner pushes rather than bounces off his toe, like the sprinter, but he shows the same straight line from his foot through his head as he drives off the ball of the foot. The athlete is Ross Bush, who holds the Pacific Coast Conference half-mile record of 1 minute 52.3 seconds.

schoolteacher timed his race so well and summoned all his strength with such determination that he came from the ruck in the last 50 meters to sprint to a sensational victory in what was then Olympic record time, 1:49.8. In winning, he forced himself to be run out so completely that it is doubtful if he could have moved another 5 meters.

In the half mile tired muscles that cry out to quit must be forced to greater effort instead of being pampered. The young man who has learned to make himself go faster when his arms and legs are deadened by fatigue has it all over the boy who has the natural physical ability but not the qualities of courage and determination to take full advantage of it.

The race is a hard one, but it is worth while. Those who really prepare themselves for it find that they are quick to recover from the most severe effort and get much satisfaction out of the self-mastery it teaches.

Training schedules should be prepared for each athlete to meet his individual needs. Here is a sample program for the average runner who is well conditioned by preseason work and is now regularly engaging in competition: a mile or more of wind sprints or distance running of from 1 to 2 miles, a good pace to be followed but no attempt made to run oneself out, on Monday; speed work of starts and from two to four 220's on Tuesday; a good 660 at a half-mile pace alternated one week with a hard quarter mile the next week on Wednesday; speed drill with the sprinters in starts and dashes of from 35 to 50 yards on Thursday; and rest on Friday for Saturday competition.

As in all events, the exercises are a vital part of each day's training. They should be taken at the start of each workout and if a great deal of this type of work is needed they should also be tried morning and night. Unless the training session stresses distance running, each workout should be finished with an easy jogging lap around the track.

VI

THE DISTANCE RACES

Distance runners in recent years have been going places with tremendous strides—and that's no pun. Within the past decade we have had four new world's records in the mile, four new marks in the 2-mile, two new times at 3 miles, and innumerable instances of record smashing in the longer metric distances that are commonly run abroad.

Speed work is the answer. Coaches and runners have learned that such things as stamina, stride, pace, wind, and heart are not everything in distance running. The athlete who stands out from the pack—or who runs away from it—is the one who has done sprinting work along with his distance training. When that important stretch of 100 or 200 yards to the tape looms ahead of him, he can momentarily become a sprinter and leave the strictly pace runners behind.

Walter G. George of England stands out as our first great star at the mile and 2-mile distances and his records made in the 1880's stood for many years. In 1882 he set a world's mark of 4:21.4 in the mile; in 1884 he established a record of 9:17.4 in the 2-mile. Most remarkable of George's feats occurred after he turned to professional running. As a pro in 1886, he ran a mile in 4:12¾, a terrifically fast race for his day. Although it did not go down as a world's record, the mark was not to be surpassed until Norman S. Taber ran the distance in 4:12.6 in 1915—29 years later.

In setting his professional record, George ran his 440 in 57 seconds, his 880 in 2:01, and his three-quarters in 3:07. These lap times are interesting to note because of their contrast with the marks that leading runners attempt to make en route today. Present-day methods call for the last lap to be the fastest one in the race and for the second 880 to be faster than the first.

Not long ago in reminiscing over his track career, the veteran George remarked that if he had known as much then about running the mile as athletes do now he believes he could have put the record much lower. He ran the first half mile much too fast and his last lap was the slowest 440 in the race instead of the fastest. Nevertheless the record was a remarkable one and for many years no runner even came close to it. In fact, it was 37 years before a miler was to break 4:12.

George's amateur mile record of 4:21.4 lasted from 1882 until 1895 when T. P. Conneff lowered it to 4:15.6. This record stood for another 16 years until John Paul Jones of Cornell shaved it to 4:15.4. Two years later—in 1913—Jones clipped a full second from his own mark, running 4:14.4 in an I.C.A.A.A.A. championship meet.

While at Cornell, Jones had a brilliant competitor in Norman Taber of Brown. In one of their races—the 1912 I.C.A.A.A.A. championships—the two great rivals ran to a dead heat. Their rivalry undoubtedly had much to do with their splendid marks and in 1915 Taber set a new world's record of 4:12.6. This mark, considered one of the most brilliant in the record books, was destined to stand eight years until a silent, tireless, smooth-striding Finn, who had won the 10,000-meter race in the 1920 Olympics, dropped down to this distance for a record try.

The expressionless athletic wonder who ran with such clocklike precision was Paavo Nurmi, and his record attempt in Sweden in 1923 sent him across the finish line in a new mark of 4:10.4. Strictly a pace runner with no great sprint for his closing lap, Nurmi negotiated the race like George by running his fastest lap first.

The era of milers who would discard old methods and finish with a sprinter's kick was approaching, and the 1930's gave us four different record holders and a number of athletes who could beat the time of the phantom Finn with marks under 4:10.

First to crack Nurmi's four-lap time was Jules Ladoumegue, a strong little Frenchman, who ran the distance in 4:9.2 in 1931.

Ruled out of track competition in an eligibility squabble, Ladoumegue saw his record fall to John E. (Jack) Lovelock. This light-footed little New Zealander's terrific sprint convinced coaches and athletes that speed training was of vital importance

98

and that the mile henceforth must be treated more like a middle-distance event than a distance run. Lovelock's mile record, made in 1933 and destined to stand only a year, was 4:7.6. Even though he lost this mark, his sensational sprinting ability at the end of a hard race sent him to a world's-record-smashing feat in the 1936 Olympics when he won the 1,500-meter race in 3:47.8. In this race, which is 119½ yards short of a mile, Lovelock ran his last 400 meters in 56 seconds.

It is significant to note that during the 1930's the emphasis upon speed work for milers had made them so much faster than in the past that the first three men to cross the finish line of the 1,500-meter run in the 1936 Olympic games all shattered the previous record for the distance.

Following Lovelock in that race were Glenn Cunningham of the United States, Luigi Beccali of Italy who had won the 1,500-meter race in the 1932 Olympics, Archie San Romani of the United States, and Phil Edwards of Canada.

Cunningham, who has had the longest career of any American distance star, brought Lovelock's mile record down to 4:6.8 in 1934 in a race in which he covered the second half mile in a shade over 2:1.

Cunningham's mark lasted but three years. Sydney Wooderson, small, slender Englishman, lowered it in 1937 to 4:6.4. Cunningham still has the distinction of the fastest mile on record, however, since he ran the distance in 4:4.4 on Dartmouth's lightning-fast indoor track in 1938.

In recent years the mile run has resulted in so many spectacular races that it has become the feature event of the big eastern indoor meets. Cunningham, despite occasional challenges from Gene Venzke, headed a fast field of indoor milers for several seasons until the winter of 1940 when the barrel-chested Chuck Fenske of Wisconsin in his third campaign on the boards went to the fore with a series of sensational victories. With Cunningham, Louie Zamperini, Archie San Romani, and Blaine Rideout competing against him in most of the meets, Fenske made a clean sweep of the principal mile championships, winning most of his victories with a terrific last-lap sprint.

Not only Fenske but also most of his leading competitors finished nearly every race well under 4:10. In one race, the

Wanamaker mile in the Millrose Athletic Association games in Madison Square Garden, four men were timed in 4:8.2 or better. Fenske won in 4:7.4, Cunningham was second in 4:7.7, and Venzke and Zamperini crossed the line shoulder to shoulder in 4:8.2 for the fastest four-man finish ever seen in mile racing.

Distance men admit that smoothness of track and lack of interfering breezes more than compensate for sharp turns, and make indoor mile running faster than turning the event outdoors. When Zamperini was timed in 4:7.7 in finishing second to Fenske in the New York Athletic Club games during the 1940 winter season, he estimated that if he had run the same race outdoors his mark would have been about 4:9.5. Milers vary in their opinion of the relative speed of indoor and outdoor miles, but all admit that indoor running saves at least a second and some claim that the boards are up to 4 seconds faster than the average outdoor track.

With all the fast marks that have been made in recent years, turning a mile in 4:12 is still an outstanding piece of running.

When John Paul Jones ran his 4:14.4 race in 1913, it was an I.C.A.A.A.A. as well as a world's record. As an I.C.A.A.A.A. record it lasted for 25 years until Howard Borck of Manhattan College clipped ½ second from it in 1938. Borck's intercollegiate mark was quickly smashed, however, when Louie Zamperini of Southern California dropped it to 4:11.2 in 1939.

Since we have been spoiled lately by sensational performances, it is a good thing to remember that even the greatest champions don't always come close to the record and that in the much publicized Princeton Invitational mile of 1939, Fenske won in 4:11 and defeated by a good margin such stars as Cunningham, Wooderson, San Romani, and Blaine Rideout.

In reviewing the accomplishments of the great milers of the past and how they have cut down the world's record, we have seen how sprinting work has more and more entered into the picture in the training methods of the best runners.

Lest the beginning runner be frightened away from the event by the talk of miles in 4:12 or better, he should be assured that many high school races are still won at around 5 minutes and that 4:25 to 4:35 is still considered very good time for college dual-meet miles.

Suppose a young man is just starting his mile-running career in high school. His object first of all is to cover the distance in 5 minutes. Since at first we cannot expect him to be overly blessed with stamina and speed, we stress pace for him. To make it as simple as possible, we divide the race into four 440's and tell him that the best way to run a 5-minute mile is to round each lap in 1:15.

Aiming for 75-second laps will teach pace to the beginning runner. When he gets to the point where he can put four of them together for the 5-minute mile, he should try to better his mark by improving his time for the second 880.

Later as further improvement is shown, he can speed up the first 880 too, always striving to make the second half mile his best. Even though he is running in time far from that of the champions, he can imitate them in this respect. When the beginning miler attempts to make the last part of his race the fastest, he learns the importance of combining sprinting with distance work at the outset of his running career.

To the man who has settled down to life in an office and who has grown therewith a bit on the portly and short-winded side, distance running probably appears a drudgery and an unnecessary waste of energy. It is nothing of the sort to the young man who participates, however. Boys take it up only because they think it is fun to run long distances. To practically all of them, their love for running over a long course started early in life. Probably they lived in the country and had a long way to go to school on foot, or they delivered papers, or their best friend lived on the other side of town. They covered long distances by walking and running, gradually built their legs and lungs up to it, and found that it was fun to go into races in which they could use their stamina and wind.

Sometimes unusual reasons are responsible for boys getting into distance events. Cunningham had his legs badly burned when a youngster. When he learned that there was danger of his never having full use of them again, he took up walking and jogging to try to build them back to normal.

Louie Zamperini, who set the N.C.A.A. mile record of 4:8.3 in 1938 and who also cracked the I.C.A.A.A.A. record in 1939, tells an interesting story about how he took up distance running.

101

He had an older brother, Pete, who in true fraternal spirit had always tried to advise and protect him. When Pete was a senior in high school in Torrance, Calif., he found that kid brother Louie, who was a freshman, was running around with a neighborhood gang of boys, all of whom smoked. When Louie confessed that he had been sneaking smokes with the gang for several years, Pete decided to do something about it. Pete was a miler on the Torrance high school track team and he made Louie go out for the same event.

Louie wasn't in very good condition at first and tried to take it easy in his workouts. Pete found a way to stop his loafing, however. He would run behind Louie with a switch and when kid brother began to lag he would give him a few good cracks that worked miracles in increasing the younger Zamperini's speed. Louie soon learned that the cigarette ads which portrayed the weed as a boon to athletic success were a trifle exaggerated. Desiring to be able to sit down at night after a workout with Pete, he found that the only way he could keep out of reach of the brotherly whacks was to give up smoking and really go into training.

Pete was the champion miler of his league but Louie could beat him a year after giving up smoking. Louie, who would now rather run than eat, says that he'll never smoke again and is quite sure that if he even tried to, it would make him sick.

Extremely simple are the training rules for getting into condition for running the distances. Just run and walk, walk and run, and then do it some more. Whenever you want to go somewhere within a reasonable distance, forget about the automobile or the streetcar or the bus. Use the old-fashioned means of locomotion nature supplied.

Conditioning should start in the fall as in the other events we have already discussed. Pull-ups to develop the torso and the regular stretching exercises that loosen the hips and crotch and strengthen the abdomen should be done daily.

Candidates should walk at least 2 miles a day and should go out on the track and run at least twice a week. Since the danger of overworking is not so great for distance men as it is for those who run the dashes and middle distances, they can stand much more running. The miler or cross-country man can run almost every day in the fall if he wishes. He should use moderation though and take a day or so of rest if the training begins to get tiresome.

He should always remember that in the fall he is just trying to get into condition, not attempting to break any records. He must not make his preliminary work so strenuous as to become drudgery or he will lose his zest for running and be spoiled entirely for the coming season.

Louie Zamperini's success in smashing college records as a miler can be traced to a large extent to the fact that, when he developed an enthusiasm for running, he went on foot everywhere possible. He used to like to swim at Redondo Beach, which is 7 miles from Torrance, and he thought nothing of jogging down there and back for a dip.

Paavo Nurmi used to run back and forth to his place of work which was 5 miles from his home. Cunningham and San Romani covered long distances on foot in going to school.

A distance runner doesn't need a set course. When he is going somewhere, that distance becomes his course.

Interspersed with the walking and jogging in the fall should be wind sprints which are so valuable for both conditioning and speed. Walk, jog, and run at first. Then when the legs are strong enough, go into the familiar wind sprint routine of walk, jog, run, and sprint 30 to 40 yards, and repeat. With two wind sprints to a lap, a distance man can go from 1 to 2 miles a day, getting invaluable training in speed, relaxation, and endurance.

In training for distance work, runners should make it a habit to finish fast. If it becomes habitual for them to turn on the speed on the last lap in every workout, they won't find a sprint so difficult at the end of a hard race during the regular season.

In discussing running form we have noted that sprinters and quarter-milers stay up on their toes all the way and that half-milers, when hitting up their fastest pace, run on their toes but allow their heels to touch in the easier stages of their race. In the distances, runners find it too tiring to run very much of their race up on their toes. The distance-running technique perfected by the Finns and demonstrated in its most perfect form by the smooth-striding Nurmi is favored by many coaches because it permits the runner to touch his heel at each stride without any flat-footed pounding. In covering long distances runners will do well to follow the Nurmi technique whenever it does not impede their own natural style. Naturalness in running is what we seek first of all, but to the endowments of nature coaches attempt to add refinements of technique that will develop more speed with less effort.

From slow-motion pictures of the flying Finn taken when he was at the height of his record breaking, we have made an analysis of the Nurmi running technique that we should like to pass on. He used a free stride of medium length with a considerable forward thrust and good knee lift, the feet never rising higher behind than the knee. His ankles were remarkably relaxed and he came down almost flat-footed, the heel touching the ground, but very lightly. He then moved forward with a rocking motion on his foot until he was high on the toe.

A flat-footed stride generally means pounding, but Nurmi did not pound at all. This was avoided by the flexibility of his ankle. The strong drive tended to throw the center of gravity forward, an item of extreme importance in relation to the body carriage. There seemed to be only a very slight hip swing.

Nurmi's body inclination was almost vertical and appeared more so than it really was because his shoulders were thrown back and his chest was thrust out. The erectness really came from the hips up.

One of the most interesting points in Nurmi's style was his method of carrying and swinging his arms. The forearms were kept parallel to the ground with the hands almost against the chest, moving back and forth across it. The swing was mostly with the shoulders, the arms moving very little in their sockets and the elbows being carried well out from the body. This type of arm carriage affords an excellent aid to breathing. The lungs have an opportunity to work freely and at full capacity. There is no waste motion or consumption of energy because the arm movement is restricted.

Everything in Nurmi's style was worked out for ease, relaxation, and the elimination of waste motion and energy.

While he aimed to set an even pace and always carried a stop watch which he ran against rather than paying attention to his opponents, he never ran in the same style for more than 3 minutes at a time. He would change his stride, lifting his knees and running on his toes, sometimes bounding, all for the purpose of relieving tired muscles by bringing new ones into play. His style proved ideal for him and is also aiding many runners today who are imitating it.

The claim is not made that it is the one and only correct way to run distances. When a runner has developed a natural style suitable to his size and build, it would be foolish for him to try to change his technique completely. From the form of a champion such as Nurmi, he can pick up many helpful features, however, and thus improve his stride, arm carriage, breathing, and general relaxation.

Zamperini was a splendid natural runner when he came to the University of Southern California from high school. Since he had several individual peculiarities, instead of trying to change him all around, as his coach I endeavored to give him the elements of the Finnish style of distance running that would be most likely to aid him.

As a result, although one can see many features of the Nurmi technique of running in his races now, Zamperini's style is distinctly Zamperini's and not Nurmi's. For one thing, he has a slight body lean as opposed to Nurmi's erect carriage. Also he usually carries his arms in a more elevated position and he runs higher up on his toes, the result of having had more sprinting work in training than did Nurmi.

In general, I believe that the longer the distance a runner covers the more nearly he should try to duplicate the Nurmi style.

Since we are making the mile more of a middle-distance event than a distance race, the best style for a championship miler today is a combination of 880 running and Finnish distance-running techniques. It must be remembered that the one weakness in Nurmi's running was his lack of a finishing sprint. To get the fast last lap that we must have for outstanding performances today, we must not only put more sprinting work into our training program but we must also vary when necessary from the Nurmi running form that stressed even pace and overlooked the modern climactic burst of speed.

To illustrate further the change in mile running since Nurmi set his world's record of 4:10.4, we can make an interesting comparison of the Finn's fastest mile with Zamperini's winning mile in the N.C.A.A. championships of 1938.

Although not the fastest race in recent years, I believe Zamperini's mile is a splendid example of the way the athletes try to run the distance in the modern manner. Also it is an N.C.A.A. record and I was on hand personally to time accurately each of his laps.

In setting his 4:10.4 record, Nurmi turned the four laps as follows: 58.6, 63.2, 64.9, and 63.7 seconds. In establishing his N.C.A.A. mark of 4:8.3, Zamperini ran his laps as follows: 61.5, 62.8, 63.5, and 60.5 seconds.

In order to visualize the difference in the races, let us try to imagine that these runners actually competed against each other in making these marks. Since in a 4:10 mile, a runner covers approximately 7 yards every second, we'll make our comparison on this basis. Had the runners been racing against each other, Nurmi would have beaten Zamperini by 2.9 seconds in the first lap, taking a lead of 21 yards. In the second lap Zamperini would have picked up $4/10$ second or approximately 3 yards, leaving him trailing by 18 yards at the half-mile mark.

The third laps of both Nurmi and Zamperini were their slowest, but the latter would have gained 1.4 seconds or approximately 10 yards, leaving him 8 yards in the rear as the final lap started.

In the last lap the difference between the two types of running becomes amazing when we consider it in matter of yards. Zamperini ran his final lap in 60.5 seconds to 63.7 for Nurmi. The former therefore picked up 3.2 seconds, which is approximately 22 yards. Zamperini thus would have made up the 8 yards he trailed and raced home with a winning margin of 14 yards.

Cutting their races in half, we find that Nurmi ran his first half mile in 2:1.8 and his second in 2:8.6. Zamperini ran his first 880 in 2:4.3 and his second in 2:4.

When one considers that a decade ago Nurmi's world's record was believed to be unbeatable, we realize how much progress has been made in running the mile in the past few years. Imagine a college sophomore gaining 22 yards on the peerless Finn in one lap and defeating him in his greatest race by 14 yards!

Because the ability of milers to sprint on the last lap varies considerably, strategy as well as pace plays an important part in running this event. In fast competition no man can run entirely against the watch. It is a good thing for him to learn as much as possible about the type of races his competitors usually run, so that he will know whether he is up against fast pace setters or great last-lap sprinters.

Changes in running strategy frequently bring about upsets in the most experienced competition. When Sydney Wooderson failed to set his usual fast pace in the 1939 Princeton mile, Chuck Fenske, whose greatest asset is his ability to run a blistering final quarter mile, was able to stay up closely enough to overhaul the field at the finish. Fenske ran his last lap in 57 seconds to defeat Glenn Cunningham, Archie San Romani, and Blaine Rideout as well as Wooderson.

Later in the 1,500-meter run of the national A.A.U. championships, Rideout tried a bit of strategy that upset another splendid field. Knowing that he was up against three runners with fast closing sprints in Fenske, Cunningham, and Zamperini, he stepped out in the third lap to pile up a 30-yard lead. Believing that he could not hold the pace, the other runners let him go, figuring to cut him down on the final lap. But although the others finished fast, Rideout had enough endurance to hold his lead and win by several yards. Ordinarily this isn't the best way to run a mile or 1,500 meters, but it shows what can be done sometimes by unusual tactics.

The beginning runner who will likely be opposing boys whose ability is unknown to him will do best by sticking to steady pace and running against the watch. He should set his own pace, paying no attention to the others no matter how far ahead they may be, and he should be particularly careful not to be affected by their stride.

It is a common error for a distance runner to drop in behind another and fall into the stride of the leader even though it may be entirely unsuited to him. Once he has planned the pace and lap times that will ensure him his best race, he should not worry about what his opponents are doing but should stick to his own methods.

It is very important to run on the pole, especially over long distances. A runner who stays in the second lane over the mile distance would have to cover some 18 yards more than the man on the pole. Of course, at the start it is better to run wide around the first turn if first position cannot be taken than it is to drop back of the pack to reach the pole.

Being boxed is not much of a factor because there is little chance that the others will maintain it. Even if they do, it is a small loss to drop back slightly and go around.

It is usually wise to speed up when a competitor tries to pass, but it is never good tactics to accept every challenge or to run very fast to prevent another runner from going ahead. When trying to pass another, one should do it quickly and unexpectedly, not by a mere lengthening of the stride.

Team strategy lies in the use of pacemakers, either to draw out opponents so that a strong-finishing team mate will find them weakened at the finish, or to "carry" a team mate so that he will have sufficient lead for the finish.

It is the coach's duty to help his runners lay their plans for the race and, if permitted, to call out their elapsed times for each lap as they run, perhaps encouraging them at the same time.

Fans have become so interested in following the time of distance races by laps that big electric clocks are now furnished for them at many fields. Runners can get information on their pace by glancing at these occasionally if their lap times are not announced or given by a timer or coach.

Mile runners can be short or tall, but they are usually of medium height and weight. At Southern California our best milers have come in a variety of sizes. Cliff Halstead, who ran better than 4:20, never weighed less than 180 pounds, and Francis Benavidez, who broke Halstead's school record, was a slight 115-pounder. Zamperini weighed 145.

Among the record smashers, Wooderson and Lovelock were small in stature, being under 130 pounds in weight. Cunningham was fairly short but was stocky and weighed between 150 and 155. Ladoumegue and Nurmi were of average height and weight, being 150-pounders.

Most American milers are slightly taller than the average athlete. Bill Bonthron, who chased Lovelock into his record-breaking 4:7.6 mile in 1933, was close to 6 feet in height. Norman Taber, John Paul Jones, Fenske, and Rideout were all taller than average men, with long ground-eating strides. Paul Moore of

Stanford, one of the fastest milers of the 1940 season, was another tall, slender runner.

Since running the mile requires much harder training than the shorter races, time as well as stamina, speed, and determination is needed by the athlete who would succeed. We have already noted how much preliminary work is necessary both in exercising and jogging. In the spring when the actual competitive season starts, the candidate must still give plenty of time to his training. Besides jogging to develop endurance, he must run enough laps in exact times so that he becomes a sure judge of pace. He must take enough starts and short dashes with the sprinters to work up speed for his finishes.

During practice fairly heavy shoes should be worn. Jumping shoes with the heel spikes removed are good for milers to run in while training, but of course the regulation lightweight shoes should be worn in competition.

Coaches and athletes must plan their training during mid-season to suit the runner's condition and temperament and must also give variety to the practice program.

Here is a typical training week for a runner who has had a good background of distance work to develop stamina and who is now attempting to increase his speed: a mile of wind sprints, two to a lap, or a run of from 1 to $1\frac{1}{2}$ miles at good speed on Monday; a lap at a jogging pace, starts and short dashes with the sprinters, one or two fairly fast 220's and another lap at a jog on Tuesday; a brisk $\frac{1}{2}$- or $\frac{3}{4}$-mile run at close to the best time that can be made on Wednesday; a lap of jogging, a series of 40- to 50-yard dashes and another lap at a jog on Thursday; and rest on Friday for Saturday's race. Naturally the daily walking of at least 2 miles and the exercises should never be overlooked.

When one wishes to run distances longer than a mile, he trains like a miler, only more so. He needs still more walking, running, and track work as a whole. Once he gets his legs in condition, pace is his chief worry. His laps are run more nearly at the same speed than they are in the mile and he must always know how fast he is going.

In the United States, long-distance races until very recently have not been particularly popular, with the exception of occasional marathons; consequently we have fared poorly in Olympic competition in races of more than 1,500 meters.

We are steadily improving in distance running, however, and in 1936 an American became the world's record holder at 2 miles for the first time when Don Lash of Indiana ran the eight laps in 8:58.4.

England was the home of the first great two-milers. Walter George, the brilliant miler, set a world's 2-mile record of 9:17.4 in 1884 that lasted for 20 years. Alfred Shrubb, another tireless British star, broke the mark with a 9:9.6 race.

Then came Edvin Wide of Sweden with a 9:1.4 record in 1926 and Nurmi with the first race under 9 minutes in 1931 when he ran the distance in 8:59.6. Lash lowered this mark in 1936, but the American's record lasted only a year, Miklos Szabo of Hungary running an 8:56 race in 1937.

In 1938 a new threat to distance marks flashed over the tracks of Europe when Taisto Maki of Finland turned in a record-breaking 10,000-meter race of 30:2, beating by 3.6 seconds the time established the year before by Ilmari Salminen, also of Finland.

American track fans, never much concerned with the performances of European runners in the longer metric distances abroad, showed little interest in this record race at the time, but Maki demanded attention the following year when he set five new world's records. One of them was at 2 miles, the one long-distance race in which Americans had begun to excel.

Maki's first record-breaking race of 1939 was in June in Helsinki where the slender Finn ran 3 miles in 13:42.4 and went on to cover the 5,000-meter distance in 14:8.8. In this race Finnish athletes showed that long-distance stars were still being produced as regularly as ever in their country when Kauko Peturi, a heretofore little-known runner, also improved on the 5,000-meter record with a time of 14:16.2. Maki's marks broke records of 13:50.6 and 14:17 that had been set by Lauri Lehtinen of Finland in Helsinki in 1932.

In July, 1939, Maki dropped down to the 2-mile distance and turned in a race of 8:53.2 to crack Szabo's official world's record of 8:56. Two months later Maki completed a clean sweep of the records from 2 miles to 10,000 meters when he added the 6-mile

110

time to his collection and lowered the 10,000-meter mark he had set the previous year. His 6-mile time of 28:55.6 broke Salminen's 29:8.4 and his new 10,000-meter record was 29:52.6.

Like all long-distance stars of Finland, Maki was a matured, veteran runner when he began to cut his time down to the record-breaking brackets. Born in Helsinki, he had Paavo Nurmi for his idol during his boyhood days. Although he spent much time running over the countryside and entered a few meets in his teens, he showed no more promise than hundreds of other young Finns who dreamed of some day winning their way to Olympic competition.

By the Olympic year of 1932, Maki was twenty-one years of age and running in regular competition. But he was far back of his countrymen in tryout meets and had no chance to make Finland's Olympic team. During the next four years he continued to train hard and by 1936 had high hopes of making the Finnish team for the 1936 Olympics. But he still could not match the speed of such veteran stars of his homeland as Gunnar Hockert, Lauri Lehtinen, Ilmari Salminen, Arvo Askalo, and Volmari Iso-Hollo and he failed to make the team.

By 1939 at the age of twenty-eight Maki was in his prime and his record-smashing races indicated that he would be as great a hero in the 1940 Olympics as his idol Nurmi has been in 1924. But hardly had his last great record-breaking race been run in Helsinki in September, 1939, than the sound of bombs instead of spikes began to be heard in the country that had been preparing for the 1940 games as Finland vainly tried to fight off the Russian invasion. Maki went to war against the Soviets and visions of Olympic glory for him or anyone else in 1940 faded as most of Europe and the Orient plunged into war.

To serve his country as a good-will ambassador and help raise funds for Finnish relief, Maki was brought to the United States early in 1940 for a series of exhibition races, with Nurmi making the trip as his coach and manager. Although there were no Olympic honors for him to win, Maki did much to stimulate interest in the long distances in this country.

Aided by Maki's tour around the country under the auspices of the Amateur Athletic Union, the distance races became a real attraction. Long neglected by American track fans, the events

111

suddenly drew considerable interest, especially when it was revealed that we had been quietly producing athletes capable of giving the flying Finns a race at their favorite distances.

Gregory Rice, the stocky, deep-chested boy from Montana who had his college competition at the University of Notre Dame, in particular loomed as the man who would bring American long-distance running to the front. Competing in the national indoor championships of 1940 in Madison Square Garden, New York, he set a new world's indoor record at 3 miles in 13:55.9, breaking the mark of 13:56.2 that had been set in 1925 by Willie Ritola of Finland.

As there is actually no official sanction placed on "world's indoor records," the term, of course, is used in its restricted sense. Although Rice's time was 13.5 seconds slower than the outdoor record of Maki that was awaiting official adoption by the I.A.A.F., it was close enough to indicate that America was very much on the upgrade in the developing of distance men.

Two weeks after setting his 3-mile indoor mark, Rice returned to the same track to run 2 miles in 8:56.2, which bettered both Don Lash's American records of 8:58 indoors and 8:58.3 outdoors. Later, Rice climaxed his 1940 indoor season with another record-breaking race at 3 miles when he defeated Maki and Don Lash and lowered his own indoor mark to 13:52.3 in the New York Finnish Relief meet. In this race Rice finished 25 yards ahead of Maki with Lash 5 yards in front of the Finn.

This was one of numerous defeats for Maki during his American tour. Another victor over him on several occasions was Walter Mehl of Wisconsin. In the Finnish star's last race in the United States, Mehl defeated both Maki and Rice outdoors at 2 miles in 9:1.8 in the Los Angeles Coliseum.

The numerous defeats of Maki in the United States did not lessen his prestige as a really great runner. Track followers realized that he went into his 1940 running campaign without sufficient conditioning and that his frequent jaunts around a strange country prevented him from training properly. The one important thing that his tour did do, in addition to raising funds for Finland, was to show that American weakness in the long-distance runs may be a thing of the past. Had there been any Olympic games in 1940, from among such stars as Rice, Mehl,

112

Lash, and Fenske might finally have emerged an American champion.

Until recent years, Americans had little chance to become proficient in the longer metric distances as there were few races at more than 2 miles for the long-winded boys to enter. In intercollegiate competition the two-mile is still the longest race. As approximately 95 per cent of the American Olympic track and field team is made up of athletes produced by the colleges and universities, it can be seen why this country has been shy of men well seasoned in traveling the long routes.

The oldest long-distance race in national championship competition was the 5-mile run. It was put on the program of the national meet in 1880, dropped in 1895, resumed in 1899, changed to the 2-mile run in 1903, replaced in 1904, and changed to the 6-mile run in 1925.

At the present time athletes may compete in national A.A.U. championships at these distances: 5,000 meters, which is 3 miles 188 yards; 10,000 meters, which is 6 miles 376 yards; 15 kilometers; 20 kilometers; 25 kilometers; 30 kilometers; the marathon; the cross-country; and the 3,000-meter steeplechase, which is 239 yards less than 2 miles. A kilometer is 1,093.623 yards, or approximately ⅝ mile.

Many of these events are still comparatively new to national competition. The 5,000-meter run was put in the program in 1932 and has brought out some of the best competition. Ralph Hill of Oregon was the first champion and his time of 14:55.7 was not bettered as a meet record until Greg Rice won in 14:50.9 in 1939. In defending his national 5,000-meter championship in 1940, Rice lowered the record still further to 14:33.4.

The 6-mile run, introduced in 1925, is now the 10,000-meter run, having been changed permanently to this distance in 1932 after a temporary switch in the Olympic year of 1928. Louis Gregory, running for St. Joseph's Catholic Club of Newark, N. J., started an auspicious series of victories in the race in 1929, winning again in 1930, 1931, 1933, and 1939.

Competition at 10 miles was started in 1889, but the event was left out of numerous meets; in 1933 it was changed to the 15-kilometer run. The 20-kilometer run was started in 1933, and the 15-mile run, which was introduced in 1925, was changed to the

113

25-kilometer event in 1933. A 20-mile run was put on the A.A.U. program in 1930 and changed to 30 kilometers in 1933. Competition in the marathon has taken place since 1925.

Two-mile steeplechasers have had their ups and downs in more ways than one. The event was instituted in 1889, dropped in 1895, resumed in 1896, dropped in 1903, resumed in 1904, dropped in 1906, resumed in 1916, dropped in 1917, and again resumed in 1919. After a temporary switch to 3,000 meters in the Olympic years of 1920 and 1928, the event was permanently set at this distance in 1932.

Cross-country, which was started in 1890, has also been staged off and on, but regular championships have been held since 1903.

One of the fastest distance men of a few decades back was Hans Kolehmainen who won the 5-mile championship in 1912, 1913, and 1915 and the 10-mile title in 1913, 1914, 1915, and 1916. Hans was a Finn running for the Irish-American Athletic Club of New York City.

Another Finn who won many American distance championships was Willie Ritola, who was titlist at 10 miles in 1922, 1923, 1925, 1926, and 1927 and who also won five national cross-country championships.

Paul S. Mundy, running for the Millrose Athletic Association of New York City in his later races, was one of American's most consistent 10-mile men in the early 1930's, while Joe McCluskey of Fordham had a long reign in the steeplechase, with seven national championships between 1930 and 1939 to his credit.

Louis Gregory was a frequent winner in national competition at 20, 25, and 30 kilometers as well as at 10,000 meters. Outstanding competitor in cross-country running in recent years has been Don Lash with six straight championships from 1934 to 1939. In 1940 he was national champion at 10,000 meters.

Although America has had occasional notable national champions, we have won small fame in distance racing in international competition. In distances of more than 1,500 meters, in which we won our last championship in 1908 with Mel Sheppard, we have registered only one Olympic victory, the win of John J. Hayes in the marathon run of 1908.

Joie Ray of the Illinois Athletic Club, who won his first national championship in the mile run in 1915 and then won seven straight from 1917 to 1923, made a game but not too successful try to shift to longer distances in the 1928 Olympics. He did manage to score for the United States with a sixth at 10,000 meters and showed his stout heart by placing fifth in the marathon. Leo Lermond also scored for the United States in the 1928 Games with a fourth place in the 5,000-meter run.

By far the best showing by an American distance runner in any of the games since 1908 was made by Ralph Hill in the 1932 Olympics in Los Angeles. This slender country lad from the Pacific Northwest had won the first staging of the national A.A.U. 5,000-meter run that year to make the American Olympic team and then he had finished first in his heat of the event in the Olympics. In spite of this, no one thought that Hill would figure prominently in the finals against the Finnish favorites, Lauri Lehtinen and Lauri Virtanen, and American fans felt that they would be well satisfied if Hill could win a point or two.

Consequently some 75,000 fans looked on in amazement in the 5,000-meter finals when Hill dogged the steps of Lehtinen lap after lap, holding a running position ahead of Virtanen who stayed a stride behind. As the rivals went into the last lap the fans were greeted by the astonishing sight of Virtanen unable to keep up with the American and Hill actually sprinting stride for stride to challenge Lehtinen for the drive at the tape.

On the homestretch Hill swung out to go around Lehtinen but the Finn moved out from the pole to keep him from passing. Hill then tried to pass on the inside but Lehtinen cut over to the inside lane and held him back. The jockeying continued as Hill again attempted to pass on the outside, and when they hit the tape the American was still vainly trying to find room to go by and being cut off whether he attempted to make it on the inside or the outside.

A loud boo went up from the stands as Lehtinen won by inches, but when announcer Bill Henry, who was also the sports technical director of the games, admonished the fans over the public address system, "Remember, these people are our guests," American sportsmanship quickly smothered resentment and the stadium became quiet.

European athletes seemed quite surprised that fans had objected to the winner's tactics, declaring that it was a common

115

and accepted piece of strategy abroad for a tiring distance runner to try to hold his lead by jockeying. Lehtinen felt very badly about the whole thing and Hill aided the situation admirably by being a perfect gentleman, not only refusing to consider the claim of a foul but also consoling the repentant Finn.

When the Olympic victory ceremony for the 5,000-meter run was held the next day—it had been diplomatically postponed to let the crowd cool off—Lehtinen in a sentimental gesture presented Hill with a Finnish emblem and the affair ended with many expressions of good will and friendly feelings all around.

Whether or not Hill could have won that race will, of course, never be known, but it still stands as the best showing of an American in international distance competition since Hayes won the marathon in 1908.

In the same 1932 games, America drew its usual blank in the 10,000-meter run, but Albert Michelson, who had been ninth in the 1928 marathon, moved up to sixth, and Joe McCluskey finished close to the leaders in the steeplechase to take third.

Incidentally, the runners in this steeplechase were the victims of a long count when the judges lost a lap somewhere and the boys had to run approximately 3,450 meters instead of the official 3,000. No one was ever able to verify the report that the foreign official charged with the job of counting the laps lost track when he took time out to count his American money instead.

America had a few faint hopes that it might make a showing in the long distances in the 1936 Olympics, but the lads were completely shut out except for Harold Manning's fifth place in the steeplechase. Finnish stars were one-two-three at 10,000 meters with Salminen, Askola, and Iso-Hollo, one-two at 5,000 meters with Hockert and Lehtinen (Hill's old pal), and one-two in the 3,000-meter steeplechase with Iso-Hollo, 1932 winner, and Touminen. In the marathon, the first American to finish, Johnny Kelly, placed sixteenth.

Undoubtedly America's poor showing in the long distances against foreign stars has been due to the fact that we have had to rely upon runners developed in infrequent club competition instead of upon those who were developed, or at least who got the start of their competition and interest, in the colleges. We can't expect the colleges to supply stars at extreme distances

116

from their teams, because the long-winded boys don't reach their prime until they are about 25 years of age, but the universities should start them out and give them an interest that will keep them in training and steadily improving after they are graduated.

With the coming to the fore of such men as Gregory Rice, who ran for Notre Dame; Don Lash, who competed for Indiana; and Walter Mehl, who ran for Wisconsin; and with the stimulus of Maki's 1940 exhibition tour, American running at the longer distances will undoubtedly show a decided pickup in the coming years.

Cross-country running and steeplechasing are important autumn sports in some colleges but for the most part they are principally conditioners for the spring track work of distance men. Steeplechasing differs from cross-country in that it has fixed obstacles such as hurdles and water jumps but the running form is the same. The runner in either of these events can do well to study the principals of the Nurmi technique and incorporate its main features into his natural style.

Some general points in the strategy of cross-country running and steeplechasing should be noted. The runner must necessarily run semiflat-footed but he should be relaxed and must not pound. He should not set the pace on a heavy course. It is always best to follow someone else on a breezy day, letting him take the force of the wind. However, running behind a man with a choppy stride is harmful if it tends to affect one's own stride.

Obstacles should be hurdled rather than vaulted. In soft ground and on hills, the runner should shorten his stride and lean forward. Running downhill he can relax and let the momentum carry him, striding a little longer but not landing on his heels. Ditches and streams should be run through rather than jumped unless they afford an easy leap. Gates and fences should be climbed rather than hurdled or vaulted unless they are low. The method of taking the obstacles that involves the least fatigue should always be used even though it may require a little more time.

The 5-mile cross-country race is a hard one even for college men and no one under twenty-one years of age should try it.

The 2-mile run is a better race but boys under fifteen should not even attempt that distance.

The training is the same in principle as for all distance running. Walking, alternated with jogging, is excellent. No attempt to sprint at the finish of long jogs should be made until good condition is reached. When the candidate is ready for regular running, he should train part of the time at underdistances and part of the time at overdistances, working up to the longer ones gradually. Like the miler, he needs speed work to develop a finishing sprint and should always remember to run well up on his toes when sprinting.

Long-distance runners should wear soft woolen socks with elastic tops to keep out the dirt. The care of the feet is an important matter in long races, for a blister may bring defeat or a serious infection. The inside of the socks should be smeared with soap or tallow, and talc should be dusted over the feet. If a blister develops during a race, it should be opened and covered with court plaster after being disinfected; this is contrary to the general rule that a blister should not be opened. The feet may be toughened by using salt water, benzoin, formaldehyde, or methylated spirits.

In regard to running form, long striding is out of the question in all distance racing. The best type of runner is usually the small man with powerful legs, good lung development, and a strong heart. Don Lash, the former record holder, and Gregory Rice, who set a new N.C.A.A. 2-mile mark of 9:2.6 in the 1939 intercollegiate championships, are excellent American examples of small, strong distance men.

Because a time schedule should be figured out ahead and adhered to rigidly, knowledge of pace is extremely important. The first part of the race should not be too fast; in the marathon this should apply to the first 10 miles.

Along with time and pace, rhythm must be learned, but it must be remembered that a steady, continual grind at the same stride tends to tire the muscles. To relieve them, change the length of the stride, bound a little, or rise on the toes from time to time.

The 2-mile pace is very even for every lap. When Rice set the N.C.A.A. record, he ran practically every lap in 67.5 seconds.

He covered the first mile in 4:30 and his second mile in 4:32.6. Nurmi ran at a fairly even pace when he set the American indoor record of 8:58.2 in 1925. His laps, omitting fractions, were 62, 66, 67, 69, 70, 70, and 67 seconds. He ran a typical Nurmi race, faster in the first part than in the last, doing his first mile in 4:22 and his second mile in 4:36.

Although distance runners require more work than those who train for shorter races, if they find themselves feeling fatigued they should not work so often. Naturally marathon runners need to accustom themselves to vast distances and by the end of 12 weeks of training they can be taking runs of up to 16 miles and walks of up to 35 and 40 miles.

Most marathon and long-distance men train almost the entire year around. Their work should be light during the week before any long race, however. Long-distance men should vary their training by having a day of sprint work to developing finishing speed, a day of underdistance stressing pace and timing, and a day of overdistance to build stamina.

Overdistances are not necessary in marathon training, however. A 20-mile run once in two weeks is ample, and runs of lesser distances are sufficient when perfect condition is reached.

Inasmuch as the 2-mile run is the most common distance event for American runners, a training schedule for it is given. Naturally the condition and needs of individuals vary widely and must be studied before their training programs can be mapped out, but here is a typical schedule of a two-miler who has reached good condition and seeks to improve his time: a run of 1 mile to limber up, or wind sprints, on Monday; three or four short sprints, two 220-yard dashes, or two good quarter miles, or one furlong and one 440, on Tuesday; a mile at a good pace, or 1½ miles at the regular 2-mile pace, on one Wednesday, and a fast 880 or ¾ mile on alternate Wednesdays; sprints of 30 to 40 yards and a few starts on Thursday, or complete rest if any fatigue is felt from earlier workouts; and rest on Friday for the long-winded competition on Saturday. And don't forget the usual body-building, muscle-stretching, and relaxing exercises, and the walks on each day of training.

119

In running long distances the athlete lands flat-footed but avoids pounding through the relaxed position of his ankle, knee, and body. He hits the ground lightly with his heel and rocks forward to his toe. There is an instant of relaxation in the foot as the weight of the body rocks forward.

The runner keeps his right knee bent and strives for an easy stride rather than a long one. Overstriding in the distance races is almost as tiring as trying to run them on the toes like a sprinter. The shoulder and arm action is easy and principally for balance. It is vigorous only in the final sprint when the athlete is running on his toes and may need to emphasize a hip swing to force tired legs to go faster.

The runner moves off his toe with a flexible foot in striding but does not attempt to drive hard. He tries to make each stride with little effort as he can prevent early fatigue in his race only by keeping well relaxed.

In full stride there is not so high a knee lift as in the middle distances and sprints. There is also less emphasis on hip swing and the shoulders rotate only moderately. The body angle here is good, being fairly erect but not so straight up in the torso as with the Finns.

The landing is made with a relaxed ankle and with the knee bent to keep from a flat-footed slap on the ground. In practice this runner uses a piece of sponge rubber on the heels of his shoes to prevent stone bruises. No attempt is being made to reach out for a long stride.

This runner is able to carry his arms higher than most distance men without fatigue because, although his build is light, he has splendid muscular development in his upper body. Many distance runners neglect exercises for the upper body and are slowed down as much by tired arms and shoulders as by tired legs.

Note the flexible ankle. The foot is still almost flat on the ground as the left leg from the knee down assumes a forward angle. The muscles in the calf of the left leg go to work as the runner swings forward for an easy drive off the ball of the foot.

The characteristic deep chest of the distance runner is noticeable here. All good distance men develop great lung capacity (vital capacity). The runner is Louis Zamperini, former N.C.A.A. and I.C.A.A.A.A. mile champion and N.C.A.A. record holder at 4:8.3.

VII

THE HIGH HURDLES

In the flat races we have seen champions in so many different sizes and shapes that we know there is no standard type of build necessary for an athlete's success. Sprinters and distance men are constructed in such variety that if you should put them all together, short and tall, light and heavy, you would probably come up with an average-sized young man of about 5 feet 10 inches in height and about 150 pounds in weight.

As we take up high hurdling, we start getting into events of track and field in which a definite type of athlete holds the advantage. The runner in this race must clear ten barriers on a course of 120 yards or 110 meters, which is 120.34 yards. The standard height for the high hurdle in college competition is 3 feet 6 inches. There is a 15-yard run to the first hurdle and, from that point on, the barriers are 10 yards apart, leaving 15 yards from the last hurdle to the finish line.

Naturally for this type of event the athlete must be physically equipped in such a manner that he can step over the obstacles with little loss of speed. This requires that the high hurdler be tall and long-legged. He also needs to be supple and loose-jointed. His hurdle jumps are fatiguing and make it necessary for him to have plenty of stamina. And since the race is run wide open from start to finish, he needs speed and lots of it.

Forrest Towns of Georgia, holder of the world's record at 13.7 seconds, was 6 feet 2 inches in height, and Percy Beard, his predecessor as a record holder, was 6 feet 5 inches.

It isn't necessary for athletes to be of freakish heights for this event, however. The average high hurdler is about 6 feet 1 inch. Fred Wolcott of Rice Institute, national intercollegiate champion in 1938 and 1939 and national A.A.U. champion in 13.9 seconds in 1940, was a shade under 6 feet. He has run the 100-yard dash in 9.5 seconds and if he lacked an inch or so in height he more than made up for it with his amazing speed between the barriers.

122

High hurdlers of the past used to sail over the sticks. They made their event a pleasant one to watch from an aesthetic viewpoint, but, although they looked artistic flying through the air, they weren't going places very fast. National championships in the 1870's and 1880's were frequently won in 19 seconds or more. Compare this with the way we now stress speed between the hurdles and lightning steps over them. Had one of those nineteenth century national champs run against Towns when the latter set his record, the old-time champion would have been somewhere around the seventh hurdle when Towns hit the tape.

When the A.A.U. was organized in 1888, the world's record for the high hurdles was 16.2 seconds and was held by A. A. Jordan, one of the most consistent performers of the old days and national champion from 1885 to 1888.

During the next decade steady improvement was shown and a whole second was cut from Jordan's mark. H. L. Williams ran the race in 15.8 seconds in 1891 and in the following year W. H. Henry cut the mark to 15¾ seconds. S. Chase, national champion in 1894 and 1895, shaved the record to 15.6 seconds in 1894 and cut another two-tenths from it the following year.

Chase's record lasted three years and then came an athlete who can well be called the father of modern hurdling form. He was Alvin C. Kraenzlein, who lowered the record to 15.2 seconds in 1898 and who proved to be one of the greatest athletes of his day when he won three Olympic championships for the United States in the 1900 games in Paris.

Up to Kraenzlein's time, the standard form for hurdlers was to crook the knee of the lead leg as the barrier was cleared. The leg was twisted in such a way at the knee joint that the lower leg was parallel to the top of the hurdle and approximately at right angles to the thigh. Thus the foot and the knee cleared the hurdle at almost the same time. This meant much lost motion in bringing the leg back to running position when the barrier was cleared and also made it difficult for the runners to stay in balance. The hurdlers made a beautiful picture floating through the air but with such outlandish form it is a wonder that they ever got home in time for dinner.

Kraenzlein apparently decided that soaring like gulls may be all right for ballet dancers, or maybe for the gulls themselves, but

123

he intended to come out of the air in a hurry and do some running. In developing a speed form over the hurdles, he abandoned the fancy bend at the knee of the lead leg. He simply went up over the obstacle with the foot of the lead leg straight out ahead of him. When his body was up and over the hurdle, he snapped his foot down and was back running at top speed without any waste of time.

Kraenzlein developed a new hurdle technique probably because he was too versatile a track and field performer to be strictly a hurdler. His first object in track was to get places in a hurry and his foundation for fast hurdling lay in the fact that he was an exceptional sprinter. His speed also made him an outstanding broad jumper. In 1899 he held the world's records for the high hurdles, low hurdles, and broad jump and he won these three events and also the 60-meter dash in the Olympic games of 1900.

Kraenzlein's mark of 15.2 seconds was in the record books for 15 years, until Fred Kelly of Southern California broke it in 1913 with a race of 15 flat.

Actually Forrest C. Smithson improved the Kraenzlein mark in the 1908 Olympics in London when he won the 110-meter high-hurdle race in 15 seconds. The metric distance is 120 yards 10$\frac{7}{10}$ inches and any record over the 110-meter course now automatically becomes the record for 120 yards.

Smithson, however, was given only the 110-meter high-hurdle mark at the time, and Kraenzlein's figure stayed in the books until Kelly's race. However, with the new form there was a general improvement in high hurdling and the 15.2-second record was equaled in 1908 by national champion A. B. Shaw, in 1909 by Smithson and also by W. A. Edwards, and in 1912 by John P. Nicholson, late track and field coach of Notre Dame.

Fred Kelly, who won the Olympic 110-meter high-hurdle championship in 1912 and set a world's record of 15 seconds flat for the 120-yard hurdles the following year, has a particularly warm spot in my heart. In those days good prospects in track and field at the University of Southern California were few and far between and Fred came as a gift from heaven to a struggling young coach.

No small amount of intestinal fortitude must be possessed by

124

hurdlers as they risk spills in skimming over the barriers at top speed and I found Kelly well supplied with courage and an ideal type to work with in the event. What he lacked in speed he more than made up for in recklessness in cutting his margin of safety over the hurdles to an eyelash. Also though he was soft-spoken and easygoing, he feared no competitor. You can imagine how I practically split wide open with pride when my pet athlete became the first University of Southern California student to win an Olympic title.

While Fred was still at Southern California, another good-looking prospect came along on the Trojan freshman team. He was Earl Thomson; later as a varsity competitor at Dartmouth and as an Olympic representative for Canada, he was to prove one of the greatest hurdlers of his day.

Kelly's 15-flat record, tied by himself in 1914, stood for three years. Then in 1916 Thomson dropped it to 14.8 seconds, but the new mark was too short-lived to receive consideration as a record. Just 2 weeks after Thomson's fast time, Bob Simpson, a rangy husky from the University of Missouri, turned in a 14.6-second record-shattering performance.

Thomson was too good a hurdler not to win official recognition in the record-breaking class eventually. In 1920 he not only won the Olympic 110-meter hurdle title in the Olympic record time of 14.8 but also cut Simpson's 120-yard mark down to 14.4 seconds.

Simpson, Thomson, and Harold Barron, of the Meadowbrook Club, Philadelphia, dominated American high-hurdling ranks for some time. Simpson was national champion in 1916 and 1919, Barron in 1917 and 1920, and Thomson in 1918, 1921, and 1922.

Meanwhile Kelly had liked flying over hurdles so well that he had turned to aviation. After serving in the American air forces during the World War, he became one of the first air-mail pilots. Flying, which was no doubt first inspired by his jaunts over the hurdles, is still tops in his life and today Fred is chief pilot for one of America's biggest air transport companies.

Incidentally, there must really be a strong connection between hurdling and flying, for we find that Thomson also turned to aviation. When he won his first A.A.U. national championship in 1918, it was as a representative of the Royal Air Force, Toronto.

Even though high hurdlers in general were running much faster in the 1920's than in the previous decade, Thomson's records held up well for some time. G. C. Weightman-Smith of South Africa ran the 110-meter hurdles in 14.6 seconds in 1928 and the following year E. Wennstrom of Sweden set a new world's record of 14.4 seconds for the metric distance. This mark also made Wennstrom a coholder of the 120-yard high-hurdles record with Thomson.

Eleven years after Thomson established his 14.4 mark, Percy Beard, a lanky, limber, easygoing Southerner who had been practically unbeatable while at Alabama Poly, joined the ranks of world's record holders when he won the national A.A.U. championships in 14.2 seconds. The same year S. Sjostedt of Finland tied the 14.4-second 110-meter record and in 1932 George Saling also tied the metric mark in winning the Olympic title. The latter was also credited with a 14.1-second race in winning the N.C.A.A. championships in 1932 but this record was never officially adopted. Jack Keller of Ohio State was another of the outstanding hurdlers of this period.

Winner of three national championships, Beard dominated the high-hurdle field for a time just as Thomson had done in his prime. Like Thomson, he eventually also became the holder of the world's records in both yards and meters, adding the metric mark to his collection in 1934 with a 14.2-second race in Olso, Sweden.

Beard combined an ideal build for his event with perfect form and when he came into possession of both records it was thought that no man would be able to challenge his supremacy for a long time. But the era of phenomenal high hurdling was at hand, for in 1935 his 120-yard mark was tied by three men. Tom Moore of the University of California equaled it first. Then the unheard-of feat of two men running a dead heat in world's record time occurred when Phil Cope and Roy Staley, University of Southern California sophomores, broke the tape together in 14.2 to tie Beard's record.

Hurdlers began working more and more for speed as well as hurdling perfection and out of a large group of star performers arose a tall, lithe Georgian named Forrest Towns, who had everything a champion needed in perfect combination. Long-

126

Twin Record Breakers

Competition within a team's own ranks is one of the greatest incentives to championship performances. Southern California team mates Roy Staley, left, and Phil Cope ran a high hurdles dead heat in 14.2 seconds when this time was the world's record.

legged and limber, with a sprinter's speed and splendid form over the barriers, Towns lowered the high-hurdle marks at both yards and meters to 14.1 seconds in 1936. Staley equaled this time and Bob Osgood of Michigan turned in a 14-flat performance, but in 1937 Towns put the record down to a new sensational figure when he ran the 110-meter hurdles in 13.7 seconds in Oslo.

Only Fred Wolcott and Ed Dugger, a Negro flier from Tufts who won the 1940 N.C.A.A. title in 13.9 seconds, have been able to break 14 flat since Towns record-slashing achievement and there are many track fans who believe that Towns has put the world's record away for keeps. Although I must admit that it doesn't seem humanly possible to run 120 yards over ten 3-foot-6 barriers any faster, I am of the opinion that the record will go still lower, and in the near future.

We are turning middle distances into sprints and long distances into middle distances through our knowledge of how to train for speed and combine it with endurance and now we seem to be making just another sprint out of the hurdles. Perfection in hurdling form is turning the clearing of a barrier into just a long step in the middle of a sprint as the modern hurdler runs his race. A far, far cry it is from the aviating 1880's when national champions sailed gracefully—and unhurriedly—over the obstacles and won races in 19 seconds. Today races in 15 seconds, world-record time a few years ago, are common in high school meets. The 1939 national A.A.U. champion was Joe Batiste, a high school boy from Tucson, Ariz. and his time was 14.1 seconds. Allan Tolmich of Detroit and Boyce Gatewood of Texas have also made sensational time in recent years.

Since proper technique is of the utmost importance in high hurdling, candidates need to work harder for perfection of form in this event than in any other on the track. Not until he has eliminated every trace of waste motion will he ever find success.

In clearing the hurdle the runner must do it in such a way that he is in the air a minimum of time and is in sprinting position when he strikes the ground. Despite the obstacles, he must always be moving forward at a steady rate of speed. Proper hurdling technique requires that the barriers be cleared by the slimmest possible margin. Occasionally in practice I like to have hurdlers place pennies or matches on the top of the obstacles. When they

127

take the hurdles so closely that they flick the objects off with their abbreviated pants, they know they are skimming the sticks properly.

A most important point in technique is that as the hurdler clears the barriers his head is never raised higher off the ground than during normal sprinting. To visualize this better, imagine that you were taking in a side view of a flight of hurdles being run across a field. Suppose that between you and the hurdles there was a 5-foot hedge, hiding the hurdles from your view. With an expert hurdler running the course in correct form you would never be able to tell from the bob of his head when he cleared the barriers.

Keeping the head on an even plane is accomplished by leaning forward as the hurdle is taken. When the athlete raises his leg to clear the barrier, he leans far forward at the waist. With practice he can do this so smoothly that all head bobbing and time-wasting upward motion are eliminated.

Usually eight strides are taken in the 15-yard opening drive to the first barrier. On the marks it is usually best to start with the opposite foot advanced that will clear the hurdle first. However, to conform to some individual peculiarity in build, starting, or pickup, a variation in the placing of the feet might be necessary. Usually right-handed people start with their left foot forward and take off at the hurdle with their left foot.

Three strides must be taken between the hurdles. If the hurdler cannot cover the 10 yards in three strides he might as well give up the event. Short athletes who either have to take five steps or must lose speed by stretching out to three abnormal strides have no chance to become champions. One extra stride above the prescribed three means that the hurdler will find himself in no end of trouble as he tries to alternate with his take-off leg at each hurdle.

The stride that clears the hurdle takes off about 7 feet in front of the obstacle and is completed about 4 feet beyond it. Fairly short hurdlers—those of less than 5 feet 11 inches in height— usually cover more than this 11-foot distance in their hurdle stride. By doing this, they do not have to stretch out with steps of abnormal length between the barriers.

It might be well to mention here that height in high hurdlers is reckoned not by the athlete's total altitude but by the length of his legs. A medium-sized boy who is "split to the ears" may be ideal material. In my experience, however, I have never seen an outstanding star in this event of less than 5 feet 9 inches in height; practically all champions have been 6 feet or better. The principal test of whether a boy can ever be expected to make fast time is, of course, not by the yardstick but by his ability to speed the 10 yards between the barriers in three normal strides.

In starting to move over the hurdle, the runner brings up his front, or lead, foot with a slight bend at the knee. The body takes such a pronounced forward lean that as the athlete clears the hurdle the chest almost meets the knee of the lead leg. The forward foot is extended only a short distance beyond the hurdle when it is snapped down to the ground. The sharp body angle furnishes a natural aid to this quick finish of the hurdle stride.

As the hurdle is being cleared, the rear leg is brought up with the thigh swinging out and on a plane parallel with the ground. The lower leg, which is also swung up parallel with the ground, is crooked at the knee. The bend at the knee is sufficient to put the lower leg and thigh approximately at right angles to each other. Some hurdlers, especially those who are extremely slender and loose-jointed, make this angle a very sharp one, and it may vary with the athlete's physical qualifications.

The rear leg is swung over smoothly. By the time the hurdler's crotch is directly over the barrier, the knee of the rear leg has swung forward to a point where the foot is about even with the crotch. The ankle of the rear leg should be turned in such a way as to lift the toe over the hurdle. This eliminates drag and the possibility of hitting the hurdle with the foot after the rest of the body is over it.

The smooth swing of the rear leg brings it naturally in position for the sprinting stride as the lead leg strikes the ground. If the runner lets his rear leg trail, he will have to jerk it over quickly and will land with a jolt. This is disastrous to smoothness and the sprinting speed that must be maintained.

Proper use of the arm swing aids balance in clearing the hurdle. If the hurdler's lead leg is his right one, as he goes over the barrier his left arm reaches straight out. This forward reach puts the left hand close to the right toe just before the foot is swung down to the ground. The hurdler carries his right arm in the same manner he would if he were sprinting. In fact, the only time the hurdler varies from sprinting form in the carriage of his arms is when he reaches out in leaning forward in clearing the sticks. Then he reaches out only with the arm that is opposite the lead leg.

While the shoulders move naturally with the swing of the arms, they should be facing forward evenly when the hurdle is cleared. If the runner overreaches with the arm opposite the lead foot, he will thrust his shoulder too far out in front and throw his body off balance.

Wild swinging of the arms in clearing hurdles is due to bad balance. The hurdler who finds himself flailing the air should work on just one barrier over and over again until he can keep his shoulders square at the instant of hurdling and fall into a natural sprinting stride as he hits the ground.

Keeping the trunk well forward as the barrier is taken not only makes it necessary for the runner to bring his front leg down quickly but also carries momentum into the next step. Hurdlers of the past lost much time by sailing through the air as they uncoiled the forward leg for the landing, and in this style of clearing barriers few of the athletes were able to carry their body weight properly into the next stride.

In handling their hurdlers, coaches continually stress smoothness. One of the most difficult things about obtaining this smoothness is picking up the sprint between the obstacles with no loss of time. When technique is so mastered that the hurdles are skimmed and the hurdle stride flows smoothly into the sprinting stride, the hurdler then reaches his objective of becoming a sprinter and his contest with the timers' watches and with his opponents depends upon old number one, which is speed.

Because of the stride of approximately 11 feet that the hurdler takes in clearing the barrier, the first stride after landing cannot help but be a recovery step and somewhat shorter than the next two strides. Candidates who have difficulty in making the 10 yards between the hurdles in three strides should work particularly on this recovery step. For hurdlers not endowed with especially long legs, this stride gives the best opportunity to compensate for an unfavorable build.

Loose-jointedness in hurdlers is very important as a man with

130

tight hips cannot snap the lead leg down quickly. For this reason, hurdlers never stop working on the bending and stretching exercises that are particularly good for relaxing and loosening the hips and crotch.

Quick acceleration is as necessary to a hurdler as it is to a sprinter. In sprinting we have seen how the runners take 30 to 35 yards in their pickup before they hit their top speed and raise their bodies up to the sprinting angle. In high hurdling the runner has only 15 yards before the first barrier is reached. Obviously he cannot hit his maximum sprinting speed by this time, but he must approach it as closely as possible because it is very difficult to increase the speed when the hurdling is begun.

The greatest hurdlers, however, develop the ability to gather momentum as they go. Forrest Towns, the present world's record holder, used to leave the pack at about the fifth hurdle and then fly the rest of the way.

The first hurdle is usually the most important one in the race. If the runner clears it as nearly as possible to full speed and in good form, he has the momentum and equilibrium that will probably last him throughout the full race. If he takes the first barrier badly, he may never be able to get into his proper groove.

Next to the first hurdle the last two or three are the most difficult because the runner is beginning to tire or perhaps to press in an attempt to catch other men who are ahead. Athletes in good condition find easy sailing throughout most of the early and middle stages of the race and they shouldn't get overconfident and try any short cuts over the final hurdles.

To compensate for fatigue in the later stages, it is sometimes a good idea to try to give the last few hurdles a little more clearance. It is well to remember that the wood used in the hurdles today just doesn't "give."

Concentration is a vital point in a hurdler's race. He can take only one obstacle at a time and consequently he should never look farther down the course than the next hurdle. He should never try to sneak a peak at his opponents as this will prevent him from concentrating on his own hurdles, perhaps throwing him off his timing just enough to cause a spill.

Once over the last stick, the athlete is a sprinter and must lean well forward and dig in to develop his maximum speed. He must try to attain in the final 15 yards his full sprinting speed, something that obviously has been difficult for him to do with a series of obstacles in his way up to this point. Although he had little chance to hit his top speed by the time he reached the first hurdle, he now has this opportunity when the last barrier is cleared. His 15-yard sprint to the first hurdle was from a standing start, but at the finish he has a final 15-yard sprint from a running start and this advantage gives him his greatest and perhaps only opportunity in the race to run wide open.

A great many high-hurdle races are won or lost in this final 15-yard drive and the hurdler who has studied sprinting form and worked often with the dash men has a big edge over the competitor who has neglected his high-speed work.

Breathing should be done in a relaxed, normal manner. Sometimes the 100-yard dash man runs his race on three long breaths, but the hurdler simply takes in his air as he needs it.

In taking up training methods for the event, it should be emphasized that great hurdlers are made, not born. Although it is true that tall, long-legged athletes have the advantage in build, no one was ever born with natural hurdling ability. A rangy boy with good speed might be excellent material for the race but only hard work and lots of it will ever give him the skill to take advantage of his physique.

Leaving the talk of character building to football coaches who have to explain a losing season, I must say that there is something about high hurdling that is certainly a revealer of character.

Has a boy got patience and stick-to-itiveness? Does he do his stretching and bending exercises over and over again each day and does he repeat and repeat the clearing of from one to three hurdles until he gets his form right?

Has a boy got will power? Does he make the sacrifices in diet and late hours and does he put in the time on the track necessary to develop endurance?

Has a boy got courage? Does he save time over the hurdles by skimming them and does he take bruises and spills with a smile, coming back to his event more determined than ever to increase his speed by eyelash margins over the barriers?

All champions have to have these qualities and one of the greatest pleasures I have had in coaching is in watching boys

132

develop into topnotchers because they've had what it takes in moral fiber.

About 15 years ago an unusually frail-looking boy reported for track at Southern California. He said he wanted to take up high hurdling, but after one look at him I wondered if he could run as far as 120 yards without any obstacles in his way. Equipped with little strength, form, or speed for the event, he made rather sad affairs of his first races and I expected him to be badly discouraged. Each defeat, however, only sent him more diligently back to work in his training and never have I seen a more conscientious candidate. For one of his slight build, he began developing amazing stamina. His speed increased somewhat, but he simply wasn't the sprinting type and I could see that this would always be a weakness. Consequently the only thing to do was to concentrate on form.

The result of two years of hard work was that Leighton Dye became one of the most perfect high-hurdle stylists I have ever seen. Entirely on determination and perfect form, he arose to the top ranks in his event. A consistent 14.6-second performer, he won the I.C.A.A.A.A. championship in 1925 and both the I.C.A.A.A.A. and national A.A.U. titles in 1926.

I am not one to do much preaching in track coaching work but I have to admit that Dye's accomplishments have been a big inspiration to numerous later Trojan hurdlers who followed his example in developing themselves into performers of championship caliber.

Early conditioning in the fall should follow closely the program of the sprinter. Daily walks of at least 2 miles should be taken, and there should be about two visits a week to the track for jogging and wind sprints. The hurdle candidate can take longer jogs than the sprinter to build endurance but he shouldn't make a practice of lengthy jaunts that build stamina at the expense of springy speed.

Extremely important in the preliminary work are the exercises. Since he must be exceptionally supple, he needs many bending exercises to stretch his muscles and tendons. The high kicking and bouncing exercises that high jumpers specialize in are also good. The deep knee bends and leaps into the air that are fundamentals of Russian ballet dancing likewise are helpful.

133

The pet exercise of the barrier man and the one he tries practically every day in the year is "ground hurdling." In this, he simply sits on the ground and takes the same leg position that he uses when he is clearing a hurdle. His lead leg is stretched out in front with his back leg bent as though it were being swung over a barrier. With his legs in this hurdling position he bends forward as far as possible, bringing his chest down to the thigh of the lead leg. At the same time he reaches far out in front with the arm opposite the lead leg. This exercise and the "splits" will do much for candidates who are troubled by tightness in the hips.

To get a smooth swing of the back leg over the barrier, the candidate should stand alongside a hurdle and swing his leg over it, attempting to get the same form that he will actually use in hurdling. Standing on his lead leg and holding something for support, he can practice this leg swing over and over again, concentrating on making the movement smooth and continuous.

Parallel-bar exercises are valuable, especially those that stress spreading the legs and stretching the hip tendons. Because candidates for practically all events can well afford to pay visits to the parallel bars during an afternoon of training, I believe that all practice fields should have this apparatus.

When the candidate is ready for actual work over the sticks, it is best not to use a wooden hurdle at first. Early in his training he should work over a piece of gauze tape or string that is stretched between a pair of hurdles and which will pull out easily if struck. In this way the candidate is given the correct hurdling height but he will be in no danger of injuries to knees or ankles or of taking bad falls if he fails to clear the obstruction. As a further protection, the ankle of the rear foot can be covered by a sponge-rubber pad or some kind of light brace to prevent bruises if the back foot drags too low at first.

There is no use in trying to run a series of hurdles until the form over one is perfected. After technique begins to be developed through practice on one barrier, the sticks can be run for a time in a series of two or three. When good form can be kept for three hurdles, the candidate is ready for the complete series of ten but he doesn't need to run the full flight often in practice.

Sprinting shoes should be worn. Some hurdlers believe that they need heel spikes, but the only time the heel should strike

134

the ground is at the take-off and the skillful athlete in this event does not want to be bothered by the heel spikes that used to be common.

Because speed is as important as correct hurdling technique, the candidate should work out much of his time with the dash men. Short sprints up to 50 yards and many starts as practiced by sprinters should be on every barrier man's training program. Jogging is helpful but should be restricted to mild amounts, not more than ½ mile at a time. The 220-yard dash can be used to build up endurance in practice and occasional hard runs up to 300 yards are also useful.

If the hurdler runs frequent 220's in training, he won't have to worry about much additional work to develop his staying qualities. Although the hurdler needs more endurance than the dash man, he should remember that he is really a sprinter with a few obstacles tossed in front of him just to add zest to his life.

At morning and at night in his room as well as in the afternoon practice session, the hurdle candidate should run through the exercises that will increase his suppleness. It is absolutely essential that the hips be loose. Otherwise the hurdler must go too high in the air to clear the obstacle.

Tightness makes the hurdler lunge instead of striding smoothly over the sticks. Boys who do not have the looseness required for high hurdling and who cannot seem to develop it should try another event. Perhaps the low hurdles, in which speed and stamina now count much more than form, would be a better race.

Hurdlers need patience not only in learning technique but also in keeping it polished throughout the season. It is easy for them to get off form by suddenly and mysteriously acquiring a small, unnoticeable fault.

When a coach finds an athlete slipping off form, he should check the hurdler from every angle, watching such factors as body lean, leg position, balance, arm action, length of stride, take-off, landing, and pickup leading to the first hurdle. In hunting for "bugs" in my hurdlers who have slipped off form, I like to get perspective by standing about 30 yards away and from there watch the boys run the barriers in series of two or three.

A typical schedule for a hurdler's training week follows: wind sprints and intensive work on the exercises, especially "ground

135

The runner approaches the high hurdle in a sprinting stride up on his toes. The right arm, which is the lead arm from a right-footed take-off, is carried fairly low. As the right arm starts to reach forward, the high knee lift of the left leg starts.

The sprinting angle of the body starts a steady change to a sharper angle as the hurdler begins a slight forward bend at the waist. The knee lift of the lead leg assists the spring off the take-off foot. As the lead leg comes up in the giant stride, the opposite arm begins to reach forward for balance.

The athlete's limberness is shown by the high position of the left thigh. While the angle of the body changes during the hurdle stride, it does so in a smooth, continuous motion without sudden bobbing or dipping. The left arm is being swung close to the side in the proper sprint carry and is not visible.

The lead leg is elevated almost enough to clear the hurdle and is still rising. At this point the lead arm could be a little lower. Some hurdlers can get better body position over the barrier if this arm is carried down closer to the lead foot. The take-off leg is starting to pull.

As the foot of the lead leg reaches its highest point in clearing the hurdle, the chest contacts the thigh. Note that there is no ducking of the head to get into this position. At this point the right arm could have been a few inches lower with the wrist about even with the ball of the left foot.

The foot starts its descent quickly and the heel is already lower than the hurdle. However, although the lead foot has dropped several inches, the spring from the take-off foot has caused the hips to continue to rise. Meanwhile the take-off leg continues its steady pull.

As the thigh of the trailing leg nears the hurdle, it is lifted parallel to the ground. The take-off foot has been steadily turned and is also parallel to the ground in order to lift the toe out of the way. The body, shoulders, and head face straight forward as the downward thrust of the lead leg continues.

The toe of the lead leg is ready for the landing in sprinting position. The take-off leg is swinging forward quickly to pick up the sprinting stride as the athlete must run in sprint form for the next three strides. The hurdler is James Humphrey, former I.C.A.A.A.A. and Pacific Coast Conference champion, who has a best mark of 14.2 seconds.

hurdling," on Monday; form work over one hurdle, or over three if the technique is correct, two 220's at three-quarter speed, and a lap of jogging on Tuesday; work with the sprinters on starts and short dashes, three or four trials over from three to five hurdles and a lap at a jog on Wednesday; short dashes with the sprinters and form practice over from one to three hurdles on Thursday; light exercises but no track work on Friday; and competition on Saturday.

VIII

THE LOW HURDLES AND 400-METER HURDLES

The Low Hurdles

Progress in low hurdling was retarded for many years because runners in this event insisted too much on being hurdlers. When coaches and athletes realized one day that the race was really a sprint with a bit of woodwork tossed in for spice, we began to develop the general level of fast times that we now have.

Of course, it can't be ignored that along the 220-yard course the low hurdler must clear ten barriers that are $2\frac{1}{2}$ feet in height and placed 20 yards apart. But the point is that, if he concentrates too much on being a hurdler and doesn't run the race as if there were no obstacles in his path, he is going to be a long way from home when the rest of the boys have sprinted across the finish line.

Prehistoric low hurdlers, meaning those who ran before the A.A.U. was invented in 1888 and even for several years thereafter, favored the same sea-gull soaring form that old-time high hurdle stars used. This technique had them crooking the lead leg as it cleared the hurdle, with the runner sailing gracefully through the air as he unwound for his one-point landing.

In tracing the improvement in low-hurdle racing we find that the event was speeded up first by developing a faster hurdle form and then by putting form in the background more or less and concentrating on sprinting.

In 1888, the world's record for the 220-yard lows was set at 26.6 seconds by A. F. Copland in winning the event in the N.A.A.A.A. championships. In 1888 there were two national championship meets, the other being held by the newly organized A.A.U., and Copland won the low hurdles in that one also.

In the nineties, champion hurdlers began to crack 26 seconds and in 1895 J. L. Bremer, Jr., dropped the record down to 24.6 seconds.

Alvin Kraenzlein, the versatile star who was so instrumental in changing high-hurdle technique to the form we have today, also influenced low-hurdle methods. In 1898 he slashed a full second off Bremer's mark by running the race in 23.6 seconds. Kraenzlein's record lasted for a quarter of a century and had one of the longest lives of any track mark ever to gain official recognition. Although it was equaled in 1913 by J. I. Wendell and in 1916 by Bob Simpson, who had set a new high-hurdle record of 14.6 seconds the same year, it was not broken until 1923 when Charles R. Brookins of Iowa lowered it to 23.2. Just as he did in running the high hurdles, Kraenzlein abandoned the fancy twist of the lead leg in going over the barriers. He changed the business of clearing a hurdle from a slow, floating aerial act to a fast high-stepping stride.

Kraenzlein, as we have seen, was an exceptionally fast man and when a successor as a record holder eventually came along it was in the person of another athlete noted for his ability as a sprinter. Brookins could run the 100-yard dash in 9.8 seconds and he packed the power of a quarter-miler along with his speed racing ability. The year after he set his 23.2-second record, he dropped the mark down still farther, putting it at 23 flat.

In 1929 R. C. Rockaway of Ohio State was timed in 22.8 seconds, using starting blocks, and in 1932 Jack Keller, also of Ohio State, was credited with a 22.7-second race, but neither of these marks saw the record books.

Normal Paul of the University of Southern California tied the 23-second record in 1933 and two years later Jesse Owens cut it to 22.6 seconds. If track experts hadn't been convinced up to this time that the low-hurdle race was primarily a sprint, the flying Negro star from Ohio State won them over with his performance. His record-breaking day was May 25, 1935, and when he smashed the low-hurdle figure it was the fourth time that afternoon he had tied or cracked a world's record. Owens started out by tying the 100-yard dash record of 9.4 seconds, then broke the broad-jump mark with a leap of 26 feet 8¼ inches, and lowered the 220-yard dash figures to 20.3 seconds. After thus proving himself supreme in speed ranks, he showed what a great sprinter could do to the low hurdles by cutting $\frac{4}{10}$ second from the world's record.

All this is by way of convincing the young man who would be a successful hurdler that the race must be treated principally as a sprint. Form over the barriers is important, but not so vital as in the high hurdles, and the most perfect technique will never make a champion out of a runner unless he also develops sprinting speed.

Fred Wolcott of Rice Institute, who combined the speed of a 9.5-second 100-yard dash man with perfect hurdling technique, cracked Owens's world's record in the Princeton Invitational meet of 1940 with a 22.5-second race. The most consistently fast man over the hurdles that the track sport has ever seen, Wolcott won the 1940 senior national A.A.U. championship in the 200-meter low hurdles in 22.6 seconds, after setting an American record of 13.9 seconds in winning the 110-meter high hurdles.

Many candidates who have been unsuccessful in the high hurdles have turned to the lows and become splendid runners because they were better able to meet the conditions of low hurdling. The man who runs the low sticks doesn't need to be so supple and limber, particularly in the hips and crotch, as the high hurdler. Although short men are at a big disadvantage in the high hurdles, they may attain success in the lows unless they are so stubby that a barrier of 2 feet 6 inches constitutes a real leap for them or the 20-yard distance between the woodwork is too great for them to cover in the normal seven strides.

Successful high hurdlers can usually turn in a good low-hurdle race but it does not follow that low hurdlers can switch so easily. Sometimes a great low hurdler is entirely unsuited to the highs. Although there are occasionally men like Fred Wolcott who can turn in championship performances in either event, it is best for an athlete to specialize in one race or the other.

It sounds confusing, but the form used in the low hurdles might be described as the same as that employed in the highs, only different. The approach is the same, the length of the hurdle stride is similar, the lead leg goes up the same, and the action of the back leg in being pulled over quickly and smoothly is almost the same.

The big point of difference to remember is this: you don't have to skim the low hurdles. Since you don't have to save time by allowing only a hair's breadth margin between yourself and the woodwork, you don't have to use the pronounced body lean of the

141

high hurdler. In other words you don't hurdle too much—you are too busy sprinting.

High hurdlers who necessarily must be specialists on form find the matter of body angle a big handicap when they try to shift to the lows. They are unable to overcome their tendency toward an extreme body lean as they go over the hurdles. If the low-hurdle candidate will keep this matter of body angle in mind, he can follow the technique of the high hurdler in most of the remaining points as he works on his form over the barriers.

As he starts over the hurdle, he brings up the lead foot with the knee bent slightly but with the trunk retaining the sprinting angle instead of bending down to the knee. This may give the appearance of sailing over the hurdle, but it doesn't result in loss of time because the sprinting stride is not broken. The forward foot is swung down quickly after clearing the hurdle.

Because the rear leg does not have to skim the barrier as in high hurdling, it is not necessary to bring the thigh up parallel to the ground as it clears the obstacle. In this point of hurdling the low-stick man, therefore, doesn't need the suppleness of the high-barrier performer. The ankle must be flexed and the toe raised so that it does not strike the hurdle, but here again loose-jointedness is not so essential.

As in the high hurdles, any drag on the rear leg or delay in bringing it over the hurdle will cause the runner to land with a jolt and a consequent breaking of his stride. It is so easy to clear the obstacle that low hurdlers often fail to swing the rear leg over quickly enough to have it in position for a sprinting stride as soon as the lead leg lands.

The length of the hurdle step naturally varies with the build and striding peculiarities of the runner. The stride when the barrier is taken may vary from 10 to 13 feet but the average is 11. Long-legged men usually take the shortest stride over the hurdle because they can practically step over it and do not need to stretch out. Short-legged athletes take a longer leap not only because they require greater effort to clear the hurdle but also because it makes it easier for them to run the 20 yards between barriers in seven steps.

The heel is used lightly in the take-off at each hurdle but otherwise the entire race is run on the toes. It is well for all track men to keep continually in mind that sprinting is always done on the toes. The instant a man drops down to a flat-footed stride he becomes a runner, not a sprinter.

Momentum for the race must be gained in a fast start and sprint to the first hurdle. The beginner should practice until he can reach this first barrier in ten strides. The 20-yard opening sprint must bring the runner to his first hurdle at very nearly top speed. If he takes this hurdle in correct form and lands in sprinting stride, he will develop his full speed by the time he reaches the second barrier.

A beginner often needs nine strides between the barriers, but this requires too much time for competition and the steps must be cut to seven as soon as possible. Some hurdlers, unable to make the distance in the required seven strides, use eight. The take-off legs must be alternated in this process. Few low hurdlers can use the eight-stride method with any degree of success because no man can take off equally well from alternate legs.

Jesse Owens showed that the low-hurdle event was a sprint rather than an obstacle race when he set his amazing 22.6-second official world's record. There are track aspirants by the thousands who wish they could run a furlong on the flat in 22.6 seconds. When Owens turned in this time with ten barriers in his path, he could have defeated many ordinary 220-yard dashers running without hurdles. Since his best 220-yard dash time is 20.3 seconds, the difference between that mark and his low-hurdle time shows that it required just 2.3 seconds for him to take the ten barriers along the way.

Lest anyone should get the idea from the emphasis on speed that no one should even try the race unless he is a natural sprinter, let us also consider how perfection in hurdling form can help a boy with ordinary speed.

Earl Vickery of the University of Southern California is an outstanding example of a runner who first learned form, then developed enough speed to go with it to make him a champion in his event. Earl ran the low hurdles a number of times under 23 seconds during the 1939 season, setting an I.C.A.A.A.A. record at 22.8 seconds. His fastest mark was 22.7 seconds, just $\frac{1}{10}$ second off Owen's record. Yet Earl in a flat 220-yard race was nearly $1\frac{1}{2}$ seconds slower than Owens.

Vickery's best 220 flat race was 21.7 seconds. This means that when ten hurdles were placed along the route it required him only 1 second more to negotiate them. We have already seen that the difference between Owens's best 220 sprint and his best 220 hurdles race was 2.3 seconds, more than double Vickery's 1-second margin.

A natural deduction is that had Vickery possessed Owen's sprinting speed he would have been able to run the low hurdles in the phenomenal time of 21.3 seconds. And of course another deduction is that had Owens had Vickery's hurdle form he would have set the low hurdles record at 21.3 instead of 22.6.

It is well to remember that Owens was no low-hurdle specialist, as was Vickery, and made no pretense at having perfect form over the barriers. With the aid of his excellent coach, Larry Snyder of Ohio State, he specialized in sprinting and broad jumping, in which he won three Olympic championships in 1936. Because of his marvelous gifts of sprinting speed and his steady improvement under Snyder's coaching, it naturally was better for Owens to spend most of his time on the sprints and broad jump instead of worrying about learning hurdle form. The fact that his low-hurdle record was set merely incidentally to his career in other events makes his accomplishment even the more remarkable.

Vickery's running career is interesting to trace because it shows what specialization can do. He first became interested in track and field as a high school sophomore at Chaffey Union high, in Ontario, Calif. Having little natural speed but being fairly long-legged he tried the high jump. He was unable to place in any prep meets and experimented with other events. Toward the latter part of the season he switched to the low hurdles. His big moment came in the Class B division of the league championships when he placed fourth in the 120-yard low hurdles and by so doing won a track letter.

The next two years found him working hard on the low hurdles and finishing his senior season by being runner-up in the state high school championships. Then he attended Chaffey Junior College for a year and worked out under Coach Ernie Payne, an excellent student of form who had won an I.C.A.A.A.A. championship in the low hurdles for the University of Southern California in 1931. In junior college Earl shaded 24 seconds. Entering the

144

sophomore class at Southern California, Earl cut his time down to 23.2 seconds and won his event in the N.C.A.A. championships. As a junior he improved his mark to 22.9 and in his senior year he cut it down to 22.7.

The interesting part of Earl's improvement is that during his last two seasons at Southern California he was given speed work almost entirely in training. He had perfected his hurdling form as a sophomore and therefore the only way to improve his time was to make as fine a sprinter as possible out of him. In preliminary work and during the first few weeks of the 1939 season, Vickery was put through the sprinter's training program and for a time we just forgot that he was a hurdler. In fact, even when he began to run the low hurdles in meets, we'd ignore the barriers in returning to the practice field the following Monday and would go back to sprint training again.

Because he was a boy who enjoyed every minute of his practice sessions and cooperated thoroughly, he developed excellent speed for one who was far from being a natural sprinter and he threatened Owens's record closely on several occasions.

Vickery's greatest rival in his final college season, in 1939, was Fred Wolcott, who, as we have mentioned, was a great sprinter as well as hurdler. The meeting between Vickery and Wolcott in the 200-meter low hurdles in the 1939 national A.A.U. championships was a classic. Neck and neck they sped over the entire ten hurdles, Vickery seeming to gain a momentary advantage as he cleared each barrier and Wolcott winning it back between the obstacles.

At the final hurdle Vickery put everything he had learned about hurdle form and sprinting into a tremendous effort and went ahead. I would like to be able to finish this by saying that Earl's long, conscientious training in sprinting resulted in a final dash that brought him victory. But the fact is that the most conscientious hurdler who ever lived can't beat a 9.5 sprinter like Wolcott on the flat. A yard or two from the tape Wolcott flashed by to victory.

The difference was slight but it told the story—a great hurdler with natural sprinting speed had beaten a great hurdler with "made" sprinting speed. The conclusion could be that no one will ever become a champion in the low hurdles unless he is a natural sprinter of unusual ability. But Vickery, a hurdler with "devel-

145

oped" speed, won many championships and came within an eyelash of tying the world's mark; some runner of his type may yet set record time.

At any rate, Vickery's accomplishments can be an inspiration to other boys who want to be outstanding low hurdlers but who are unduly worried about the lack of natural sprinting speed. Their progress must be made the hard way, but they can get to the top by saving time over the hurdles with perfect form, developing stamina that will catch tiring competitors, and then creating as much sprinting ability as bodies not naturally endowed for high-speed work can hold.

Despite my emphasis on speed throughout the discussion of the low hurdles I have to admit that Kenny Grumbles, Bill Carls, Ernie Payne, and Earl Vickery, all intercollegiate champions while running for the University of Southern California, and Norman Paul, who tied the world's record when it was 23 flat, were all boys who won their honors much more on hurdle technique than on natural speed.

Like the quarter-miler, the low hurdler has to develop both speed and endurance. Since their main problem in general conditioning is the same, their training schedules in preliminary work should be much alike. Preseason conditioning for the low hurdler should be like that of the quarter-miler—exercises in the gymnasium and later in the fall a couple of days a week on the track for jogging and wind sprints. Endurance work should not be overdone by running many laps because the hurdler must eventually develop the sprinter's springiness and fine edge.

Although the low hurdler does not need the limberness of the man who runs the highs, he can profit by the same type of bending and stretching exercises. The "ground hurdling" exercise, with the lead leg stretched out in front, the trailing leg placed out at the side at right angles to the hip and bent at the knee, and the trunk bending forward and returning to an upright position, is one of the best.

During the training for the regular competitive season in the spring, the low hurdler when not concerned with practice on form should divide his time between work with the sprinters and drill with the quarter-milers. He needs the starts and short sprints of the dash men to develop his speed. He also can use the numerous

220's and 330's and even an occasional 660—all popular training distances for 440 men—to build his stamina.

In developing hurdle technique, the beginner should work for a long time on only one hurdle. Then he should perfect his step from the start to the first hurdle. It is extremely important for him to gain full speed in this opening 20-yard drive and to clear the first obstacle in the proper form. Then when he has full confidence that he can take the first hurdle in perfect step and with good speed and form he can work on his technique over three hurdles. As in high hurdling it isn't necessary to run the full flight often in practice.

In early hurdle training, the low hurdler should protect himself from spills by stretching a light tape or string between the tops of two hurdles. He should hurdle over this instead of trying to clear wooden barriers.

When the candidate starts running three hurdles at a time he will find that he must develop not only a sprinting stride but one that is uniform in length. A sprinter's stride should not vary to any appreciable extent but it could do so without any harm to his race. A hurdler's stride must never vary. His seven strides between hurdles should bring him up to the same take-off distance at every barrier.

When he loses his step through irregular running and is forced to try to regain it by shortening his stride just before the take-off or by broad-jumping the hurdle, his chances for fast time are gone. The race is a continuous sprint, fractions of a second are important, and he who hesitates at the hurdle is last.

Running the low hurdles in series of three is such valuable training in creating a uniform stride that pole vaulters and broad jumpers, athletes who must hit take-off points with exactitude in order to be at their best in their events, are often trained over three barriers.

Here is a typical training schedule for a low hurdler during the regular season of competition: Monday, form work over one hurdle, starts with the sprinters, and a jog of ½ or ¾ mile; Tuesday, two 220's, starting with full speed and finishing with full speed, or heavier work up to 660 yards with the quarter-milers, a lap at the start of practice and one at the finish, a few starts if speed work is greatly needed; Wednesday, jog a lap at

147

As the low hurdler springs off his left toe, his right thigh comes up high enough to be parallel to the ground and the left arm goes forward for balance. The body moves forward to a more acute angle than the sprinting angle but not so far forward as in clearing a high hurdle.

This hurdler is taking the barrier with little margin although it is not necessary to skim the obstacles as in the high hurdles. The right arm of this runner, which is swinging back in an exaggerated sprint position, could have been bent more at the elbow, as in normal sprinting.

For good balance the left hand is carried fairly low and almost alongside of the right foot. The left leg has already started its fast, steady pull and the foot is turning to raise the toe. When the athlete is clearing the low hurdle, his thigh and chest do not contact as they do in high-hurdle technique.

As soon as the lead foot clears the hurdle, the leg starts an immediate downward drive to prevent time-wasting sailing through the air. As the knee of the trailing leg clears the hurdle, it is carried fairly low, no attempt being made to bring the thigh up parallel to the ground as in the high hurdles.

Swinging the lead arm down helps to bring the right leg back to the ground quickly. As the trailing leg clears the hurdle, the thigh is in line with the top of the barrier. The knee of this leg remains fairly low. The foot is now turned parallel to the top of the hurdle to keep the toe or instep from dragging and striking the obstacle.

As the right leg is ready to strike the ground, the left knee from its continuous pull has reached a point slightly in front of the right thigh. The foot position insures a toe landing that will be ready to propel the athlete forward in his regular sprinting stride. Taller athletes than this runner could bend the right knee and land closer to the hurdle.

The athlete here is about average in height. The short-legged hurdler would have to sail out beyond the point of this landing in order to reach the next obstacle in seven strides. This runner is landing firmly with no loss of forward momentum, avoiding the common fault of "caving in."

The pull of the left leg has been timed perfectly to swing into the sprinting stride on the first step after clearing the obstacle. Good body balance over the hurdle has automatically put the athlete back into his sprinting angle. The hurdler is Earl Vickery, former N.C.A.A., I.C.A.A.A.A. and Pacific Coast Conference champion who has a best mark of 22.7 seconds.

the start, warm-up practice over one hurdle, two 70-yard races over five hurdles, a medium-fast lap at the finish; Thursday, five or six 40-yard dashes over two hurdles, or starts and dashes with the sprinters and no barrier work if further practice is not required on hurdling form; Friday, limbering-up exercises but no track work. Exercises, of course, are always on the program except on the day of competition.

400-METER HURDLES

Once upon a time an ogre of some kind noticed with surprise that boys were running long distances and thriving on the work and sprinting over hurdles and growing hardier every minute. Something should be done to end this race of happy, healthy athletes, he figured with a fiendish sense of humor, and he thought up the 440-yard hurdles in which the runner has to clear ten 3-foot obstacles while running an already severe distance. Clearly invented with homicidal intent, the 440-yard or 400-meter hurdle race is the man-killer of track and field. Although I have never seen anyone give up the ghost entirely in this race, more than once I have observed the boys in such a condition that I thought the event would end with a wake at the last hurdle.

Whether the race is 440 yards or 400 meters, which is $437\frac{1}{2}$ yards, the hurdles are the same distances apart. From the starting line to the first hurdle the distance is 45 meters, or 49.23 yards. Between barriers the distance is 35 meters, or 38.29 yards.

The race has never had much popularity in the United States and has never been a regular event in the colleges. Even though it is run in the Olympic games and the low-hurdle race is not an Olympic event, we still stick to the lows in high school and university meets and run the quarter-mile barriers only in A.A.U. competition.

Comparatively few Americans excelled in this event in the early days of track and field. One of them, Harry L. Hillman, now highly successful head track and field coach at Dartmouth, turned in a remarkable performance in the 1904 Olympic games in St. Louis, winning the 400-meter barriers in 53 seconds. His regular event was the low hurdles, which he won in the same Olympic meet. The Olympics, incidentally, programed the 200-meter low hurdles in only the 1900 and 1904 games.

150

C. J. Bacon, another American, won the 400-meter hurdles in the 1908 Olympics in London in 55 seconds, but the event was not run in the 1912 meet and there was no more international competition in it until the 1920 Olympic games in Antwerp.

Meantime because the 440-yard hurdles were not introduced into national A.A.U. championship competition until 1914, the best records at the 440 distance were held by British athletes. G. Shaw of England set a record of 57.2 seconds in 1891 that stood for 19 years until a countryman, G. R. L. Anderson, lowered it to 56.8 seconds.

First national A.A.U. champion in this event was W. H. Meanix of Boston. He won the race in 57.8 seconds the first time the A.A.U. put it on its program in 1914; the following year in repeating his championship victory, he cut far under the record with a time of 52.6 seconds. This mark was not allowed because of a wind but during the same year he bagged the 440-yard hurdles world's record with a performance of 54.6 seconds.

During the 1920's, star hurdlers at this trying distance were much more numerous in the United States, among the standouts being Johnny K. Norton, F. F. Loomis, F. Morgan Taylor, and John A. Gibson. Norton lowered the 440-yard hurdles record to 54.2 seconds in 1920. Loomis won the national title at that distance and took the Olympic 400-meter championship during the same year.

Taylor reigned as national champion in 1924, 1925, and 1926 and won the Olympic championship at Paris in 1924 in the fast time of 52.6 seconds. This record was not allowed, however, as he had knocked down a hurdle during the race. Gibson won the 440-yard hurdles national championship in 1927 and set a new world's record of 52.6 seconds in doing it. Taylor was not to be kept out of the record-breaking class, however, and in 1928 he broke the world's record for the 400-meter hurdles by running the race in 52 seconds flat.

Taylor couldn't repeat his Olympic win that year though, and Lord Burghley of Great Britain took the event to mark the first time in six Olympiads that America had suffered defeat in this race.

American runners were also doomed for defeat in the following Olympics, the 1932 games in Los Angeles, where Robert Tisdall of Ireland won in the record-smashing time of 51.8 seconds. Once again the Olympic winner failed to get credit for the world's record because of knocking down a hurdle and Tisdall's mark did not count. Instead, the runner-up, who was Glenn Hardin of the United States, was credited with 52 seconds flat and went down in the record books as joint holder of the world's mark with Taylor.

Hardin proved to be a brilliant prospect in this event and for several years he was outstanding in national competition. In 1932 before the Olympics he had finished first in the national championships only to be disqualified for stepping out of his lane, but in 1933, 1934, and 1936 he took the A.A.U. crown without dispute. In 1934 he reached his peak in a world's-record-breaking 400-meter hurdle race of 50.6 seconds in Stockholm; in 1936 he climaxed his career with an Olympic victory in Berlin. Although Hardin now holds the world's record for the hurdles in meters, he never had much opportunity to crack Gibson's record of 52.6 for yards as all national A.A.U. competition has been over the 400-meter course since 1932.

Hardin is a perfect example of what it takes to be an outstanding quarter-mile hurdler. He had endurance and speed, having run 47-flat quarter miles and having been timed in 23 flat in the low hurdles. With his stamina and ground-eating stride he could also run an exceptionally fast half mile. Besides these qualifications, he was long-legged and limber, possessing the suppleness of a high hurdler.

High hurdlers find plenty of hard work ahead when they shift to this tiring race because they are usually men of the sprinting type and lack endurance. Hardin, although a high hurdler in his rangy type of build, developed stamina as a quarter-miler. Later he ran both the low hurdles and the 440 flat; finally he stepped up to the 3-foot hurdles of the quarter-mile obstacle race.

Tom Moore, who had tied the world's record for the 120-yard high hurdles when it was 14.2 seconds, is an example of a high hurdler who took on the added distance successfully. He won the national title in 1935.

Jack Patterson of Rice Institute, who was national champ in 1937 and 1938, was a good performer in both the high and low hurdles. Roy Cochran of the University of Indiana, who won the national A.A.U. title in 1939, was Western Conference low-hurdle champion the same year. In the indoor season of 1940, he proved one of the country's fastest runners at the grueling distances from 440 to 600 yards. Carl McBain of U.C.L.A., a good but not outstanding low hurdler, won the 1940 national A.A.U. 400-meter hurdle title in 51.6 seconds to tie the American record.

In taking up the technique of hurdling the 3-foot barriers, we find that candidates must spend much more time on form than they have to in the low hurdles. The style of the high hurdler must be used since the height of the obstacles is too great for them to be taken in the easy low-hurdle stride. Runners must use a pronounced body lean in going over the obstacle. They also need the looseness in the hips and crotch that will enable them to skim the sticks with the lead leg straight ahead and slightly bent at the knee. The trailing leg should be parallel to the ground and at right angles to the hips when the barrier is cleared.

Because the runner becomes much more fatigued in this race than he does in the high or low hurdles, it is more difficult for him to maintain a definite number of strides between barriers. Fifteen strides should be taken between the hurdles and the outstanding men in this event usually hold to this number right up to the finish. Eighteen steps to the first barrier are standard. It is easier for beginners to meet this requirement than it is for them to stay down to fifteen strides between the sticks.

With the fatigue that wears down a runner toward the end of this race will come a tendency to shorten the stride. Since the champions themselves occasionally tie up to the point where they miss their step, it is wise for all competitors in this event to know how to take off from either foot.

The runner should always keep his eyes on the hurdle just ahead. If he cannot maintain a uniform stride between hurdles so that he will automatically arrive at the proper point of take-off, he must make allowances in his last few steps in coming up to a barrier. In these steps he should increase or decrease his stride in order to arrive at the proper take-off spot. This take-off, as in the high- and low-hurdle races, is about 7 feet in front of the barrier; if the runner is tiring badly at the final hurdles, he will want a shorter distance.

Often it is better to take off with the wrong foot than to broad-

153

jump the hurdle to try to maintain the stride or to put in two extra steps and then high-jump the obstacle.

For the beginner there are many ifs, ands, and buts because the race is so fatiguing and hazardous, but if he is intent on excelling he should always bear in mind that the best men in this event are those who hold to a uniform stride and make the 38-yard distance between hurdles regularly in fifteen normal steps.

Much starting and sprinting to develop speed and plenty of work with the half-milers to build up endurance are involved in the training of this event. A strong finish must be developed as most races are won or lost in this final sprint. In the closing burst of speed, the quarter-mile hurdler must remember that he is now a sprinter. Like the dash men he must run on his toes, use a good arm action, and carry his body at the sprinting angle.

A point always to be considered when a coach starts training a man for the 440 hurdles in this: what did he do first?

No innocent child ever starts life wanting to run a quarter mile and ten hurdles at one and the same time, but when in his youth for some unexplainable reason he gets the idea that he wants to try this man-killer, one must consider his past track work.

Was he a quarter-miler or middle distancer who has built up such endurance that he thinks he can tackle anything, or was he a hurdler now seeking a form of suicide? If he has had the background of endurance, then he must be worked with the sprinters and high hurdlers for speed and form. If he has been a hurdler, then he needs to start chasing around the track with the middle-distance boys to build up his wind and stamina.

First of all, however, I think some kindly soul should take him to one side and say, "Listen, son, what's this I hear about your wanting to take up the 440-yard high hurdles? Be reasonable, my boy, life is a beautiful thing after all; why risk ending it all right in the bloom of youth? . . . " etc.

If nothing can be done to change the young man's mind, here is a sample midseason training schedule: jog a lap, work for form over one hurdle, finish with two or three laps with the distance men if stamina is needed, or practice sprint starts and jog a lap, on Monday; take four dashes over three hurdles, or short

154

sprints on the flat if hurdle practice is not needed, and finish with a fast 330-yard dash, on Tuesday; work on one or two hurdles if better hurdle technique is needed and finish up with a good 660 with the quarter-milers, or run three 220's at close to top speed and finish with a lap, on Wednesday; practice starts and limbering up, with no hurdle work and no dashes of more than 35 yards on Thursday; stay away from the training track on Friday to store up energy for the man-killer on Saturday.

IX

RELAY RACING

Most spectacular of all events in track and field is a good relay race. When four-man teams are fighting it out so closely that positions are shifted with each exchange of the baton, the fan is treated to as hair-raising a thriller as he can find in any sport.

The mile relay is often the deciding event of a college dual meet and is kept for the last as the feature of the program. High school meets are usually topped off by a sprint relay.

Relay carnivals, in which baton-passing events are served up as the main course of a track meet instead of the dessert, have become among our most popular track and field spectacles. The University of Pennsylvania was one of the first institutions to foster a big meet featuring relays. Now in addition to the Penn relays we find that the Drake, Texas, Kansas, and West Coast relays are attracting more interest than most championship meets.

During the 1940 track season, at the suggestion of Coach Brutus Hamilton of the University of California at Berkeley, California and Stanford held a relay meet in addition to their regular dual affair. The event was so successful that it may be copied by other institutions, and relay racing, which now has only a small part on the dual meet program, may become prominent enough to stand on its own in intercollegiate and even interscholastic competition.

There are two relay races on the schedule of the Olympic games. They are run at 400 and 1,600 meters. In the United States, the relay races we see most often are the four-man mile in college meets and the four-man half mile in high school competition. Occasionally high schools stage a four-man two-mile or an eight-man mile instead of a four-man 880.

Baton-passing races are run over a variety of distances. World's records are recognized for the four-man teams at 440 yards, 880

156

yards, 1 mile, 2 miles, and 4 miles and in their metric equivalents of 400, 800, 1,600, 3,200, and 6,000 meters.

Sprint and distance medleys, shuttle hurdles, and sometimes makeshift medleys in which there is no attempt at standardization are found on most relay carnival programs. The shuttle-hurdle race is for 480 yards with the athletes running back and forth over a 120-yard high-hurdle course. The distance medley is usually divided into runs of a quarter mile, half mile, three-quarter mile, and mile. In the sprint medley there are usually a quarter mile, two 220's, and a half mile. Another popular medley starts the race with a mile which is followed by a 220, 440, and 880.

In early relay racing a runner would start the next man by touching his hand. In the confusion of several athletes being touched off at the same time it was impossible for judges to determine whether or not there had been proper contact between the team members and the plan of passing a stick was adopted.

Success in relay racing in the events up to one mile depends as much upon the speed with which the baton is passed as the fleetness of the runners. Fractions of seconds count in the short races and often championships can be won and records broken by teams whose individual personnel is not outstanding. A relay squad that by perfect technique can pick up 2 or 3 yards at each pass of the stick can often defeat a team of stars doing mediocre work at the exchanges.

Relay racing at the shorter distances has been my own particular hobby for many years. One of my assignments as a member of the coaching staff of the American Olympic team in the games of 1928, 1932, and 1936 was to handle the American 400-meter relay team. Working with boys who were not only fast runners but also willing to put in much time in order to perfect their team work, I had some of the biggest thrills of my life in seeing the 1928 team win and tie the world's record, the 1932 team win and set a new world's mark, and the 1936 team win and set a still faster world's record.

At the University of Southern California I've also had a lot of fun working with relay teams. At present, Trojan teams hold the official world's record in the 440-yard and mile relays and American records that are up for adoption as new world's records in the 440-yard, 880-yard, and 800-meter relays.

157

In seeking to increase speed in the sprints we are always striving to cut tenths of a second from a runner's time. In working with relay teams, I use a watch that shows hundredths of a second and drill the boys over and over again in baton passing until the last $\frac{1}{100}$ second of speed can be squeezed out. Relay racing has shown steady improvement during the past twenty years and I believe that the marks will continue to go down for some time to come, as we are nowhere near the limit of our possibilities.

Sprinters from Great Britain were victorious when the 400-meter relay was introduced in the Olympic games in 1912. In the next games, in 1920, an American team won, and in 1924 the United States quartet anchored by Loren Murchison finished first in the fast Olympic and world's record time of 41 seconds flat.

One of the first great American sprint relay teams consisted of Bernie Wefers, Jr., F. K. Lovejoy, H. Ray, and Ed Farrell, who established two world's records in a national championship meet July 5, 1921. Their times were 42.4 seconds for the 440-yard relay and 1:27.4 for the 880-yard distance.

A University of Southern California team, anchored by Keith Lloyd, brought the 440-yard world's record down to 42 seconds in 1925, but this mark had a second lopped off in 1927 by another American foursome anchored by H. H. Cumming, Jr. This time of 41 seconds also tied the 400-meter record, and the latter mark was equaled twice more in 1928. A German team anchored by Salz hit 41 flat that year and the American Olympic quartet of Frank Wykoff, James Quinn, Charley Borah, and Henry Russell made the same time in winning the event in the games at Amsterdam.

After the 1928 Olympic games, a German 400-meter team anchored by Kornig reduced the 400-meter record to 40.8 seconds and the following year another German squad, with Kornig leading off and H. Schlosske running anchor, tied this mark.

Americans returned to the record class at this distance in 1931, however, when a University of Southern California foursome consisting of Roy Delby, Milton Maurer, Maurice Guyer, and Frank Wykoff dropped the 440-yard mark to 40.8 seconds. This record was also officially adopted as equaling the 400-meter time, since 400 meters is $2\frac{1}{2}$ yards shorter than 440 yards.

158

This 40.8-second 440-yard record is still in the books, but as a 400-meter mark it has been beaten by American Olympic squads. In the 1932 games in Los Angeles the United States foursome left the 400-meter relay field far behind in the world's record time of 40 seconds flat. Frank Wykoff of Southern California ran anchor on that team which included Bob Kiesel of California, Emmett Toppino of Loyola University of New Orleans, and Hector Dyer of Stanford.

The 400-meter record took a further beating in the 1936 games in Berlin. The American squad of Jesse Owens of Ohio State, Ralph Metcalfe of Marquette, and Foy Draper and Frank Wykoff of Southern California took it down to 39.8 seconds. Some idea of the speed of these boys in this race may be obtained when you divide this figure by four and find that the average per 100 meters was 9.95 seconds.

The world's record for 100 meters, held by Owens, is 10.2 seconds. If Owens as leab-off man for that foursome had equaled his world's record for his opening 100 meters, it would leave 29.6 seconds for the remaining three runners to cover the distance. This means that Metcalfe, Draper, and Wykoff ran their respective laps in the average time of 9.87 per 100 meters, or approximately 9 seconds per 100 yards. This is really flying and shows how fast boys can travel when they are off to perfect running starts.

Already accepted as an American record is a 440-yard relay mark of 40.5 seconds set by Leland LaFond, Mickey Anderson, Payton Jordan, and Adrian Talley of Southern California in the West Coast relays at Fresno, Calif., in 1938 and this mark is up for adoption as a new world's record to supplant the 40.8-second time held at present by a Trojan team.

The baton-passing timing of this 1938 foursome was so precise that, even though Talley was the only sprinter of any national reputation in the group, the boys averaged 10.125 seconds for every 110 yards, which would be approximately 9.2 seconds for every 100 yards.

Probably because there is no 800-meter relay in the Olympic games, the half-mile event has not been shaved down so finely. The 1:27.4 record made in 1921 was dropped down to 1:25.8 by a Southern California quartet composed of Charley Borah,

159

Herschel Smith, Ed House, and Willie Lewis in 1927; this mark was also recognized as the world's 800-meter record for 10 years.

Meantime in 1934 another Southern California team comprised of Foy Draper, Al Fitch, Ed Abbott, and Charley Parsons, Jr., had cut off a second in a 1:24.8 race. This was officially recognized as an American 880-yard and 800-meter record, but A.A.U. officials claim that the application blanks for world's records were lost and that international recognition now awaits new applications.

In 1937 a Stanford University foursome composed of Jimmy Kneubuhl, Stan Hiserman, Ray Malott, and Jack Weiershauser ran the 880 relay in 1:25. This figure is down as the present world's record while the Southern Californians are awaiting recognition of their 1:24.8 mark.

Records in the mile and 1,600-meter relays have been lowered infrequently but in good-sized chunks in recent years. American Olympic team men took the metric record down from 3:16 to 3:14.2 in 1928 and also lowered the 1-mile mark from 3:16.4 to 3:13.4. The team of George Baird, Fred Alderman, Emerson (Bud) Spencer, and Ray Barbuti bagged the metric record in winning the 1,600-meter relay in the Amsterdam games. A month later in a post-Olympic meet in London, with F. Morgan Taylor, the 400-meter hurdler, substituting for Alderman, the same group set the 1-mile mark.

A university foursome took the mile relay record from this all-star group in 1931 when Stanford's team of Maynor Shove, Alvin Hables, Leslie Hables, and Ben Eastman covered the distance in 3:12.6. The 1,600-meter record underwent a terrific slashing in the 1932 Olympics when the American quartet of Ivan Fuqua of Indiana, Edgar Ablowich of Southern California, Karl Warner of Yale, and Bill Carr of Pennsylvania hacked off 6 seconds, putting it down to its present figure of 3:8.2.

In 1936 the University of Southern California added the mile relay to its record collection when a team of Estel Johnson, James Cassin, Harold Smallwood, and Al Fitch cut off a second and put the time at its present offical 3:11.6. Four years later, in 1940, a Stanford foursome consisting of Charles Shaw, Ernie Clark, Craig Williamson, and Clyde Jeffrey covered the distance in 3:10.5. This mark is now awaiting consideration as a new record.

Other present world's records are as follows: 2 miles and 3,200 meters, 7:35.8, set in a post-Olympic meet in 1936 by an American national team comprised of Charles Hornbostel, Robert Young, Harry Williamson, and John Woodruff; 4 miles, 17:16.2, made by the 1937 University of Indiana team of Mel Trutt, James Smith, Tommy Deckard, and Don Lash; and 6,000 meters, 15:55.6, established in 1930 by a Great Britain nationa team of Harris, Hedges, Cornes, and Thomas.

In the 3,200-meter relay event the official record was broken by an American quartet in Paris in 1939, and this mark of 7:35.2 is now up for adoption. The American stars on a tour of Europe just before the war broke out were Roy Cochran of the University of Indiana, Ralph Schwartzkopf of the University of Michigan, Blaine Rideout, formerly of North Texas State Teachers College, and Charles Beetham, formerly of Ohio State University.

Fast sprint-relay time is made possible principally by expert stick passing, as we have seen that even the record-holding teams, except for Olympic foursomes, have rarely had more than one outstanding star on them. Coaching opinion varies on the best technique for exchanging the baton and there are several good methods in use. The one I like for the sprints places the burden on the incoming man to make a good pass to the outgoing runner so that the later can give his full attention to a fast start and pickup.

Baton passing in relay races must be done in a zone 20 yards in length which is marked on the track. The passing zones give the runners a leeway of 10 yards on each side of their finish line.

In the sprint relays the exchange of the stick should be made while the team mates are running as closely as possible to top speed. To get a good run, almost the full length of the passing zone should be used, with the exchange being made just inside the last restraining line. In order to make full use of the passing zone and to avoid fouling by failing to complete the pass before crossing the last restraining mark, relay runners need both long practice and good headwork.

In the actual passing of the baton the incoming runner carries it in his left hand and places it in the right hand of the outgoing man. The receiver, with his attention centered on gaining momentum in the passing zone, makes a pocket, or cup, of his hand. The hand that will receive the stick should be cupped and carried closely to the hip. The elbow should be bent out and the finger tips or knuckles should touch the hip lightly. The incoming man reaches out as far as possible with his left hand and delivers the baton into the cupped hand of the outgoing runner who does not look back to receive it.

It is a good plan for the incoming runner to deliver the stick with a little force so that his team mate will know the instant he has received it. A pass that is too gentle and ladylike may not be immediately noticed by the outgoing runner in his concentration on getting a fast pickup.

Since the outgoing man once he starts to sprint does not watch the runner delivering the baton, the burden of making a good pass is therefore placed mainly upon the incoming sprinter. The important thing for the outgoing athlete is to time the start of his run so that he will be close to full speed just inside the far end of the passing zone when his team mate, running at his maximum speed, reaches him.

Let us see how this timing is worked out. The incoming man may be called A and the outgoing sprinter B.

In order to get the best timing for the exchange, B must know when to start running. He takes his position at the first line in the passing zone. He cannot use a crouching start from starting holes but he should be leaning well forward so that he can pick up speed quickly. His head must be turned so that he can watch A as he approaches the passing zone. As a rule, the best time for B to start running will be when A is from 6 to 9 yards from B's position at the restraining line.

If the coach is really anxious to get the maximum amount of speed out of each exchange, he therefore must consider A's speed as he comes in and B's pickup as he leaves, varying the distance to suit the requirements of each twosome. If A is a slow finisher and B is a fast starter, the distance must be shortened. If A is a fast finisher and B is a slow starter, the distance must be lengthened.

In working with the American Olympic 400-meter relay team during the 1936 games, I found that a distance of $7\frac{1}{2}$ yards

162

could be used in the Owens to Metcalfe and Metcalfe to Draper passing combinations. However, because of Wykoff's unusually fast pickup the distance was cut to 6½ yards in the Draper to Wykoff combination.

In the 1932 games the distance had to be cut down for both Toppino, who ran the second leg of the relay, and for Wykoff, who ran anchor.

In the 1928 Games the problem was of another kind. The anchor man was Henry Russell of Cornell, a tall, long-legged sprinter who had a terrific finish but who was a little slow to get going. In our workouts Charley Borah, running the third leg, would come in so fast that he would overrun Russell in passing the stick. We finally found that if Russell started off when Borah was 9 yards from the restraining line the exchange could be made at top speed just before Russell reached the end of the passing zone.

When the various A-to-B distances are determined by experimentation in the workouts, the runners should measure off these distances and mark them in front of the restraining line. Nothing should be left to chance and the proper mark should be closely watched by B as A approaches the passing zone. If B starts while A is still 1 or 2 feet from the mark, he may overrun the zone before the pass is made and cause his team to be disqualified. If B starts just a bit too late, A will reach him in the passing area before he has the proper momentum and the result will be a bungled, time-losing pass.

Experience has shown that in the quarter-mile relay, in which the runners are traveling wide open, the A-to-B distance should be about 7 to 7½ yards. In the half-mile relay, in which runners may be tiring although still trying to sprint at top speed, the average A-to-B figure is about 6 to 6½ yards.

When B sees that A has reached the mark, B should turn his head forward and sprint hard with the same vigorous arm action he would use if he were coming out of starting holes. After he has dug in for about 10 yards, he should then stop the action of the right arm and drop his hand to his hip in a cupped position ready to receive the pass. Until he receives the baton, he must keep his right hand as steady as possible to make it easy for A to place the stick in it.

The outgoing man in the sprint relay never looks back after he has started to run. Since A knows that B is no longer watching him and won't wait for him if he slows down, it is up to A to continue at his greatest possible speed until he delivers the stick.

In order that B may quit worrying and unconsciously holding back until A catches him, it is a good idea for A to yell "go" or "hike" at the instant he contacts B with the baton.

All runners but the last man should carry the baton in the left hand. The athlete who runs first starts with the stick held by his thumb and supported by his little finger while he uses the other three fingers for balance in the starting crouch. If he is afraid of losing the baton while carrying it in this position, he may grasp it firmly in his hand although this may upset his starting balance a little. The second and third men shift the stick from the right hand to the left as soon as they receive it. The anchor man carries it just as he has received it in order not to go through any waste motions.

Runners should remember to keep a firm grip on the baton throughout the race. Dropping the stick en route or inadvertently throwing it away while pumping furiously with the arms does not endear one to one's team mates.

The order in which a coach runs his athletes in a relay sometimes requires more than a little thought. All other things being equal, it is usually most advantageous to start the man who is third best, with the slowest man running the second leg. The next to the fastest man follows in third position and the speediest man runs anchor.

Certain conditions may call for a different line-up. The lead-off man should be a fast starter; if the third best man doesn't qualify in this respect, he is not the right runner to open the race.

Another point for a coach to consider is whether his boys run better when they are ahead or behind. Most athletes can force themselves to greater effort if trailing and faced with the necessity of making up ground, but some are overcome by a defeatist complex or tighten up in such a situation.

With a group of good front runners, the best strategy is to start the fastest man to build up a lead and use the second fastest for the anchor leg.

If the boys have the ability to come from behind, then it might be best to open with the slowest runner and work up to the fastest for the final lap. It is always well for a coach to consider the individual personalities he is dealing with when he is determining the running order of his athletes.

Nearly all sprint relays are run in lanes throughout the entire distance. If a relay is run in which there are no lanes after the first straightaway, the fastest man should be started in an attempt to take the pole and get away from the scramble. If the man used at the start is not the fastest, he should at least be the biggest and strongest to withstand all the jostling that will go on in the battle for the pole position.

There are still other factors to consider in the relay line-up. For instance, in the 1928 Olympic games I put Frank Wykoff in the starting position on the American 400-meter relay team because he was just out of Glendale, California, High School where he had been used in the opening relay lap to put his four-some out in front. He was not accustomed to receiving the baton and felt more at ease in the starting role. Later through practice Frank became adept at taking the baton from another runner and his tremendously fast pickup going into the final lap made him a valuable man to use at anchor. Consequently on Southern California relay teams and in the 1932 and 1936 Olympic games I used him as anchor man.

Another point in arranging the order for the American Olympic 400-meter team in 1936 was the ability of the men to run on curves. Jesse Owens and Foy Draper could run a curve almost as fast as a straightaway. Ralph Metcalfe and Wykoff would lose a little speed on the turns. Therefore I placed Owens at No. 1 to run the first curve, Metcalfe at No. 2 to run the back stretch, Draper at No. 3 to run the far curve, and Wykoff at No. 4 to run the homestretch.

When a relay man has to run farther than 220 yards he will be tired at the finish and probably slowing down. Therefore in longer relays another method of baton passing is used, in which the burden is on B, the outgoing man. In relays of a mile or more, B must keep his eyes on A, who will be fatigued at the finish, in order to help him make a good pass. Instead of cupping his right hand on his hip, as in the sprint-relay pass, B simply runs with his right hand reaching straight back in a palm-up position. His

In the sprint relay the responsibility for a fast exchange lies mostly upon *A*, the incoming runner, as *B*, the outgoing man, does not watch him after starting to run. *B* must time the exchange right by starting at the proper instant. *B* must also hold the correct hand position for receiving the stick.

A keeps his eyes on *B*'s right hand and hip. *B* has his right hand properly cupped with his finger tips against his hip bone and his elbow out. In this exchange, *B* started to run when *A* was 7 yards from the passing zone. *B* sprinted 10 yards before placing his hand on his hip. At this instant *B* has covered about 14 yards of the 20-yard passing zone.

A places the stick in *B*'s cupped hand. *A* has carried the stick at one end to give *B* plenty of room to grip it. *B* has now run about 15 yards in the zone. *A* is sprinting on the right side of his team's lane to avoid spiking his teammate during a fast pass. Once *A* has placed his cupped hand on his hip he does not change the hand's position until the stick is placed in it.

Both runners are driving hard as *B* grips the stick. *A* is sure that *B*'s grip is firm before he releases the baton. The runners have now covered between 16 and 17 yards in the passing zone.

At about 18 yards the pass is completed. The instant that *A* places the baton in *B*'s hand he may yell "Go" or "Run" to discourage any tendency that *B* may have to hold back for the pass. If *B* has started to run too soon or is running away from *A* in the passing zone, *A* should yell "Slow" or "Wait." In the fast action of the exchange, conversation is limited to one syllable.

A well-timed exchange should be completed at a point from 16 to 19 yards inside of the first restraining line of the passing zone. To be sure that he does not slow down before completing the pass, *A* drives hard until *B* is on his way with the stick. Since *B* never looks back once he has started to run, *A* must undertake most of the responsibility for a good pass.

The outgoing man immediately shifts the stick to his left hand to be ready for the next pass. This not only prevents him from absent-mindedly arriving with it in the wrong hand for the next exchange but also gives him free arm action for his entire race. Changing hands during the peak of his sprint would upset his running form and cause him to lose speed.

Before the completion of two strides, the outgoing runner has the stick in proper position for the next pass. The incoming runner continues in his own lane as he slows down to keep out of the way of athletes behind him. The runners here are Howard Upton (left) and Harold Smallwood, quarter-milers who have also run on sprint relay teams. Both have marks of 47 seconds for the 440 and 21.4 seconds for the 220.

right arm is turned outward so that the thumb points back to the incoming runner. This is opposite to the twist of the arm for the sprint pass, in which the elbow is out and the arm is turned inward to hold the cupped hand.

The outgoing runner judges his own pickup by the speed with which his team mate is finishing. Naturally he does not need the full run of the 20-yard passing zone as the sprint-relay man does. Until the instant *B* takes the stick, he keeps his eyes glued on *A* to watch for any faltering in his stride or for any emergencies that may arise from *A*'s fatigued condition. If *A* is finishing strongly, *B* can take a good long run and have plenty of speed himself when the pass is made. If *A* is extremely tired and faltering badly, *B* must meet him almost at the restraining line and forget about a fast start of his own.

In the mile relay and in relays of longer distances, headwork on the part of the runners is just as important as baton-passing technique. Bearing in mind that *A* is coming in tired and cannot take the burden of responsibility for a fast pass, *B* must be ready for anything and effect a quick exchange through his own efforts.

When the University of Southern California mile-relay team broke the world's record in 1936, the boys saved time by meeting passing problems with quick thinking. The lead-off man, Estel Johnson, was a pace runner with little finishing sprint and came in badly tired. The second man, Jimmy Cassin, noted his condition and met him almost at the back line. Taking only two or three steps to provide his own momentum, Cassin completed the pass about 5 yards from the first restraining line.

Cassin, in turn, ran himself out and had little left at the finish. Observing this, Harold Smallwood, the third man, also waited at the restraining line and effected the exchange about 5 yards from it.

Smallwood came in with a beautiful sprint and Al Fitch, anchor man, immediately saw the chance for a fast exchange. Starting at the restraining line, Fitch sprinted 15 yards before taking the pass, thereby beginning his final quarter mile with excellent momentum.

Theoretically in the mile relay each member of the team runs 440 yards. Yet we have seen how the boys in this world's record-breaking race saved time by varying this distance within the

168

limits of their 20-yard passing zone. Johnson actually ran 435 yards, Cassin 440, Smallwood 450, and Fitch 435. Approximate times for each quarter mile were 48.6 seconds, 48.2, 47.8, and 47 flat.

Normally the exchange in the mile relay is made just about on the finish line, which is midway between the boundaries of the passing zone. In the record race none of the exchanges was made in the normal location. Headwork varied the spot and saved at least a full second, which was the margin by which the old record was broken.

When Stanford's 1940 mile-relay team ran its 3:10.5 race, the approximate times for each 440 were Charles Shaw, 47.5; Ernie Clark, 48.3; Craig Williamson, 47.4; and Clyde Jeffrey, 47.3.

It is customary for teams to draw for lanes before a relay race. As a rule the lane in which the start is made is also the one in which the exchanges must be effected. There may be local rules on this point, however. Sometimes to even up things, officials decide to alternate lanes. For instance, if there are nine teams in the race, the team that starts on the pole makes the first pass in the ninth lane, the second exchange back in the first lane and the final pass again in the ninth lane.

Naturally in the mile relay the teams in the outside lanes have to run farther. However, if the runners start angling off to their proper passing lane as soon as they enter the homestretch they will not have to cover much extra ground.

With relay men being required to find their proper lane for the exchange of the baton, confusion sometimes is unavoidable. In the I.C.A.A.A.A. championships of 1939 at Randall's Island, New York City, a spectacular pile-up occurred as the three leaders on the next to last lap approached the passing zone and turned toward their proper lanes.

Twenty yards from the passing zone, Clyde Graf of Pittsburgh, Harold Bogrow of New York University, and Howard Upton of Southern California were running one-two-three almost shoulder to shoulder with Graf on the pole and Bogrow in the middle. Upton on the outside suddenly spurted with the terrific sprint that was characteristic of his finishes and began to swing slightly to his right to finish in the fourth lane where he was to make the pass to Erwin Miller.

Just as he started to pass Bogrow, the latter turned out to his right to finish in the sixth lane which was N.Y.U.'s passing lane. Pittsburgh had an inside lane and Graf continued straight ahead. In crossing over toward his sixth lane, the N.Y.U. man hit the foot of Upton and the Southern Californian sprawled flat on the track. The collision also upset Bogrow and he fell across to his left in front of Graf who likewise took a dive.

The remarkable feature of the spill was that despite their unpleasant tangle with the cinders none of the runners dropped the stick. All scrambled to their feet and Upton started Miller off in the lead ahead of the trailing teams even after losing from 4 to 5 seconds.

In a powwow after the race the judges decided that the three boys who spilled were all minding their own business at the time and trying to follow the regulations. The official ruling was that the accident was unavoidable and not to be blamed on anyone.

Sometimes competitors are unfairly delayed when runners do not finish properly in the passing zone. The incoming man after passing the baton should continue straight ahead while slowing down in order not to obstruct others behind him. The passer should stay in his own lane and not try to leave the track until he can do so without causing interference to those behind him.

In the 480-yard shuttle high-hurdle race, the athletes run back and forth and there are no batons to pass. As the incoming man arrives, an official standing behind the outgoing hurdler taps him on the back as a signal that he may start. The shuttle hurdle race is a spectacular event and it is unfortunate that it is not run more often. There is no world's record for the event but the American intercollegiate mark is 59.8 seconds and is held jointly by two Southern California teams, the 1932 foursome of Joe Bills, Al Vignolo, Jimmy Payne, and Jeddy Welch and the 1936 quartet of Gene Culp, Bill Brown, Roy Staley, and Phil Cope.

Since relay men are specialists in their own field—sprinting, quarter-miling, long-distance running, etc.—often they are so busy with their various training problems that they go into relay meets without sufficient baton-passing practice. Coaches and runners should realize that there is no use entering a relay race unless they have prepared properly. To get the exact timing will require many practice exchanges and much running over and over again.

These practice passes provide wind sprints and short speed dashes that are always beneficial, and baton drill can thus successfully replace another type of workout.

A team well schooled in passing the baton can pick up from 1 to 5 yards at each exchange. That means a lot of valuable time in a sprint or mile relay. It also means that boys of only ordinary running ability but of superior passing technique can often go out and trim athletes of greater natural speed, thereby adding welcome points for old Alma Mammie and perhaps in major relay carnivals winning a few gold watches for themselves.

A, the incoming runner in the mile relay, extends the baton with more than three-quarters of it available for the grip of *B*, the outgoing man. *B* reaches back with his palm up. *A* comes in on the right side of his team's lane and *B* takes his position on the inside of the lane in order to avoid a collision or spiking.

As *A* reaches forward for the exchange, *B* holds his hand steady so that there will be no sparring for the stick. *B* watches both the runner and the stick as the responsibility for a good pass rests upon him. If *A* is finishing fast, *B* digs in for a quick pickup. If *A* is tiring, *B* waits for him.

At the instant of the exchange, both runners have their hands on the stick and both are watching it. The incoming man makes sure that the outgoing runner has a firm grip on it before he lets go. Tired runners finishing laps in the longer relays have a tendency to reach too far forward with the stick. This may cause a loss of balance and a bad spill.

As *A* is releasing the baton, *B* is turning his body ahead quickly. The incoming runner has not ceased to drive hard up to this point in order that the outgoing man may work up good momentum during the exchange. *A* is coming down on his inside foot and would have spiked *B* if each runner had not stayed on his own side of the lane.

The outgoing runner has turned ahead and is starting his drive. His left hand is already getting into position to take the stick from his right hand. As B has an exchange to make at the end of his lap, he makes sure that he will bring the baton in with his left hand by putting it there as soon as he gets it.

B's body angle compares with that of a sprinter in his first 30 yards as he drives hard to develop speed. Since A has just released the stick, he has not yet checked his speed and will not do so until his next stride.

Although the outgoing man has run only one stride since A has let go of the baton, he is already shifting it from his right hand to his left. With the pass completed, A is putting on the brakes.

As A slows down, he stays in his lane and runs straight ahead to keep out of the way of runners that are behind him. The incoming runner in this series is Howard Upton, the outgoing man Harold Smallwood. The latter was national 400-meter champion in 1936 and a member of the American Olympic team.

X

THE POLE VAULT

Pole vaulting requires more all-round athletic ability than any other event in track and field. In the vaulter must be combined the speed of the track man, the upper body strength of the weight thrower, and the gymnastic ability of the tumbler, topped off by a dash of the aviator's daring.

When a track coach has a good vaulter on his squad, he knows that in a pinch he has in this same man a better than average jumper, discus thrower, flat racer, and hurdler. Probably the school's gymnastics coach is also interested in the vaulter and would like to lure him off to gym meets as a rope climber or horizontal-bar performer.

Pole vaulting as a pastime, and often as a utilitarian accomplishment, can be traced back for many centuries. Foreign words for "vaulting" hint strongly at its origin. The Greek word for pole vaulting is translated literally as "spear high jump." The German word *Staubhochsprung* means "staff high jump."

From the Greek word it is easy to visualize the soldiers of the constantly warring Hellenic states using their spears to hurdle hedges and jump streams as they pursued one another with homicidal intent. From the German word, one is taken back to the days when boys and young men of Teutonic tribes tended their flocks and used their staffs as an aid in jumping stone fences or other obstructions. Through the use of the spear and staff in clearing heights or making jumps, a vault technique was developed.

When track and field first inherited vaulting as an event it came in two kinds. There was the pole jump for height and the pole jump for distance. The latter has been given up by the sport of track and field, and the pole jump now is a specialized vault for height only.

Vaulters have made remarkable progress in heading for the stratosphere since G. McNichol of the Scottish-American

174

Athletic Club of New York City won the first national championship in 1877 at 9 feet 7 inches. The official record today is 14 feet 11 inches, held jointly by Bill Sefton and Earle Meadows of the University of Southern California, but Cornelius Warmerdam, formerly of Fresno State College, was credited with a height of 15 feet 1⅛ inches in winning the national A.A.U. championship in Fresno, Calif., June 29, 1940, and this mark will probably be accepted as the new world's record. In every major meet we expect at least one man to reach 14-foot heights.

Two things have contributed to our vaulting progress—the switch from fairly heavy wooden poles to limber, lightweight bamboo, and the development of new techniques.

When H. H. Baxter of the New York Athletic Club set the world's record of 11 feet 5 inches in 1887, he turned in a remarkable performance. His pole was a solid staff of cedar and he used the accepted technique of holding the hands in a set position which means that his lower hand had to be approximately at the height of the crossbar when he cleared it.

Pits in the early modern vaulting days were just the bare ground dug up and loosened a little. Between hard, jarring landings and the constant danger of a pole splitting during a vault, the early competitors in this event were necessarily a hardy and daring set of athletes.

Baxter reigned as national champion from 1883 to 1886 and his record lasted from 1887 to 1892 when W. S. Rodenbaugh of Philadelphia, who had been national champ in 1890, raised the mark to 11 feet 5⅜ inches.

Yale, which has produced more individual I.C.A.A.A.A. pole-vault champions than any other university, developed an outstanding star in 1898 in R. G. Clapp, who raised the world's record that year to 11 feet 10½ inches. In the I.C.A.A.A.A. championships of 1898 he engaged in one of the greatest vaulting duels that had been seen up to that time when he met W. W. Hoyt of Harvard, who had been America's Olympic winner in 1896 at Athens at 10 feet 9¾ inches. The boys fought it out all afternoon and finally tied at the new intercollegiate record height of 11 feet 4½ inches.

Six years after Clapp set his world's record, Norman Dole of Stanford University brought the West into the limelight in this event by clearing 12 feet 1.32 inches. Then came steady improvement in the record, with Leroy Samse raising the mark in 1906 to 12 feet 4⅞ inches, and W. R. Dray of Yale putting it up to 12 feet 5½ inches the following season and up to 12 feet 9½ inches two years later.

During this period following the turn of the century, coaches and athletes were experimenting with bamboo poles sent over from Japan, and as they came into general use vaulting marks steadily grew higher.

One of the topnotchers of the day was A. C. Gilbert of Yale, who tied for the Olympic championship in 1906 with E. T. Cook, Jr., of New York City. An enthusiastic follower of vaulting ever since his competitive days, Mr. Gilbert frequently now takes time off from his manufacturing business to give pointers to athletes at his Alma Mater. His assistance has done much to keep Yale track teams to the fore in the production of championship vaulters. So well has this Olympic champion of more than thirty years ago kept abreast of technical progress in the event that I believe no man in the world knows more about vaulting today than he. Vaulting is the Gilbert hobby and he has shown how a man can continue to enjoy his event long after he has ceased active participation in it.

After the West won back the vaulting record in 1910 with a mark of 12 feet 10⅞ inches by L. S. Scott of Stanford, heretofore unbelievable 13-foot heights came definitely into sight. H. S. Babcock of New York almost hit the 13-foot ceiling in winning the Olympic title in 1912 at 12 feet 11½ inches; during the same year M. S. Wright went over the hump with a record of 13 feet 2¼ inches.

The greatest vaulter during the ensuing decade was Frank K. Foss of Chicago, who added an inch to the record in 1919 and then set a new world's mark of 13 feet 5 inches when he won the Olympic championship in Antwerp the following year. Foss was probably better trained for vaulting than any man up to his time. He had worked on gymnasium apparatus as a boy, building up his upper body by exercises on the horizontal and parallel bars, the rings, and rope. Later he developed speed on the track so that when he went into vaulting he had a perfect background for a championship performer.

A few years later another outstanding competitor in the event came along in Charley Hoff, a tall, rangy Norwegian. Whereas Foss had had specialized training to develop himself as a vaulter, Hoff took up vaulting after first proving adept in many other events. His versatility was another proof for coaches and athletes that to be a good vaulter an athlete must possess more all-round athletic prowess than any other track and field performer.

Hoff was an excellent competitor in the high jump, broad jump, sprints, and hurdles. Although slender, he used to play around with the weights, too, and this developed a strong, wiry body on speedy, springy legs. In 1923 he sent the vault record skyward with a leap of 13 feet 9¾ inches and two years later he barely missed the 14-foot mark with a vault of 13 feet 11⅜ inches.

Before Hoff could become the first vaulter to hit 14 feet, he ran afoul of the A.A.U. while on an American tour. He was disqualified from amateur athletics when he went on the stage in a dancing act and gave exhibition vaults on the side.

Lee Barnes of Southern California and Sabin Carr of Yale started a rivalry about this time that brought more record smashing and the first 14-foot leaps. Barnes had tied for the Olympic title in 1924 with Glenn Graham of California Tech, but in Carr he found a formidable opponent in national intercollegiate competition during the next few years. Carr won the I.C.A.A.A.A. championship for three straight seasons, beginning in 1926, and in the 1927 meet he became the first man to clear 14 feet when he took the record up to that height.

Encouraged by Carr's performance at what had been considered a practically impossible height, Barnes steadily soared higher and in 1928 he broke Carr's mark with a new record of 14 feet 1½ inches. Barnes was an amazing vaulter for his size. Rangy boys have a decided advantage in this event because of their reach and Barnes was only 5 feet 8 inches tall. He was well developed for his size and an excellent gymnast. He could run the low hurdles and throw the discus well and, like Hoff, was fond of trying a variety of events during an afternoon of training.

Combined with this all-round ability was technique as nearly perfect as I have ever seen. Lee and I learned a lot together during our long sessions on the Southern California practice field. Pointers which we worked out and which his vaults demonstrated so splendidly were to be used later by Bill Graber, Earle Meadows, Bill Sefton, "Bud" Day, Kenny Dills, and other Trojan aerialists to whom 14-foot heights became commonplace.

Barnes was the ideal type of athlete to work with—physically well developed, mentally keen, conscientious and enthusiastic in his training. When a coach has such a man who can take the coach's ideas, add some of his own, and then have the physical ability to demonstrate them, the lucky "teacher" really has a gem. I don't mind admitting that Barnes taught me more about vaulting than I taught him and I can thank him for championships and records that were bagged by later Southern California vaulters.

Barnes's record lasted until another Trojan, Bill Graber, came along in the national championships of 1932 to take the mark up to 14 feet 4⅜ inches. In the summer of 1932 Bill Miller of Stanford won the Olympic title at 14 feet 1⅞ inches, and this mark, having been made in Olympic competition, went down as a record until Graber's record could be officially recognized by the I.A.A.F. in 1934.

Yale returned to the record-breaking picture in 1935 when Keith Brown won the I.C.A.A.A.A. championship with a vault of 14 feet 5⅛ inches. Defeated in this meet were two Southern California sophomores, Bill Sefton and Earle Meadows, who were close friends of Graber. When they saw their pal's record smashed, they determined that some day they would get it back themselves.

Brown's mark, however, never saw the record book because George Varoff of the University of Oregon won the national A.A.U. championship in 1936 with a mark of 14 feet 6½ inches, a figure that received the recognition of the I.A.A.F. that year. Although he had boosted the record in the national championships, Varoff lost out a week later in the final American Olympic tryouts when the three Southern California buddies, Sefton, Meadows, and Graber, won the right to go to Berlin for the 1936 Olympics.

Meadows won the Olympic title at 14 feet 3¼ inches, and the following season he and Sefton went on the greatest record-breaking rampage in the history of vaulting.

178

On April 10, 1937, in a dual meet between Southern California and California at the Los Angeles Coliseum, Sefton cleared 14 feet 7⅜ inches for a new world's record. There was such a hubbub of picture taking, measuring, and general backslapping that Meadows, whose turn it was to vault next, had to wait half an hour and was too cold to have a fair trial at the same height.

Later in a Southern California dual meet with Stanford at Palo Alto, May 8, Sefton raised the record again, going to 14 feet 8½ inches. This time officials saw to it that Meadows should have a fair crack at the same mark and 5 minutes later Earle also soared over the bar to become joint holder of the new record.

Three weeks later back in the Los Angeles Coliseum in the Pacific Coast Conference championships the boys went to work on the record again. Once more Sefton was the first to hit new heights, clearing 14 feet 11 inches. Again finding himself on the spot, Meadows came through a few minutes later with a tying vault. The boys might have gone on up to 15-foot heights that day but the pole-vault standards could not be raised higher. They were already stretched out to their maximum height, the manufacturer having probably figured that constructing standards that would go 15 feet high would just be a waste of lumber.

Never in the history of track and field have world's records taken so thorough a beating in such a short space of time and with two boys sharing in the record breaking. And, of course, let's not forget little Lee Barnes. What we had doped out together ten years before was worked into the form of Sefton and Meadows as they sailed into altitudes never before reached by young men with bamboo poles.

Although it is hardly more than a decade since 14 feet was first cleared by Sabin Carr, vaults well over that figure are fairly common now. Sefton, Meadows, Varoff, and Warmerdam all soared over 14 feet 7⅝ inches in the National A.A.U. meet of 1937.

"Bud" Day of Southern California and Dick Ganslen of Columbia, recent winners of N.C.A.A. championships, have respective marks of 14 feet 7 inches and 14 feet 5 inches. Milt Padway of Wisconsin and Rod Hansen of Oregon have marks of 14 feet 4 inches. Kenneth Dills of Southern California, 1940

179

N.C.A.A. champion, reached 14 feet 8 inches that year. With such vaulting the 15-foot leap, first made by Warmerdam, may eventually become common. Where it will go from there I dare not guess. The boys are getting so good these days that they may not stop short of the clouds.

When W. W. Hoyt won the first Olympic vaulting championship in Athens in 1896, like other men of his day in the event, he used a solid cedar pole. There was no box in which to place the pole at the start of the vault as there is now. Instead the pole simply had a spike in the bottom of it. If the spike caught a firm place in the ground and held while the vault was being made, all was well and good. If it didn't, there was usually some fancy skidding by the vaulter, often climaxed by a nose dive either in or out of the pit.

Landing in the pit in the early days of vaulting wasn't much of an advantage because it was scarcely more comfortable than hitting the ground. Pits, so-called, were either holes filled with sand or merely a small section of the ground dug up a little. In either case after a few vaults they were soon just as hard as the ground. In Europe today vaulting pits are still about as soft to land on as a cement sidewalk. Officials abroad seem to take a sadistic delight in seeing vaulters bounce. When American coaches at Olympic or other international meets request a truck load of shaving for the pits, foreign officials take it as a huge joke and never think of complying. Apparently they believe that flops on hard surfaces are a major part of the fun of vaulting, or at least of watching a vault.

If you have followed the competition of Americans in meets abroad, outside of the Olympic games, you have probably noticed that the pole vault is usually won at mediocre heights. This is because Europe has been unable to develop vaulters in their leg-wrecking pits and Americans on tour will vault only high enough to win. If 12 feet will take first place, after two or three unhappy landings the American athletes have no desire to go any higher.

The European pole-vault record of 4.35 meters, which is 14 feet 3¼ inches, is held jointly by Sefton and Meadows, who are also the world's record holders. While on tour with an American team in 1935, Sefton took as few vaults as possible during most of the meets and rarely went higher than 13 feet. In the final meet, in Budapest, he decided to risk a broken leg and cleared the 4.35-meter height for the new European record.

The following year Meadows tied this mark in winning the Olympic championship in Berlin. Sefton tied Nishida and Oye of Japan for second, but the hard pit was too much for a weak ankle that had been bothering him and he took fourth in the jump-off.

Bill Graber, the third member of the all-Trojan American Olympic vaulting combination, had all the spring taken out of his legs in his first workout at a cementlike German pit and was lucky to take a fifth at a height nearly a foot lower than his best mark.

In view of the horrible example set by European pits, coaches should see that there is always a generous pile of shavings for their vaulters' landings. Besides being deep, the shavings should be spread over a good-sized area so that vaulters who make bad take-offs and go sideways will still have a soft spot for their descent.

The selection of a pole is important. Beginners do not need to be so particular, the main feature that they require in their bamboo being strength to withstand the strain of poor vaults. Poles come in 12-, 14-, 16- and 18-foot lengths. There are no rules, however, to govern their exact length and vaulters may cut them down to whatever size they like.

Lee Barnes's pole was 14 feet 1 inch in length. When he placed it in the take-off box, which is 8 inches in depth, it was shorter by 8½ inches than the world's record height of 14 feet 1½ inches that he made with it. Sefton and Meadows used 16-foot poles and this length is the most common today. Sefton, weighing 180 pounds, always had to have a much heavier stick than Meadows, who was 163.

In selecting a pole, the vaulter should look for one that is aged and cured sufficiently so that it will be springy enough to snap back to position when depressed. If a green pole is bent, it won't always spring back to its former straight position. If strength is the main consideration in picking out a pole, the vaulter should get one with the joints close together. Poles with joints farther apart will be springier, but only boys possessed of a reasonable amount of skill or who are light in weight should use them.

181

Bamboo poles will warp or crack if subjected to changes in weather. Rain or hot sun will damage them. They should not be allowed to drop. When champion vaulters get a pole that has just the right "feel" to it, they protect and care for it as tenderly as a mother with a newborn babe.

Aluminum poles are official and are finding general use. The 14-foot length is of uniform thickness throughout and is lighter than bamboo, weighing less than 6 pounds. The 16-foot length is tapered and shaped like a bamboo pole. The chief advantage of the aluminum pole is that it is much more substantial than the bamboo. It won't break, crack, or check and will withstand a lot of tossing around. The disadvantage of aluminum poles is that they do not have the springiness of bamboo. The snap of the pole near the top of the vault is a big help in clearing sizable heights. At Southern California our freshmen use aluminum poles while training; when they graduate to varsity ranks, they select the choicest bamboo.

In the early 1900's when bamboo poles were being experimented with by vaulters for the first time, Eastern athletes had the first crack at them. Western men now have this advantage. Getting the pick of the crop of bamboo poles when they arrive from Japan may have had something to do with the supremacy of Western vaulters in the past few years.

Small pole-vaulting champions, like Lee Barnes, are rare because the tall boy has several advantages. His reach makes it easy for him to use a hold considerably higher up on the pole than the short man can take. With a higher handhold he does not have to pull up his body so far as a shorter man must with a lower hold. Also, if he is a champion vaulting at great heights, his long arms make it possible for him to lift his body higher. Vaulting at the same height as a tall man, a short athlete might have to grip the pole 6 inches higher in order to lift his body as high as his lankier opponent.

Of America's three vaulters in the 1936 Olympics, Sefton was 6 feet 3 inches in height and Meadows and Graber were each 6 feet 1 inch. All the 14-foot vaulters of the past few years—among them Varoff, Warmerdam, Ganslen, Padway, Day, and Dills—have been six-footers.

Physical requirements for a vaulter include strong shoulder,

182

arm, chest, and abdominal muscles. The gymnast's timing, coordination, and sense of balance are also possessed by those who do well in this event.

There are many steps to the technique of pole vaulting but the beginner should not be discouraged because sailing high over a crossbar at first looks like a complicated process. Many of the items of procedure in vaulting will soon become automatic. A young man who is enthusiastic over the event and anxious to work at it can become fairly proficient in a short time and will get much enjoyment out of it right from the start. Careful training and rigid attention to fine points will then carry him up to greater heights.

The first step in preparing to make a vault is to locate the point at which the take-off foot will leave the ground. This is done by standing on the runway facing the take-off box and placing the base of the vaulting pole in the slot. The vaulter then raises the pole over his head and holds it there with both hands. If he is right-handed, his right hand will be the top one, that is, the one that is farthest from the base of the pole as it rests in the take-off box. The left hand should not be tight against the right, a little space of from 4 to 6 inches being a good distance to keep them apart.

As the athlete stands facing the take-off box with his hands holding the pole overhead, the point for the take-off foot is found by following a straight line from the right hand down past the back of the head to the back of the heels. It is important to find this take-off point with a reasonable degree of accuracy. A few inches either way will not make much difference but there will be trouble if this point is very far off. If a vaulter takes off too far back, he loses power. If he takes off too near the pit he will be thrown directly into the air and the beneficial body swing will be lost.

Vaulters who have developed their technique to the point where they are regularly clearing good heights usually allow 1½ feet for their pull-up, their grip on the pole being this distance below the altitude they are making.

Beginning vaulters, however, should grip the bamboo at a point even with the crossbar or slightly above it. This will help them because at first they will have difficulty lifting their bodies higher than their hands in clearing the bar. Tall men because of their reach can always take a higher grip than short athletes. The maximum height for the grip of a short boy may be a little over 11 feet but a tall vaulter of no more ability may be able to hold a foot higher.

As a vaulter enters the elite of championship ranks, he begins driving his body far above his hands. Again lanky men because of their reach have an advantage since they may clear greater heights with lower grips than shorter athletes. When Sefton and Meadows cleared their world's record height of 14 feet 11 inches, their grips on the pole were at 12 feet 2 inches. Thus they lifted their bodies 33 inches higher than their hands in making their vaults.

Upon feeling an uncomfortable jerk as the take-off is made, the vaulter knows that one of several things is wrong. Either he has his take-off too close to or too far from the standards or he is trying to grip too high up on his vaulting pole. It is a common fault for vaulters, particularly those in the beginner class, to try to hold too high. The vaulter must determine his limitation in the height of his grip, and although he should try to raise this limit gradually as he progresses, he must be careful not to go beyond it in attempting to clear normal heights.

As the crossbar is raised during the progress of vaulting competition, the hand grip will be moved up higher and this may require a slight variation in the point of take-off. Full speed is not necessary with lower handholds, but as the grip raises higher on the pole greater momentum must be obtained from the run.

After the vaulter has located his take-off point properly, he must measure off his approach run. A uniform stride must be developed for this approach in order that the same number of steps from a given point will always land the athlete at the place he has determined as the correct spot for him to leave the ground. Sprinting over low hurdles in a series of two or three is one of the best means of developing steps of uniform length. The beginner is likely to have trouble in this respect but low-hurdle practice will overcome this difficulty.

A system of two check marks will ensure reaching the take-off properly. The checks are measured back from the standards so that the mark that becomes the second check is determined first.

184

"HEAVENLY TWIN"

When team mates Bill Sefton and Earle Meadows were breaking world's records in the pole vault together, the press called them the "Heavenly Twins." Here Sefton is caught at the top of a record-breaking vault.

THE OTHER TWIN

Five minutes after Sefton raised the world's pole vault record to 14 feet 11 inches, Earle Meadows, the Olympic champion, equalled it. Cornelius Warmerdam broke the Sefton-Meadows record in 1940.

The first check to be marked is placed at a point between 60 and 70 feet from the uprights, depending on the length of the vaulter's stride and on the number of steps he wishes to use from this check to the take-off. The next check should be farther back from the standards and should indicate the start of the run. This mark is usually approximately 30 feet from the other check. Both checks should be so located that the vaulter will hit each with his take-off foot. As the athlete will not be able to use a full sprinting stride while carrying his vaulting pole, he should have the pole with him in the trial runs he takes to determine the check marks.

Once the marks are definitely established, they should be carefully measured off with a steel tape on the practice and competitive runways. They should not be left to chance by trying to step them off. The rear check mark, which shall be called the first since it is the first that the vaulter hits on his run, may be anywhere from 85 to 110 feet from the standards. The length of the run naturally depends on the vaulter's ability to gather momentum.

At Southern California we found that Meadows, Sefton, Barnes, and Day needed 105 feet, but Graber wanted only 100, and Dills required only 85. A few preliminary steps are used to help the vaulter hit the first check with his take-off foot, but these steps require no more than 8 or 10 feet.

Right-handed vaulters take off with the left foot and swing up on the right side of the pole. The top hand gripping the pole is the right which is usually the last to leave the pole as the vaulter makes his final thrust.

The beginning vaulter can learn the fundamentals of technique on a suspended pole or rope. Hanging to this piece of apparatus and facing an imaginary crossbar, he should pull his body into the air, twisting it at the top of the pull in such a way that his chest faces the imaginary bar. When he first visits the vaulting pit, it isn't necessary for him to have a crossbar at all, for a bar is a hinderance when a boy makes his opening efforts at learning vaulting technique. One should have the "feel" of vaulting before one attempts any heights.

Long runs should never be made at the pit until one has mastered the form on short take-offs. In the first season of Meadows and Sefton at Southern California their timing was perfected by limiting them for a long time in practice to a take-off run of only 55 feet. With this reduced run, which was actually less than 15 yards to the point where the take-off foot left the ground they finally progressed to the point where they could clear 13 feet. Having learned and perfected timing in this way, they found it easy to go much higher when they added the momentum of their full run.

In carrying the pole, the vaulter holds it with the back of the left, or lower, hand up and the back of the right, or upper, hand facing toward the ground. The pole should be carried in a comfortable manner and the distance between the hands may be anywhere from 18 inches to 3 feet. The beginner should adopt a hand spread that suits him physically or one that his coach works out for him. Lee Barnes, smallest vaulter ever to reach 14-foot heights, had to use a spread of nearly 36 inches but taller athletes at Southern California were able to use much less.

The distance between the hands gripping the pole during the run should not be too great because the vaulter does not want to have to move his lower hand very far in making his hand shift just before his take-off. The pole must be carried out to the side in such a way as not to interfere with the running. It should be pointed straight toward the center of the bar with the forward point of it raised a little.

The vaulter should try to hold correct sprinting form down the runway despite the weight of the pole, but because of his burden the angle of his body will usually not be so acute as it would be if he were running a dash without the stick. He should never let the weight of the bamboo cause his body to turn at the waist and he should be facing straight ahead during the entire run. A firm grip on the pole is required but the vaulter should not make the mistake of squeezing it and developing tenseness in his arm and shoulder muscles.

The last few steps to the take-off must be normal. If the vaulter has to stretch out to long strides or choke up to short ones in order to hit the mark, the smoothness of his swing will be upset.

As the vaulter prepares to go into the air, he slides the base of his pole into the trough, brings his left hand up close to his right, and swings his arms over his head. The position of the hands is important, as a good smooth swing is impossible if they are not

186

close together. Old-style vaulters whose top heights were around 10 and 11 feet did not shift their lower hand at the take-off and had no chance to soar to the heights that the present-day stars reach. Beginning vaulters often fail to move the lower hand and perform with old-style awkwardness until they change. The hands are brought so closely together by some of our best present-day vaulters that they touch. This isn't advisable for everyone but the space between the hands should never exceed 6 inches.

When the arms go over the head, they should be slightly bent at the elbows. This flexed position acts as a cushion when the pole stops against the take-off box and the body starts to swing into the air. It also gives the athlete better control of his vault.

Assuming that the vaulter is right-handed and takes off with his left foot, he continues a striding motion with his right leg as the pole strikes the back of the box and starts to swing upward. This movement of the right leg in a stride as though the vaulter were continuing to run on air aids in the swing of the body and in maintaining the upward momentum of the pole.

During the swing the athlete holds his body close to the pole. This also aids the stick's momentum, which would be disastrously checked if the body got out of control.

At the completion of the swing the vaulter elevates his feet, kicking them straight up. One of the secrets of championship vaulting is elevating the feet into this handstand position on the vaulting pole. As the feet are kicked high into the air, the body is turned so that the chest is toward the crossbar. The bar should never be cleared with the back toward it unless the athlete yearns to be an acrobat instead of a vaulter.

The kick at the end of the swing is up, not out and over the crossbar as is often erroneously done by the beginner. The feet may or may not be together at the top of this kick. The left foot may be brought up even with the right, which has taken the lead by the striding motion at the take-off, but usually the left trails all the way.

In elevating the feet at the top of the swing the vaulter has to give a tremendous pull with his arms. The arm pull, leg kick, and turn of the body with the chest to the bar at the top of the swing must be coordinated into one continuous motion. It must be executed quickly but without jerkiness.

187

The vaulter retains his hold on the pole until it is straight up and down to get the full benefit of the final push on it. With the vaulter in a handstand position, this thrust is downward. This push not only helps the final thrust over the bar but also may even give the body momentum to go higher. Bill Sefton and Lee Barnes had such tremendous power in their leg kick and final thrust that they used to fly off the end of their vaulting poles.

Until comparatively recent years the body was jackknifed over the bar at the end of the swing. The legs would hang over the bar on the pit side with the hands still maintaining a grip on the pole on the approach side of the crossbar.

Lee Barnes tied for an Olympic championship at 12 feet 11½ inches when just out of Hollywood High School but that was his limit with the jackknife style he used at that time. I have referred to Lee as one of my principal teachers in pole vaulting, for we were dissatisfied with the standard jackknife method and together worked out the monkey-on-a-stick style that he later used to set a world's record of 14 feet 1½ inches.

When the vaulter in his handstand position makes his final push on the pole, he swings his legs down and releases the bamboo stick. The downward leg swing, if done vigorously enough, helps to throw the arms up and clear of the bar. Usually the vaulter releases the pole with his lower hand first, which would be the left if he is right-handed. The arms are swung up quickly over the crossbar. More speed can be obtained in this motion with the elbows bent slightly than with the arms held perfectly straight.

Since the body has been pulled up and thrust over the bar at a point higher than the grip on the pole, the movements in bringing the arms and hands up and over are extremely important. Vaulters attempting unusual heights often can thrust their bodies over the bar but lose out at the last instant when they are unable to throw their arms and hands clear of it.

The delayed pull-up is one of the secrets of clearing great heights. Those who really get up into the ozone hug the pole to get every ounce of momentum out of it before starting their pull.

At the end of his try, it doesn't make much difference how the vaulter comes down as long as he doesn't break his neck. Once over the bar, he should relax and let gravity do the rest. It is not wise to fall straight down feet first, for the entire jolt of the landing must be taken by the legs and knees. Even though they may be relaxed, a few long falls will take some of the spring out of them for the high vaults to come.

If a vaulter falls at an angle, he can relax as he lands and take some of the shock on his shoulder. Earle Meadows, a very slender boy, was exceptionally clever at this. Even in the hard pit in the Berlin Olympic games he was able to save his legs in his falls and this enabled him to conserve his leg spring and power for the winning vault. Meadow's vaulting mate, Sefton, was a gymnast, however, and couldn't seem to get over the gymnast's formal dismount of landing on both feet with the knees flexed. In pits well piled up with shavings, Sefton's gymnastic landings didn't injure his sturdy legs, but the hard European pits gave them a bad beating.

As in all events of track and field, tension must be eliminated every step of the way and the old cry from the coach of "Relax!" is a familiar one at the pole-vault runway. Tension at the take-off will interfere with the upward swing of the bamboo stick. Tenseness during the vault will upset the smooth coordination that is necessary for the the proper technique.

Straining at unusual heights upsets the form of most vaulters, but the real stars can be technically correct right to the finish. The champion looks good even when he misses.

Breathing is no problem at all to the vaulter. If it helps give him a general feeling of relaxation, he may take a few long breaths before he begins his jaunt down the runway. If breathing deeply makes him dizzy, then he should forget about it and let nature take its course.

Speed is important but should not be overemphasized. An athlete may run so fast that he cannot control his body in the air.

In 1936 Earle Meadows went sour in midseason after doing better than 14 feet in several meets. It was a difficult case to figure out because Earle was in perfect condition and never felt better in all his life. For two days we experimented at the pit trying to take the bugs out of his form which had so mysteriously gone haywire. Finally we found that Earle was getting too fast and too strong for his own good. He had too much speed at the take-off and that forced him to start his pull-up too soon. After

189

a little work on his run, we found that all he needed to do was shorten his take-off dash by 5 feet. This was just enough to keep him from overspeeding and throwing his body out of control during the vault. Immediately he swung back to his correct technique, and just a short time after he had had so much trouble at ordinary heights he won the Olympic championship with a new Olympic record.

The ability to concentrate, especially in his early season work, is a vital item in a vaulter's make-up because of the many movements that must be coordinated in a vault. Champion vaulters are usually found to be intelligent boys who had the ability to study out their problems during practice and get themselves into a vaulting groove that would carry them through competition with no further worry. Concentration in practice will develop good vaulting habits. It is essential for technique to be learned so well that it becomes habitual. The day of competition is no time to be worried about whether or not the form is going to be correct.

In competition one of the chief concerns of the vaulter is to hit his check marks correctly. He watches these closely; when he hits the second check with his correct foot, he can proceed with confidence that he will reach the take-off properly. His eyes should always be focussed straight down the runway and upon the take-off box after he has passed the check marks.

If he has learned his form correctly in practice and has the proper determined attitude, he can automatically make a smooth vault without worrying about all the steps in it and can concentrate upon putting an explosion of energy into the pull-up and thrust that will give him height at the top of his vault.

Work at the practice pit should never be for the maximum heights. Timing and technique must be mastered with the bar at easy altitudes. When the vaulter enters competition and is stimulated by his urge to win, it is time enough for him to start reaching for the moon.

During a meet a vaulter should not expend unnecessary energy taking his turn at every low altitude. After the athlete is warmed up, it is not necessary for him to enter every new height if he knows that he can safely wait for greater altitudes. A vaulter who knows that he can do 13 feet shouldn't waste his strength making a half-dozen vaults at heights between 12 and 13.

190

During the Sefton-Meadows record-breaking campaign of 1937, the boys saved their energy by taking as few vaults as possible. I remember that Sefton went up to a world's record in the Southern California-Stanford dual meet in only six vaults. They were 12:6, 13, 13:6, 14, 14:4, and 14:8½. He made each on his first vault. In the same meet Meadows tied this mark, which was a world's record when it was established although the boys broke it a short time later, but Earle missed his first tries at two heights and had to take eight vaults.

Vaulting poles are usually properly taped at the time of purchase to give them strength. They are strong enough at the base so that no tape is required on the lower 6 or 7 feet. Each vaulter must see that the points where he grips the stick are well taped in order to keep his hands from slipping. Poles are usually wrapped with tape at the top end to keep them from shattering or cracking when they strike the ground.

The pole vault is an event that a youngster can take up at any age. The course of preliminary training is a splendid body builder for a growing youngster as well as for the young man who has already shown some athletic prowess.

Much apparatus work should be on the preliminary training program of the vaulter. He can get much good out of exercises on the horizontal bars, flying rings, and the rope and pole climb. Work on the rowing machine, chinning the bar, and tumbling on the mats—anything that will help him to develop a strong torso—all are good. Handstands will help arm and shoulder development and will also assist in balance.

Vaulting is more closely allied to gymnastics than any other track and field event. In this connection, the case of Bill Sefton is interesting to note. At the age of twelve years, Bill was 5 feet 10 inches in height and weighed less than 100 pounds. Because he was so thin and frail, his doctor ordered him to take corrective gymnasium work in junior high school. This work eventually made Bill a fan for gymnastic apparatus, especially the horizontal bar. Never possessed with an urge for competitive athletics, Bill took up indoor vaulting at Polytechnic High School, Los Angeles, purely as a gymnastics event. When Eddy Leahy, the Poly track coach, saw Bill clear 10 feet 6 inches indoors in a gym class, he persuaded the tall boy to go out for the track team.

191

But although Bill became a champion vaulter, it was always just a gymnastics event to him. He liked to vault just as he liked to do giant swings on the horizontal bars—not because he wanted to beat somebody but because it was fun to fly through the air. Even at the height of the track season Bill would do more training in the gym than on the field. During the season when he was breaking world's records before huge track crowds, on the side Sefton was also participating in gymnastics, his first love, and having fun winning first places in the rope climb at gym meets that never drew a fan.

Pull-ups constitute one of the vaulter's most important exercises. They are good for all track and field men but they are of such special benefit to vaulters that at least six pull-ups should be done every day in the year. The boy who doesn't have access to a gymnasium can rig up some kind of horizontal bar or find an overhanging limb of a tree for this exercise. The pull-ups should always be made with the backs of the hands toward the face.

In doing handstands the vault candidate should learn to stand for 10 seconds without moving. Walking on the hands is also beneficial. Push-ups from the floor are also good for the vaulter and he should develop strength at this to the point where he can some day do at least fifty in succession.

The 25-foot rope climb is a gymnastics event that is especially good for the vaulter. This is another form of exercise that he can undertake every day. During his fall campaign to prepare his body for the track and field competition of spring, he will progress in strength on the rope until he can climb it hand over hand five times in succession with very little rest between.

The old admonition to walk at least 2 miles a day is repeated here. Gym work will build up the back, chest, shoulders, arms, and hands but outdoor training must be added to put speed and strength in the legs.

Jogging and wind sprints two or three days a week are useful in the preliminary work of a vaulter just as they are for a candidate in any of the track events. Once in a while, a quarter-mile jog should be taken carrying the pole. Occasionally, also, the candidate can visit the pit after a good warm-up and take a few vaults, but any work like this should be easy and should be for form and not for height.

If one engages in other sports out of season, he does not need much additional training. There are many forms of out-of-season athletics that aid conditioning, among them basketball, volley-ball, baseball, softball, badminton, handball, squash, and tennis.

Football tends to create heavy leg and shoulder muscles that will tie up in vaulting. Swimming also does not mix with vaulting. Skating, skiing, and dancing do no good either. About the worst thing for vaulters, or any other track men who must do some run-ning, is horseback riding. This tightens the muscles on the inside of the thighs. Does anyone know of a cowboy—the bronco-riding kind of the pre-V8 ranch days—who could even walk, much less run?

Bill Graber was one of our vaulters who found that riding and vaulting didn't mix. On his parents' ranch in Ontario, Calif., Bill had a pet horse and he used to gallop around considerably during the summertime and nurse the secret ambition of some day becoming a great polo player. Until I learned what Bill was doing in the summer, I never could figure out why he had such a wobbly stride down the runway early in the season and why it took him so long to get into shape for vaulting. When I found out about Bill's horse, we had a little talk about whether he was to be a champion vaulter or polo player. Vaulting won.

During preseason training the athlete should limit his activ-ities to a reasonable amount of daily exercise. He shouldn't play or exercise to the point where he finishes up tired out every day or he will have little energy left for a long track and field season.

About 6 weeks or two months before the first meet in the spring the candidate should start a schedule with the idea in mind of getting into perfect condition. The autumn work can be done at will, except for the walking and pull-ups which should never be missed, but the early spring schedule calls for work at the pit to form correct vaulting habits.

Vaulters should work often with the sprinters and low hurdlers to develop a uniform stride. In the hurdle work it is not necessary to have the barriers separated by the standard distance of 20 yards. The space may be varied from 16 to 20 yards to suit the size and striding habits of the vaulter. If the athlete is right-handed, the take-off at each hurdle should be from the left foot just as it will be in vaulting. Two or three hurdles are enough to take at a time in working out a uniform stride.

If the vaulter can combine upper body strength with light

weight, he has an advantage. Heavy men must carry big poles to support themselves and they also have more weight of their own to lift over the crossbar.

Sefton was so well developed from his constant gym work that his weight of 180 pounds was always greater than he wanted even though he did not carry an excess ounce. If he was to compete in a meet on a Saturday afternoon, he would take no liquids from Friday noon until after the meet in an attempt to lose a few pounds by drying himself out. I can't say whether this skrinking of a few pounds just before a meet did him any good or not, but he thought it did and I never interfered with the psychological effect by questioning the wisdom of his action.

On the other hand, Meadows couldn't have gained beyond 165 pounds if he had eaten lead biscuits, so weight was never a worry to him. Most boys do have to be careful to avoid excess weight, however, for every pound that does not go into energy either in the run or at the top of the vault adds to the load that must be pulled up in the supreme effort at the crossbar.

Probably more than competitors in any other event in track and field, vaulters are made and not born. Coaches usually don't need to worry if they have no ready-made material among the candidates who report at the beginning of the season. High school coaches can usually find material for the pole vault among their gym classes. The boy who likes to work on the apparatus and do handstands will take to vaulting quickly. His gym work builds up just the right muscles for vaulting. Furthermore, if he is at all serious as a gymnast, he will be a stylist and this will help him in an event in which perfection of form is all-important.

Sometimes a coach has a man of all-round track and field ability whom he can make into a champion by having him specialize in vaulting. Charley Hoff started out this way and so did Earle Meadows.

Meadows and Sefton, the present official coholders of the record, offer an interesting contrast in the background of their vaulting careers. Sefton was the gymnast, purely and simply, a boy who enjoyed apparatus work and individual stunts with practically no yen for competition.

Meadows came to Southern California after showing all-round track and field ability in high school. His favorite events were the high jump, low hurdles, and pole vault and he thought that

194

because of his slender build he should specialize in either the jump or the hurdles. He had a perfect competitive temperament, combining determination and a conscientious attitude with self-confidence. I knew that he would stay with whatever he went into until he excelled, and I suggested that he team up with Sefton in the pole vault and forget about jumping and hurdling.

The combination was interesting to watch. Sefton liked to vault because it was a gymnastics stunt and the higher he went the more fun it was. Meadows liked to vault because he had Sefton to work with and he ate up such brilliant friendly competition. So we had Sefton the gymnast combined with Meadows the competitor, Sefton setting the world's records first because he was a truly magnificent and powerful stylist and Meadows digging in and tying the records as fast as they were made because he was an amazing competitor who wouldn't let team mate Sefton or any one else beat him.

Because boys cannot watch their own form while vaulting they need constant attention from a coach. The coach must also be the judge on the relative amount of gymnastics and outdoor work that is needed, for individual requirements naturally vary a great deal.

Bearing in mind that individual needs must be met, here is a typical training week for a vaulter during the middle of the season:

Monday, vaulting at low heights to correct weaknesses revealed in the meet of the previous Saturday, work for form and upper body development on a suspended pole or rope, jogging a lap at the start and finish of training; Tuesday, wind sprints or short dashes with the sprinters or work over two or three hurdles for uniform step, no vaulting, jogging a lap at the start and finish of the workout; Wednesday, vaulting for form only, using greater heights than on Monday but not maximum altitudes, take-off runs to perfect step, a lap before and after; Thursday, mostly work in the gymnasium on the bars, rings, and rope, a little work with the sprinters in starts and short dashes if more speed on the runway is needed, jogging a lap at the finish; Friday, no gymnasium and track, light setting-up exercises at home, or complete rest for Saturday competition. Exercises, of course, are on the program of Monday, Tuesday, and Wednesday, but the amount depends on the condition of the athlete.

195

The vaulter is shown here at the instant of take-off. The point of the pole has been thrust in the box and the bamboo has been swung directly over the head. The hands are fairly close together on the pole. As this vaulter, who is right-handed, takes off from his left foot, his right leg continues a running stride. There is a pronounced knee lift in this leg as though the athlete were taking off for a hurdle.

A good swing with the pole is shown by the vaulter here. To get full benefit of the momentum of the pole, the athlete is riding it closely. However, he is careful not to hit it with his legs or body and interfere with his own momentum. The right leg is swinging out far enough to allow the left leg to clear the pole. If the body touches the pole at this point in the swing, the contact will be made just to the left of the breastbone on the lower ribs.

With the pole approaching a vertical position, the vaulter starts his pull. Note the muscular action of the athlete's arms and shoulders. The legs remain relaxed as they are pulled up by the abdominal muscles. In this series of pictures the athlete is vaulting at 13 feet 6 inches. At a greater height he would delay his pull-up more than he has here.

Nearing the finish of his pull the vaulter turns his body so that he will clear the bar with his chest toward it. To aid his body turn, he is making a scissors kick in which he throws his right leg across his left. The legs are still rising but remain relaxed.

Although it looks from this position as though the vaulter will never get his body over the bar, he is continuing to lift his torso higher and to elevate his legs in a near handstand. While his left arm still pulls, he is starting a push with his right. The body is still turning to face the bar.

The vaulter is almost at the end of his pull-up, which at this point becomes a push-up as he thrusts down hard on the pole to force his body still higher in the air. The right leg has just reached its highest point in the vaulting action and the left leg has already started to drop on the pit side of the bar. He is in excellent position on the pole here, with his right shoulder close to it and his hands a few inches apart ready for a final powerful thrust.

The right foot starts down and at this instant the vaulter straightens out his arms in the final push. The tremendous body lift at this point can be better appreciated if one notes how much higher his head is than in the previous picture. The vaulter has already released his left hand, and the right hand, which is still giving a final thrust, will follow quickly. The thumbs are down, showing that the arms are in good position for their final throw over the crossbar.

The left arm, with the thumb still down to ensure the proper bend in the elbow, is thrown across the face and over the head and the right arm will also be tossed over the head. Through lifting his body high over his hands, the vaulter has cleared 13 feet 6 inches with several inches to spare even though the grip of his lower hand on the pole was at 11 feet 6 inches. The vaulter here is Kenneth Dills, former N.C.A.A. and Pacific Coast Conference champion who has a mark of 14 feet 8 inches.

XI

THE HIGH JUMP

The key word in high jumping, as in a young married couple's budget, is "economy." Victories are won and records are raised by fractions of an inch. Lifting power must be distributed scientifically; therefore, it is a waste of energy to raise one part of the body higher than another in clearing the crossbar.

In modern high jumping a layout is essential. When a jumper executes a layout, he swings himself into a position parallel to the crosspiece as he clears it. All his body that is next to the bar—his shoulders, hips, and legs—are an equal distance above it. That's high-jump economy.

All high jumpers start with the scissors kick form, the simplest possible method of clearing a bar. But an economical layout is difficult to attain with this method and in the championship bracket of high jumping the scissors form is becoming rare. Replacing the old technique among most coaches and athletes is the rolling type of jump.

With large numbers of high school leapers now reaching 6 feet, it is hard to believe that national A.A.U. and national collegiate championship meets were once won at heights barely over 5 feet. J. W. Pryor of Columbia won the first I.C.A.A.A.A. high jump in 1876 at 5 feet 4 inches and J. L. Geyelin of Pennsylvania took the event the following year at 4 feet 11 inches. H. E. Ficken of the New York Athletic Club, who was national champion from 1876 to 1878, never had to go beyond 5 feet 5 inches to win the American crown during those three years.

One of the outstanding jumpers in early championship competition was W. B. Page, Jr., of the University of Pennsylvania, who was both I.C.A.A.A.A. and national A.A.U. champion in 1885, 1886, and 1887. In 1887 he cleared the unheard-of height of 6 feet 4 inches for a world's record, setting a mark that stood for seven years.

198

The coach works, too! "Kick that left leg!" yells Coach Cromwell during a workout to Duncan McNaughton, 1932 Olympic high-jump champion. Track coaches bark, implore, and gesticulate almost as much as football mentors in driving home points of technique.

199

During this time jumpers were developing the scissors style to its most efficient degree, but they were still going over the crossbar the hard way, for at the top of their leap their bodies were high in the air and practically in a sitting position. With this form, Page's record height was just about the ceiling, and as a matter of fact, there were very few topnotchers who could reach the 6-foot class.

It took a young man who suspected that some sort of flat position should be attained at the top of the jump to boost the record and to revolutionize high-jumping form. The young man of ideas was Michael F. Sweeney, now coach at Hill School, Pottstown, Pa., and his tinkering with the scissors method brought about the layout that we seek to perfect in every type of jump today.

National champion for four years—from 1892 to 1895—Sweeney was the first man since Page to reach 6 feet in the national A.A.U. meet. Like most of the leapers of his day, Sweeney used a scissors as he cleared the bar, but gradually he worked a twist and a flattening out of his body into his jumps and this new layout form took him up to 6 feet 5⅝ inches for a world's record in 1895. This prodigious mark was destined to stand for 17 years until Western athletes were to come along with a new-fangled roll that would make greater heights possible. In the meantime, champion jumpers took up Sweeney's technique and developed a standard method that is now usually referred to as the Eastern style.

At the age of thirteen, I remember reading an article on high jumping by Sweeney in a boy's magazine. It aroused my interest in the event and I lost no time rigging up a crossbar in the back yard and trying to follow the technique as he described it. It was my first attempt at a field event and it kindled an enthusiasm for this type of athletics that I have never lost.

Sweeney's technique still has many followers not only in America but also abroad. Nearly all European high jumpers use this Eastern style and even Japanese and Philippine leapers favor it. Simeon Toribeo of the Philippines, who placed in the Olympic Games of 1928 and 1932, went to excellent heights with it.

In the Eastern style the jumper runs straight at the crossbar. After kicking his lead leg straight into the air, he executes a scissors with his take-off leg. Like the Western roll, this style features a layout at the top of the bar. I have not tried to teach this form to my high-jump candidates for many years as I believe a more efficient layout can be developed from a rolling jump.

However, the Eastern style is used by many excellent jumpers and I would not like to try to discourage athletes who are making a go of it although it is always easy for jumpers to try another method. One of the best features about high-jump coaching is that a teacher by making just a few simple revisions in such things as take-off or direction of the run can soon change the style of the athlete. Whenever a boy becomes dissatisfied with the method he is using, he can be quickly switched to another.

Because the method popularized by Sweeney is one of the simplest styles in use, it is often the first technique developed by a jumper after he passes the stage of the fundamental and primitive scissors.

In the Eastern style it is not necessary to use a long run, a total of 36 feet being sufficient. The take-off distance from the bar varies considerably with different jumpers and it may grow greater as the height of the bar increases.

The run should be long enough to ensure relaxation. By giving himself enough for an easy trot to the bar, the athlete has a chance to give his arms a shake to be assured of a general feeling of looseness or to perform any other little characteristic act that will be his guarantee that he is free from tension.

Some jumpers in this style use a take-off mark of a length equal to the height of the bar. For instance, if they are jumping at 6 feet, their take-off spot will be 6 feet in front of the crossbar. The take-off has to be far enough away from the bar to permit the lead leg to swing forward and up to elevate the jumper without hitting the crosspiece. There have been jumpers who could clear 6 feet 6 inches with this style from a 4-foot-6 take-off, but most athletes need more room for the swing of the lead leg. Also the take-off distance varies with the speed of the take-off run.

At the instant before the jump on the last step there is a settling of the body and a gather to aid in the upward spring. The forward momentum of the body is converted into an upward drive. This obviously makes it impossible for the jumper to be

201

running up on his toes like a sprinter and generating great speed in the approach.

Just as the jumper gathers for the leap from the take-off foot, he usually turns the toe of the jumping foot slightly outward. If the take-off is from the right foot, the toe is turned to the right.

In making the jump the athlete executes a vigorous swinging kick with the leg opposite the take-off foot. This lead leg is kicked high and straight ahead with the knee bent. The take-off leg springs from the ground following the lead leg and cuts in under it. In cutting under it, the action of this take-off leg causes the body to take a turn in the air so that when the height is reached at the top of the bar the stomach and chest are facing the crosspiece. This kick and turn of the body result in the layout of the body which becomes parallel to the ground as the bar is cleared.

Considerable distance is traveled through the air in this Eastern style of jump. An important point of difference in the Western roll is that in this latter method the take-off and landing points are much closer together. This means that most of the athlete's energy and momentum go into an upward spring rather than a forward one, thus indicating that the Western roll is the more economical type of leap.

There are many variations in use by the jumpers who favor the Eastern style. For some athletes clearance is easier if they run at the bar from a slight angle instead of from straight on. Right-footed jumpers who like to use an angle run make their approach from the left, and vice versa. One of the cleverest exponents of this style of jumping in recent years was George Spitz of New York University, who tied for the national championship in 1932 and who had an indoor mark of 6 feet 8½ inches.

Following Sweeney's regime as national high-jump king came I. K. Baxter of the University of Pennsylvania, who used the layout style to such advantage that he won five national titles and the Olympic championship of 1900. His winning height at Paris was 6 feet 2⅘ inches. The first Olympic title in this event had been won in Athens in 1896 by E. H. Clark of the United States at 5 feet 11¼ inches.

After Baxter, American prowess in this event fell off somewhat and the United States dropped the high-jump title in the Olympics for the first time when Con Leahy of Cork, Ireland, won the championship in the 1906 games in Athens at 5 feet 9⅞ inches. H. F. Porter brought the Olympic title back to the United States in 1908, and Alva Richards, a tall, raw-boned high school boy from Salt Lake City, was one of the big surprises of the 1912 games in Stockholm when he won with the new Olympic record of 6 feet 4 inches.

About this time a new form was being developed in the West as athletes tried clearing the bar with a layout on their side, the turn of their body to get in such a position resulting in a rolling movement. For 17 years Michael Sweeney's world's record of 6 feet 5⅝ inches had been scarcely challenged, but in 1912 George Horine of Stanford University brought the new Western roll into prominence when he took the record up to 6 feet 7 inches.

The honor of originating this Western roll style belongs, I believe, to "Dad" Moulton, Horine's coach. A great hubbub in jumping circles was created by the introduction of this method, but even though it was decidedly different from the style then universally popular nothing could be found in the rule books against it.

Horine held the record only two years, for another Western roll exponent, Eddie Beeson of California, raised the mark to 6 feet 7⅝ inches in 1914. From Horine's time on, every holder of the world's record has used one of the rolls.

With the introduction of the Western roll, the level of jumping hit a new high plane and the days of winning important meets at 6 feet or less ended. The Eastern technique had to improve to keep up with the new Western form and a number of athletes won prominence with consistently outstanding performances.

One of the top-flight men was Clinton Larsen of Brigham Young University, who is said to have jumped more than 6 feet 8 inches, although he never held the record. Larsen was national champion in 1917. Another splendid competitor was R. W. Landon of Yale, an I.C.A.A.A.A. champion for three years and the Olympic winner of 1920.

Most technically perfect of the rolling school of jumpers was Harold Osborn of the University of Illinois. In the 1924 Olympics he proved one of the heroes of the meet by winning both the high jump and the grueling decathlon. In the latter event he was the first American ever to win a championship. During the same year Osborn broke the world's record with a leap of 6 feet 8¼ inches. Not so tall as the average jumper, he had tremendous spring in his legs, excellent technique, and a trick of keeping the bar on even when hitting it that made him practically unbeatable.

Eastern stylists for some time had been criticizing the Western roll as a "trick jump" since it was possible to touch the bar, sometimes with considerable force, and still have it remain on the standards. This was because the roll of the body pushed the bar backwards against the standards. The crosspiece at that time rested on 3-inch pegs in the sides of the uprights. If the jumper's rolling body, shoulder, or arm shoved the bar along the pegs against the standards, it was likely that the bar would stay on even though it may have been depressed several inches. Naturally the scissors jumpers had no such advantage. Their bodies were always moving forward and if they did much more than touch the crossbar, it would fall from the pegs.

Whatever tricks some of the Western roll experts may have tried, they became of no more use when track and field officials decided to do away with the 3-inch pegs. Now the rules state that the crosspiece must rest on a platform 1½ inches wide on top of the standards. Anything more than a light touch is enough to knock the bar off.

Osborn, who was 5 feet 10 inches in height, was the last of the comparatively short men to win in Olympic competition. In 1928 Bob King of Stanford, who was 6 feet 2 inches, won the event. In 1932 the winner was 6-foot-2 Duncan McNaughton, a University of Southern California student who represented Canada. In 1936 the champion was Cornelius Johnson of Los Angeles, who was 6 feet 4 inches tall.

Following Osborn nearly a decade later as a record holder came Walter Marty of Fresno State College. In 1933 Marty raised the mark to 6 feet 8⅝ inches, but before this record could get in the official books he set a better one of 6 feet 9⅛ inches in 1934.

With colored boys dominating this event much of the time in the last few years, it was to be expected that the Negro race would finally bag this mark. When the time came, the record breakers arrived in a pair. In 1936 in the final American Olympic tryouts at Randall's Island, New York City, Cornelius Johnson, a junior college boy from Los Angeles, sailed over 6 feet 9¾ inches, and a few minutes later David Albritton of Ohio State equaled the new world's record height.

All the Negro champions of recent years have used the roll and have had great success with it because of their excellent relaxation. Besides Johnson and Albritton, there have been such outstanding colored stars as Ed Burke of Marquette, who holds the American indoor mark from a board take-off of 6 feet 9¾ inches, and Mel Walker of Ohio State, who holds the American indoor record from a dirt take-off of 6 feet 9¾ inches.

Johnson, Albritton, and Walker took turns in winning the national championship for the colored race, except for Walter Marty's tie with Johnson in 1934, every year from 1933 to 1938. But in 1939 they finally lost out when Albritton and Walker tied for third behind Les Steers of the San Francisco Olympic Club, who cleared 6 feet 8⅛ inches, and Bill Stewart of Torrance, Calif., who was second. Steers had an unofficial mark of 6 feet 10⅛ inches in 1940 and was again national champion, raising the A.A.U. meet record to 6 feet 8¾ inches.

Throughout 1940 white jumpers threatened the supremacy of the colored stars. Johnny Wilson of the University of Southern California and Steers tied at 6 feet 9⅜ inches to set a new high mark for white men in a Southern California-Olympic Club-U.C.L.A. meet. The excellent present-day quality of high jumping was well demonstrated in this little triangular meet when out of twelve entries in the high jump, ten of the contestants cleared 6 feet 4 inches and six of them went 6 feet 5 inches or higher.

This probably does not mean the end of the Negro's supremacy in this event, however, for the lithe, pantherlike spring of the colored stars combined with their complete freedom from tenseness will always make them outstanding.

Jumpers vary so much in the angle of their take-off and in other minor points that to the spectator there appear to be as many different styles as there are athletes in the event. However, there are really only a few main classes.

The plain scissors jump is the fundamental leap, the one that the youngster first tries when he refuses to enter by the gate and

205

goes over the fence. The scissors jumper runs at the obstacle from the side, springs from the outside foot, throws the inside foot over, follows with the other leg and lands on either the inside foot or both feet.

The next type of jump in ease of performance finds the jumper running straight at the bar and using a modified scissors kick to get out a layout. This is the Eastern style.

Then there are two Western rolls, one in which the bar is cleared on the side and one in which the roll is more complete and the crosspiece is cleared by the stomach and chest. There is no official name for this latter type of jump. Although it is usually known as a Western roll, like Horine's side clearance, in order to differentiate it from the original Western roll it may be called the "barrel" or "belly" roll.

Good layouts on the bar can be obtained in other ways besides clearing it on the side or belly. Clint Larsen, the great Utah jumper, used a unique style in which he obtained his layout on his back. Instead of facing the ground, like the barrel rollers, when he went over the bar, he looked up at the sky.

Alma Richards, who preceded Larsen as a Utah jumping star, came close to this back clearance in going over the bar and seemed to be about half on his back and half on his side. Richards, Larsen, and a long line of stellar high jumpers from the state of Utah were produced by Coach Eugene L. Roberts, who is now a professor of physical education at the University of Southern California and who is kind enough to assist our Trojan jumpers with his advice.

Richards, incidentally, showed that high-jump spring can last a long time. Winner of the Olympic games high-jump championship in 1912, after he dropped out of competition he continued to leap for his own enjoyment and for 20 years he could clear 6 feet 2 inches.

There may be some argument as to which of the two types of the Western roll is the better. Although I teach the side roll to most of the jumpers at Southern California, I like to switch an athlete to the belly roll when I think it will be suitable for him. This full roll undoubtedly gives the greatest result for the least effort. Jumpers should be warned, however, that it can be used only by a completely relaxed athlete. Although it looks simple, it can get its user into lots of trouble if he slips the slightest bit in his timing.

Jim Stewart of Southern California was the first outstanding athlete, as far as I know, to use the belly roll successfully in major competition when he won the N.C.A.A. high jump in 1930. Like other users of this form, Jim could jump with either of the Western rolls. Jim picked up the belly roll so quickly that I asked him if he had ever tried it as a youngster. He said that he had been raised on a ranch and had needed considerable agility at the fences whenever the cattle went rampaging. At first he took the barbed-wire fences with the scissors high-jump form, but he found this dorsal clearance both destructive for the seat of his trousers and unpleasant anatomically. Finally, he said, since the cattle didn't get any more peaceful and the fences didn't get any lower, he was forced to use the technique of the belly roll, for with this form he could hold down the barbed-wire as he rolled over it. I never believed Jim's yarn either.

One really can't prove anything conclusively in arguing the respective merits of the two Western styles, for Johnson, using the side roll, and Albritton, using the stomach roll, set the present world's record jointly. Albritton and his team mate, Mel Walker, were about of equal ability at Ohio State. Yet the former used the belly roll and the latter went over the bar on his side.

Les Steers, the outstanding high jumper of 1939, changed from the side roll to the belly roll during that season. He was consistent at 6 feet 6 inches with the side form, but went up to 6 feet 8 inches and better and to the national championship with the belly roll. Perhaps he would have improved that much anyway using his regular side style, but I believe that Steer's successful switch shows that the belly roll is a shade the better if the jumper can master it.

The take-off for either of the Western rolls is considerably closer than that for the Eastern style. Because of this close take-off and because the jump is made from the side, the bar may be slightly touched without displacing it. In the Eastern style from the front of the bar, the same amount of force contacting the crosspiece would knock it off since the jumper has much more forward momentum.

In preparing to high-jump with the Western roll, the athlete can usually find his take-off distance by standing erect facing the bar and extending an arm at full length until his fingers just touch the stick. The spot on which he is standing will usually be found to be the proper point. Since athletes approach the bar with varying speeds and each has his own peculiarities, there should be no attempt to standardize the take-off spot for all jumpers.

The angle at which the athlete approaches the bar also varies greatly. Some jumpers run almost parallel to the bar. Others approach it from almost directly out in front and swerve as they go in for the take-off.

A system of double checks in the approach may be used but it is not absolutely necessary as the run is slow enough for the jumper to hit the take-off without too much difficulty. If double checks are used, it is well to walk or barely trot to the first check to make sure that the run to the crossbar is not overemphasized. Most high jumpers run too far and too fast and their energies in the leap are thus dissipated in moving forward instead of being properly used in going upward.

Johnny Wilson, who won the N.C.A.A. high-jump championship for Southern California in 1939, tying with his team mate Clarke Mallery for the I.C.A.A.A.A. and Pacific Coast Conference titles the same year, used a slow run of only 22 feet. Few men that I have coached have found that they needed more than 30 feet.

A right-handed person usually takes off from his left foot because it is easier for him to kick up in starting the jump with his right leg. The athlete who takes off from his left foot starts his run on the left side of the standards. At the point of take-off, the foot from which the jump is to be made is the inside foot. At the moment of the take-off there is a final gather of the body. The athlete must be careful at this point not to be leaning into the bar or swaying away from it.

The secret of attaining good heights is keeping the take-off leg directly under the body as the jump is made.

In making the jump the athlete kicks high with his lead leg, which is the right one for a left-footed jumper. Simultaneously he springs with all the explosive power he can command from his take-off foot. The swing of the right leg carries up the hips and turns the body to the left. The head and shoulders seem to come down to the level of the hips and legs, but actually they are driven into the air, too. As the hips go up, the take-off leg is brought up fast to aid in the upward drive of the body. The left leg, which is next to the bar at the top of the jump, is flexed and tucked under the right leg. In this tuck the left foot is usually brought up with the toe touching or almost touching the back of the right knee. The right or lead leg on reaching the layout should be elevated well above the bar. This helps to keep the hips up. The hardest part of the body to get over the bar is the hips. That is why they are rolled over the crosspiece.

Until recent years jumpers were disqualified for "diving" if one foot did not precede the head as the bar was cleared. Now any jump that is made off one foot is permitted and there are no more arguments about illegal dives.

In throwing the right leg up high to lift the hips well over the bar, many jumpers drop into the pit with their head and shoulders landing ahead of their feet. A good layout will usually cause the jumper to hit in the pit with his hands and feet simultaneously.

The belly-roll variation of the Western style calls for a faster turn of the body as it starts upward toward the bar. With the right leg kicked up in such a way as to aid the body in making a more rapid turn, when the layout is reached the stomach instead of the side is toward the bar. The head and shoulders frequently precede the legs in this barrel roll. The right leg goes over the bar well ahead of the left and naturally there is no tuck. One of the advantages of this type of jumping is that the take-off leg at the point of bar clearance is pulled over and not tucked under the lead leg.

The timing of this kind of jumping is what causes most of the difficulty when athletes attempt to change to it. Naturally the belly must be down exactly at the high point over the bar, otherwise the whole purpose of the style is lost. Only athletes who are able to jump without any tension whatever can master this technique.

Usually the run is even slower than in the side roll and this easy approach aids the relaxation. Jim Stewart, Les Steers, Ed Burke, Gil Cruter—all men who won championships with this form— showed very slow runs. An exception was Albritton, who had a fast approach but perfect coordination to time it just right.

Good high jumping is so much a matter of form that a coach could spend at least half of his working hours with his candidates at the pits. When an athlete gets a little off through some slight fault in his technique, he needs help since it is difficult for him to analyze his own run, take-off, and leap in order to find the difficulty.

Because a coach has fifteen events to handle and can't give all the time to the high jumpers that he would like to, it helps if there are at least two candidates for the event in order that they may train together. Early in the season the coach should spend all the time possible with them to give them the correct form and to call attention to technical flaws so that later when he is occupied elsewhere they can advise each other.

Improvement in the high jump is made by fractions of an inch and the men in this event become sticklers for the smallest details. Often they learn to analyze each other's work with the critical eye of the most experienced coach and team mates who work together constantly develop the knack of coaching one another to greater heights. That is why on high school and college track teams we so often see high-jump stars developed in pairs or three-somes. Albritton and Walker at Ohio State form one outstanding example.

At Southern California we have had a number of interesting instances. In the season of 1932 we started out with four high-jump candidates and the man who was fourth best in the early meets finally proved to be the champion of them all.

A few years earlier, a slender boy named Duncan McNaughton had come to the university from Vancouver, British Columbia, to study petroleum geology. He reported for track and wanted to go out for the high hurdles as he had run the event close to 16 seconds in high school. He had also high-jumped for his team, once having cleared 5 feet 10 inches, but he considered the hurdles his best event. Duncan didn't have sufficient speed for fast hurdle competition and I persuaded him to specialize in high jumping. His progress was steady and by his Junior year in 1932 he was consistent at 6 feet 2 inches and was occasionally good for 6 feet 4 inches.

During that season we had an unusually high-class crop of jumpers. Jim Stewart, a one-time N.C.A.A. champion, was still

210

THE LAYOUT'S THE THING

Whether the high jumper has his back or his front to the bar when he clears it, his body must be flat over the crossbar. Bob Van Osdel, former national cochampion, almost had his back to the bar in clearing it.

on the squad, and he had a team mate, Will Brannan, who also used the belly roll and who went up to 6 feet 5½ inches. We also had another ace in Bob Van Osdel, who turned in consistently good performances and who reached his peak in the combined national championship–Olympic tryout meet when he tied George Spitz and Cornelius Johnson for first at 6 feet 6⅝ inches.

With such competition on his own team, McNaughton was just another jumper to track followers during the season. With the conclusion of the college meets, fans forgot him completely, but he liked to jump and continued to work out on the Southern California practice field with Van Osdel, who had made the American Olympic team. Somewhat timidly and expecting to be turned down, he sent a request to Canadian Olympic officials to see if he might enter the games on their team. To his surprise they put him on the squad.

During their varsity careers, Van Osdel and McNaughton had trained together and now they worked out with new enthusiasm. We continued to meet together at the Trojan training grounds as though the Olympics were merely a continuation of the college schedule, but I soon found that the two boys didn't need me much because by this time they knew all the angles of high jumping and were eagerly coaching each other. They were still Southern California team mates and the fact that they were to meet in international competition for rival nations didn't mean a thing to them. Both used the Western roll with side clearance. They used opposite take-off feet, Van Osdel approaching from the left and McNaughton running at the bar from the right, but otherwise their style was identical. Thus they knew exactly what the other should be doing and were able to analyze each other's form and give helpful suggestions.

On their day of competition in the Olympics, they were still university team mates, criticizing, advising, and encouraging each other after every jump, and finally they found themselves tied for first at 6 feet 5⅝ inches with Cornelius Johnson of the American team and Simeon Toribio of the Philippines.

On the jump-off, McNaughton, supposedly the fourth best Trojan high jumper, won the Olympic championship, and Van Osdel finished second. It was a great victory for the modest, good-looking Canadian boy and he was the first to say that it

211

would have been impossible if he hadn't had Van Osdel to work with and help him.

Once when this point was being discussed in a fanning bee, I heard the criticism that an American athlete had no business aiding a competitor representing another nation. This is about as narrow-minded a crack as I have ever heard.

Sport is organized for health and recreation. But these features are no more important than sportsmanship, friendship, and good will. That's why leaders in the realm of athletics hold the hope that sports competition some day can help to break down ridiculous international jealousies and hatreds and delusions of racial grandeur.

High jumpers as a general rule are tall and slender. Those in the championship class who are not above the average in height will always be found to have unusually long legs for their size. The high jumper has to be "split." Naturally he must also be streamlined, for every extra pound increases the load that he must lift into the air.

Prep school boys who can jump as high as their head or an inch or two higher are very creditable performers. College athletes in the championship class are rarely expected to clear more than 5 inches above their head. Jumpers like Harold Osborn and Clinton Larsen who were under 6 feet in height and who cleared the bar 8 or 9 inches higher than their own altitude are extremely exceptional.

Considering the present world's record holders, Johnson's height is 6 feet 4 inches and Albritton's is 6 feet 2. High-jump fans who have wondered if a 7-foot record will ever be attained can be sure that it will be. It awaits only a streamlined athlete who is about 6 feet 6 inches in height and who combines with his altitude the spring and coordination of the present record holders.

When a prep school coach seeks material for the high jump, he should look for a tall boy with a funny walk. Since this seems to take in a lot of territory, let me add that the walk can be of the springy variety or it can be gangling and shuffling. Boys who come up on their toes when they walk do so because they possess natural spring. Walter Marty, Bob King, Les Steers, John Wilson, and Bob Van Osdel were of this type.

Vastly different in walking appearance, the shuffler is often

212

the perfect high-jump type because he is loose-jointed and re-laxed. Most of the great Negro stars in this event—Johnson, Albritton, Walker, Burke, and Cruter—had a shuffling gait that completely camouflaged the springs in their legs and gave them the appearance of being too tired to get their feet off the ground. The shuffling itself was the tip-off, however. It was not due to laziness but to the complete relaxation of all the muscles and tendons. The thighs seemed to dangle from the hips, the lower legs dangled from the knee, and the feet dangled from the ankles.

This freedom from tension is one of the most important characteristics of the high-jumper type of athlete, and a coach can often get surprising results from a young man who looks when he walks as though he is falling to pieces just because he is "loose."

After the high-jump type is obtained, the next thing is the selection of a jumping style. The candidate will probably already have jumped with the straight scissors, for this seems to be the natural way to leap and usually starts from the time a small boy sees his first low obstacle.

Unless the jumper has developed the scissors to an efficient Eastern style, it would be well to change him over to the Western roll. Although the two methods are vastly different, the change can be made easily. All the scissors jumper needs to do to get started on the new form will be to change the direction of his approach run so that he will be taking off from his inside foot instead of his outside.

For instance, if the candidate is left-footed, he will run at the bar from the right side for a scissors jump. As he leaps, his left or take-off foot will be on the outside. To change to the Western roll the jumper needs only to approach the crossbar from the left side. When he reaches the bar from this new angle, his left or take-off foot will be on the inside. As he throws his right leg up from this angle, he will turn his body and automatically get the start of a roll.

A good argument in favor of the belly-roll style of jumping is that a given height can be cleared with a lower center of gravity than is necessary in other methods. The athlete does not have to raise his body so high off the ground to get his stomach to the bar as he does to get his hip to it. However, notwithstanding the

213

advantages of the various rolls, it is not wise to make changes in the form of experienced jumpers if they are doing well with a style that is natural to them.

Regardless of the jumping style, athletes should not worry about the action of their arms and must not make unnatural motions with them. It is no trick at all to get the arms over the bar and they will be a natural aid to the body in its spring and turn if the jumper does not even think about them. If the jumper wishes to concentrate on getting any one particular part of his anatomy over the bar, he should think about his hips. If they are driven upward high enough, the legs and torso will go along.

Many athletes give the take-off foot a severe stamp in starting the jump. This stamp can easily be overemphasized. The athlete must remember that in making the leap he transfers the forward momentum of the run to an upward drive through the medium of the kick of the lead leg and spring of the take-off leg. He does not try to bounce himself over the bar by a resounding stamp of the take-off foot.

Until a step or two before the jump is made, the athlete should fix his eye upon the point of take-off. Then, as he is about to jump, he may look up to the bar and imagine a target several inches above it.

It is well for the jumper to get frequent advice from some one standing alongside of one of the uprights as to whether he is going up or coming down when he clears the bar. If he is going up, the take-off check mark should be moved away from the crosspiece. If he is coming down, the take-off should be moved closer.

Crossbars are usually painted with black and white or colored sections in order that they may be easily distinguished. If because of the lighting or background the bar is hard to see, it is permissible to lay a handkerchief or a piece of cloth on it.

Officials staging night meets should take care in the placing of lights as high jumping and pole vaulting are very difficult when the crossbar is dimly illuminated or when the competitors have to run into a glare.

Like all competitors in track and field events, the high jumper will do well to start his conditioning in the fall, or even the summer. To a great extent he can get his conditioning by the usual pull-ups and walks of at least 2 miles a day and by games that

214

require lightness of foot such as tennis, badminton, handball, and volleyball. The last named sport is exceptionally good for high jumpers because of the leaping into the air for spiking at the net.

Jumpers lose the bounce and spring in their muscles if they are bumped around in contact sports such as football. Athletes who have been able to combine successfully the gridiron sport with jumping have usually played end where they were a little out of the path of most of the bone-bending mass play.

Only two football players at the University of Southern California in recent years could combine jumping with the gridiron game with even a fair degree of success. One was Ambrose Schindler, a ball-carrying back. Amby was 5 feet 9 inches in height and once jumped 6 feet 4 inches, which was 7 inches above his head and very creditable leaping for his build. Doyle Nave, another backfield star at Southern California and the hero of the 1939 Rose Bowl game when his passes in the last minute of play won a Trojan victory over Duke, also was fairly successful in combining football and jumping, since he could clear 6 feet 2 inches, which was 4 inches greater than his own height. As a general rule though, the rough stuff on the gridiron makes a football–high jump combination just about impossible.

In the early conditioning period, a great deal of running is not necessary if the athlete is faithful in taking his daily 2-mile walks. Occasional visits to the track if the weather is mild enough will be helpful. Long runs are out, but light jogging and wind sprints are good.

The high jumper should avoid distance work since this type of training often interferes with the rubbery and springy muscular structure of his legs. A certain amount of endurance for an occasional long afternoon of jumping is necessary but it can be acquired by a lighter type of training along other lines.

In the preseason training period in the fall, the athlete may do some jumping, but not more than two or three times a week, after he has first put his legs into good condition. The fall training period is a good time for the candidate to perfect his form while working on easy heights. If he develops correct jumping habits at this time, it will relieve him of worry over technique in the spring and will allow him to concentrate on getting into perfect competitive condition. However, if the candidate gets no coaching or good advice from an experienced jumper in this fall work, it will probably be best for him not to jump until the proper help is available.

The notion that practice makes perfect is sometimes misleading. There is a saying about the persistence of error that the jumper should keep in mind. If the fall jumping practice is not of the right kind, the candidate would be better off without it.

In his early enthusiasm the jumper must be careful not to overwork. He must beware of mental as well as physical staleness and quit jumping if it ceases to be fun.

In the running part of his preseason training, the jumper should keep up on his toes and emphasize bounce. He may run short distances with a bounding stride, but 50 yards of this at a time is enough. The jumper should remember that he only wants his legs to get him 6 feet or so up into the air and not to carry him on a marathon run. If he covers 150 to 200 yards occasionally at a good clip, he is working his legs hard enough.

The intensive training of the spring season usually starts about 6 weeks before the first meet. A good deal of jumping can be done during the first half of this period, as this is the time to perfect the technique. Jumping in training should never be done at maximum heights. The bar should be put at an altitude that can be cleared comfortably while concentrating on style.

At the height of the season the jumping part of the training program is cut down to the point where not more than two days a week are spent at it.

During competition the athlete should keep comfortably warm between jumps and should stay off his feet. He should give each try at the bar his serious attention. There should be no misses through carelessness as strength must be conserved for the difficult heights to come. If the bar is knocked down, the athlete should try to relax until his next turn. High-strung athletes usually are better off if they can make an almost immediate try at the height just missed before a case of jumpy nerves sneaks up on them, but competitors have to go by turn and they must learn to be calm and relaxed while waiting.

High jumpers usually find it most satisfactory to wear regular sprinting shoes in competition. The danger of bruising the heels can be eliminated by putting a pad of soft rubber at this spot.

The padding can either be placed inside the heel of the shoe or taped to the outside of it, or both.

It is natural for the athlete to feel that he must run faster at the bar as it is raised to heights he is not accustomed to clearing, but there is a danger of overdoing this. The approach should be at a reasonable speed not only because the momentum is wanted upward and forward but also because a run that is too fast might cause the jumping leg to give way at the take-off instead of taking on added spring.

Jumpers can overcome this tendency to speed up the approach at new heights by developing a uniform run during practice. In practice or in competition, at easy heights or high ones, it is advisable to keep the speed of the approach the same. The difference between clearing 5 feet 6 inches and 6 feet 6 inches is in the explosive effort of the legs at the take-off, not in the speed or length of the run. Best results will be obtained if the take-off mark, like the approach run, remains constant at all heights.

It is not wise to watch an opponent too intently during competition. One may unconsciously start imitating him, just as a runner sometimes falls in with the stride of the man ahead, and this upsets his own style.

Determination should be combined with the ability to relax mentally as well as physically. The ideal high jumper temperamentally is the one who doesn't worry about his opponents or his own misses in between jumps but calmly concentrates on overcoming his weaknesses, stepping up for each try filled with determination and self-confidence.

After the season is under way, the jumper must remember that the spring in his legs must be developed and conserved. He must not jump too much because it is asking a great deal of a leg to lift the body higher than the head and too many leaps will wear out the spring.

Although his approach run is short, the high jumper needs the uniform stride that pole vaulters and broad jumpers must have in order to hit check marks. Running low hurdles in a series of two or three will help to standardize the stride and will also give the athlete about all the stamina building he needs.

Extreme limberness is required in high jumpers and occasional practice over the high hurdles will assist in developing this looseness. If the jumper doesn't have some skill at the high barriers, he will be better off leaving them alone, however, as skinned knees and bruised ankles from awkward high hurdling will certainly be no help at the jumping pit.

The usual exercises given the barrier men are valuable in training, particularly the "ground hurdling" stunt. In doing this, the jumper takes a sitting position on the ground and extends his left leg out in front. He places the right leg at right angles to his body with the knee bent in such a way that the toe is opposite the hip. With his body thus straddling the ground as though it were clearing a hurdle, he bends his trunk forward until he touches the extended leg with his chest. The exercise should be repeated with the leg positions reversed. The high hurdler uses this exercise more than any other, but he finds it necessary for form as well as stretching and the leg that he places at the side is always the take-off leg. The jumper uses the exercise only for attaining limberness and therefore disregards the factor of a take-off foot and alternates the leg positions.

Some work should be done by the high jumper on the gymnasium apparatus but he shouldn't get a muscle-building yen and overdo it. The high jumper should have a good all-round physique but he needs mainly to keep his physique normal, which for his type of build is usually lean and light.

Few championship jumpers have excelled in track and field events other than their own. Present record holders, Cornelius Johnson and Dave Albritton, were purely high-jumping specialists. Of course, there are exceptions. The most notable one was past record holder Harold Osborn, who could run, jump, vault, and throw things well enough to be Olympic decathlon champion. Past record holder Walter Marty could run an acceptable 220, and broad-shouldered Les Steers was a good javelin thrower. Jim Stewart had all-round track and field ability, like Osborn, and starred in the decathlon.

Unless the jumper believes he can successfully combine other events with his leaping, he needs only moderate gymnastic work to develop his torso during out-of-season training. Pull-ups on the horizontal bar and push-ups from the ground are splendid general conditioners and a reasonable amount of work on the parallel bars, rings, horse, and rope will also help.

218

The most important are the exercises for the legs. Knee bending exercises, high kicking, and the "splits" are very important. In fact, the high jumper can well follow some of the training routine of the chorus girl and ballet dancer.

Loose hips are essential and twisting exercises while straddled on the parallel bars are good. The bicycle pedaling exercise also helps develop this limberness. In doing this exercise, the athlete should first lie on his back on the ground, and then by holding up his hips with his hands, support his weight on his elbows and shoulders. From this position the feet can be revolved rapidly as though a bicycle were being pedaled.

From the same position the high jumper can take another good exercise, one that resembles an upside-down split. One leg is brought toward the jumper's chest and down so far that the toe touches the ground. The other leg meanwhile is stretched with little bending at the knees. Then the legs are reversed and stretched out the other way. The process is frequently repeated, resulting in a scissorslike kick in mid-air in between the upside-down splits.

Another good exercise for high jumpers is done from a crouch somewhat similar to a runner's starting position. The hands are about a foot farther out in front of the feet than they are in a starting crouch. One foot is about 18 inches ahead of the other. Keeping his hands on the ground, the jumper springs his legs into the air and reverses the position of his feet, straightening out the back leg with each spring and repeating often.

The simplest exercise of all and probably the best is just plain bounding up and down on the ground, first on one foot and then on the other. Any simple exercise such as this that will strengthen the feet, ankle, and toes is helpful.

Walking, of course, should be done with the athlete coming up on the toes with each step. When he thinks about his "spring" muscles in daily life enough to give them frequent workouts in little ways, he will find himself feeling as light as a feather when he dons track shoes and takes off in competition.

Although high jumpers usually come in long, slender sizes, those who are naturally built a little heavier don't need to starve themselves in an attempt at streamlining. Although tall, willowy Negro stars dominated high jumping during most of the 1930's,

The high jumper has approached the bar from an angle with a short easy run. Dropping his arms and shoulders as he "gathers" for the spring on the last stride, he has them in position to swing upward as an aid to his lift. The take-off foot, which is hidden by the shavings in the pit, hits the ground flat. The right foot has left the ground for a quick, powerful upward kick.

The right leg, which is the lead leg, kicks up fast with the knee bent at the instant the jumper springs from the ground. Most of the weight is over the jumping leg. There is a slight lean so that the head, which never goes high in the air, can be a pivotal point for the rest of the body as it swings up for the layout.

At the instant the right leg was kicked up, the left arm was swung high for balance and lift. Now the take-off leg pulls up fast and the right arm is raised to aid the lift. Note that the spring from the ground has been practically straight up. This jumper is using the Western roll, side clearance.

With the legs coming up, the body starts to turn for the layout. The left arm has already been thrown over the crossbar and the head and shoulders will not go any higher than they are here. The take-off leg has come up very fast and the foot is swinging into position to be tucked under and behind the right leg.

The jumper's head is over the bar and his right leg is also starting over the bar. From this point on, extremely fast action will be necessary to raise the hips over the obstacle. The left shoulder and arm are beginning to thrust downward even though only a small part of the body is over the height. The left foot is almost in position for the tuck.

Although the head and shoulders have started to drop, the hips are not yet over the bar. The body is in excellent layout position but in the next split second a final lift must be given the hips. This final lift is aided by straightening out the right leg. The left foot is tucked out of the way behind the right leg.

In the fraction of a second since the previous picture, the jumper has straightened out his right knee and has ducked down farther with his head and shoulders. Simultaneously he is turning his body to lift his hips over the bar with a rolling motion. The left leg is starting down and is also helping with the roll of the hips. Note how much higher the right hip is than the head when it is at the top of the bar.

The head still leads the rest of the body as the jumper relaxes for his drop into the pit. The roll of the body will bring him down on all fours. The jumper in this series of pictures is John Wilson, former N.C.A.A. and Pacific Coast Conference champion, who has a best mark of 6 feet 9⅜ inches.

Steers, who won the national title for the white race in 1939 and 1940, looked like a discus thrower and weighed close to 180 pounds.

Weight should be kept normal and on a fairly even plane during the competitive season. In order to check on his condition, the jumper should keep a weight chart from day to day.

The matter of diet is no problem. The athlete should eat a normal amount of good food at regular mealtimes. He should avoid fattening and indigestible foods such as gooey pastries and fried foods which are greasy. The weight charts will tell him whether or not he is overeating.

In his social life the high jumper should stay out of swimming pools and away from dance floors. Swimming develops the wrong muscles and absorbs his bounce. Dancing takes away the jumper's spring since it requires too much shuffling and scuffling around on a hard floor. If the jumper likes the old-fashioned square dances in which the participants trot around on their toes with bouncing steps, he can go to it and substitute the "grand right and left" for his bounding exercises. I have an idea though that there won't be many boys who will be interested in making this substitution.

Day-by-day schedules for training must be drawn up to suit the condition of the athlete. Here is one that can be taken as typical for a jumper who has reached proper competitive condition:

Monday, jogging a lap, light jumping for form at easy heights, bouncing exercises stressed, a few short dashes well up on the toes, finished with a jogging lap; Tuesday, no jumping, plenty of exercise work particularly high kicking, pull-ups, and leg stretching on the parallel bars, work over low hurdles in series of two or three and a few starts and dashes with the sprinters, a lap at the start and at the finish; Wednesday, the main jumping practice of the week, working for form and checking take-off, several jumps within 2 or 3 inches of best height, more short sprints, laps before and after; Thursday, light work consisting principally of exercises, a few bouncing dashes, and a lap; Friday, rest, off the feet as much as possible to have the legs full of pep for Saturday competition.

XII

THE BROAD JUMP AND HOP, STEP, AND JUMP

THE BROAD JUMP

According to A.A.U. records, the first national championship in the broad jump was won in 1876 by a gentleman from Yonkers, N. Y., with a leap of 17 feet 4 inches. If the automobile age has done nothing else for athletics, it has at least forced a development in the race that has brought new high standards in this event.

In our present enlightened era, even the most anemic non-athlete wouldn't be allowed in a pedestrian zone unless he could beat the mark of the Yonkers gentleman by at least a foot. The minimum for a beginning jaywalker carrying shopping bag and umbrella is 20 feet, and big-city taxi drivers manipulate their four-wheeled weapons under the assumption that par for pedestrian with girl friend is at least 2 feet farther.

Undoubtedly because there was little necessity for this particular type of agility in the pre-gasoline buggy days, broad-jump championship marks and records weren't very terrific. The first I.C.A.A.A.A. championship, won by a Pennsylvania athlete in 1876, went at 18 feet 3½ inches, which seems a far cry from the present 24- and 25-foot leaps that are now fairly common in intercollegiate meets.

Best of the jumpers in early national competition was M. W. Ford of New York, who won five national championships and who in 1888 established a world's record of 23 feet 3 inches. A. F. Copland added ⅛ inch to this mark in 1890. Previously Copland had established the best amateur mark on record in the low hurdles at 26⅗ seconds.

As we go further into the consideration of the broad jump, we are going to find that skill in this event goes hand in hand with low-hurdle prowess as well as with sprinting ability. Alvin Kraenzlein of Pennsylvania, the first man to exceed 24 feet in the broad jump, was the record holder in both the high and low hurdles at the time. Norman Paul of Southern California, a coholder of the low-hurdle record a few years back, was consistent at better than 24 feet in the broad jump. The broad-jump record holder today is Jesse Owens, who also holds the official world's marks in the low hurdles and both sprints.

The reason, of course, that broad jumping, low hurdling, and sprinting are closely linked together is that speed is a first requisite for broad jumping as well as for sprinting and that the combination of speed, uniform stride, and spring in the take-off foot is essential both in broad jumping and low hurdling.

Following Copland as record holder came C. S. Reber of St. Louis, national champion in 1891 and 1893, who set a new mark of 23 feet 6½ inches in 1891. Then came two outstanding stars in Myer Prinstein of Syracuse and Alvin Kraenzlein. The former took the record up to 23 feet 8⅞ inches in 1898. Kraenzlein increased it to 24 feet 4½ inches in 1899 and won the Olympic championship in 1900.

Prinstein regained the record in 1900, however, with a leap of 24 feet 7¼ inches and continued to rank for some time as the outstanding international star, winning the Olympic titles in 1904 and 1906. Previously, in 1900, he had won the Olympic hop, step, and jump championship, and in 1904 he won this event as well as the broad jump in the games at St. Louis.

Despite the fact that Prinstein was one of the world's greatest competitors in the event over a long period—he won national championships in 1898, 1902, 1904, and 1906—his second world's record was as short-lived as his first. The mark he made in 1900 was broken the following year by P. O'Connor of Ireland, whose record of 24 feet 11¾ inches lasted until Ned Gourdin of Harvard, one of the first of the great Negro broad jumpers, came along in 1921 with a leap of 25 feet 3 inches.

In 1920, Sol Butler, a colored athlete from Dubuque College, Iowa, had won the national championship, and Negro prominence in the event in America really started from that time. Out of twenty national championships competed for during the period from 1920 through 1939, the American broad-jump title was won seventeen times by Negro stars. The victories of Ed Hamm of Georgia Tech in 1928 and Alfred H. Bates of Penn State in

1930 and 1931 were the only interruptions in the string of Negro wins.

White jumpers have never been far out of the picture, however, and twice in recent years they have set world's records. In the Olympic games of 1924, three years after Gourdin's record-breaking leap, Robert L. LeGendre of Georgetown broke through Negro domination of the event by sending the mark up to 25 feet $6\frac{3}{16}$ inches. LeGendre established the record while participating in the Olympic pentathlon.

The Olympic broad-jump championship that year was won by DeHart Hubbard, University of Michigan Negro, who succeeded LeGendre as record holder the following year when he leaped 25 feet $10\frac{7}{8}$ inches. Hubbard had followed Gourdin as national champion in 1922, and he held this title for six straight years.

In 1928 the supremacy of the American Negro was once more interrupted in this event when Hamm won the national championship and followed with the Olympic title at Amsterdam. Prior to the Olympic meet he had also added the world's record to his collection of jumping honors by setting a mark of 25 feet $11\frac{1}{8}$ inches.

Hamm's mark never reached the record books, however. Two months after he set it, Silvio Cator, a great Negro athlete from Haiti, leaped 26 feet $\frac{1}{8}$ inch, a record that became the official successor of Hubbard's mark.

Meanwhile, following the First World War, Japan was becoming athletic-minded and its sons were finding the broad jump and hop, step, and jump the most suitable of track and field events to their stocky build and powerful legs. Three years after Cator's record effort in 1928, Chuhei Nambu of Japan set a new standard of 26 feet $2\frac{1}{8}$ inches in a meet in Tokio.

This mark stood until Jesse Owens's brilliant record-smashing day in the Big Ten championships of 1935 when he set the present figure of 26 feet $8\frac{1}{4}$ inches. The Ohio State Negro also added the Olympic record to his collection with his victory at 26 feet $5\frac{5}{16}$ inches in the Berlin games of 1936.

In spite of the record breaking of Cator and Nambu, American domination of the event in Olympic competition did not drop off, as Ed Gordon, a tall Negro from the University of Iowa, won

225

the championship in 1932, filling in the gap between the Olympic victories of Hamm and Owens.

In Olympic competition the broad jump has been one of America's best events. From the time that E. H. Clark won the first modern Olympic title in 1896 at 20 feet 9¾ inches, the United States has suffered only one setback in eleven Olympiads. The one defeat came in 1920 when William Petterssen of Sweden won the title.

The superiority that Negro athletes have shown in broad jumping during the past two decades is due principally to their high degree of relaxation. We have seen how their relaxation and limberness in competition have helped them to championships and record marks in the high jump. The same faculties, combined with their natural speed, make them excellent broad jumpers.

Most of the Negro stars in this event have also been outstanding sprinters. The majority of them have been men of medium height, with long legs that were strong but not large, tapering up to well-developed and usually broad-shouldered trunks. Their legs, which were full of spring without being knotty, differed a great deal from those of the outstanding Japanese stars, Nambu, Mikio Oda, and Naoto Tajima.

The legs of these short, chunky athletes were large and got their spring from highly developed power rather than from the natural relaxed bounce of the Negro jumper. Because of their sturdiness, Japanese legs are well suited for the hop, step, and jump and in that event the Oriental athletes have proved unbeatable in the past three Olympiads.

The first requirement for a broad jumper is speed and until the candidate develops sprinting ability there will be little chance of his excelling in the event. Natural sprinters, of course, have the edge, but those who are not naturally fleet can develop enough speed to be successful jumpers. Athletes with little natural sprinting ability should undertake the same course of training as the dash men in early season work and forget about jumping until real speed is attained.

Every outstanding jumper in the past has been a good 100-yard dash runner and most of them have been better than 10-flat men. Conversely, practically all star sprinters are much better than the average athlete at broad jumping although most dash men usually give up the event because of the danger of a pulled muscle. Frank Wykoff of Southern California, coholder with Jesse Owens of the world's record in the 100-yard dash at 9.4 seconds, was a prep champion in the broad jump. Clyde Jeffrey of Stanford, the leading sprinter of the 1939 track season who equaled the Wykoff-Owens 9.4 century record the following year, was also an exceptional broad jumper in high school and junior college.

Nearly all the great Negro jumping stars also excelled in the sprints. Owens, of course, was always as sensational a performer in the broad jump as he was in the dashes. During his college days his greatest rival in the broad jump was Eulace Peacock, a brilliant Negro athlete from Temple University, who in 1935 not only won the national A.A.U. title at 26 feet 3 inches but also took the 100-meter dash in the same meet. Butler, Gourdin, and Hubbard, who first brought the colored race into prominence in the broad jump, also used to represent their teams in the sprints. Bill Lacefield of the University of California at Los Angeles, 1938 and 1939 national broad-jump champion, also was a valuable point winner for his team in the sprints and hurdles.

Although speed is continually stressed as of paramount importance in broad jumping, the young man who wants to excel in this event should not be discouraged if he is only a mediocre 100-yard dash runner. Perhaps he can generate a burst of speed for 30 or 35 yards. Since this will be the length of his take-off run, only a flash of speed and not the sprinter's continued fast pace is required.

In the approach run two check marks are used. These are located so that the first one the jumper hits with his take-off foot is about 90 feet from the board and the second, which is also touched by the jumping foot, is about 40 feet from the board. Naturally the location of these marks must be worked out for each individual. The length of the run and the position of the checks depend on the striding habits of the athlete and his ability to accelerate to full sprinting speed.

Among leading Southern California jumpers we have found quite a variation in the check-mark locations. Dick Barber, who placed in the 1932 Olympics, hit his checks at 95 feet and 42½ feet from the board. Al Olson, one-time N.C.A.A. champion, and

Jesse Hill, who held the I.C.A.A.A.A. record for a time, used identical checks of 94 feet and 41½ feet. Marvin Crawford, a small athlete who approached 25 feet on several occasions, hit his marks at 89 and 40 feet.

The generally accepted method of establishing checks is to use eight strides between the first and second marks and six steps between the second mark and the board. In order to hit the first check with the take-off foot while on the run, the jumper requires a preliminary approach of from 15 to 20 feet.

To find the proper distance for his run, the jumper can sprint down the runway in the opposite direction, starting about 20 feet on the pit side of the board. He should hit the board with his take-off foot and gradually increase his pace until he is running at full speed at approximately the 90-foot mark. At that point an observer can mark the spot where the take-off foot strikes the ground. Then when the jumper reverses his run, hitting the check with his take-off foot, he will arrive at the board with his jumping foot.

The runs, of course, must be similar in stride and speed. After some experimentation, the jumper puts in his second check mark, which is an aid to uniform running and an assurance to the athlete that he is approaching the board in such a manner as to hit it right. There should be no guesswork or attempts to mark off the distances with strides when the distances between checks and board are determined. A steel tape should be used to measure the distances accurately.

Constant vigilance is necessary to keep the check marks right, for broad-jump runways vary in construction and speed. When the athlete leaves his home field for competition, he should remember that the surface of the runway and weather conditions may cause him to vary in the length of his own stride and this will change the location of his checks. Several practice runs should be made at the board to be sure that the marks are properly relocated, if necessary, to suit the runway.

It is very important from a psychological as well as physical standpoint for the checks to be right. A runner can never do his best until he is certain in his own mind that his marks are so located as to bring him to the board in perfect step. When he gets a feeling of confidence in his step, he can concentrate on developing full speed in the run and on the spring from the board.

The uniform running necessary to hit the check marks consistently is difficult to develop at first but striding over low hurdles will correct uneven steps. By running the hurdles over and over again in series of two or three, the jumper will gradually fall into a sprinting stride of uniform length and will at the same time be building up his endurance for the many speedy dashes he must take during an afternoon of competition.

In working on his approach run, the jumper should frequently test his accuracy in hitting the checks. This can be done by placing a small rag or piece of paper on the runway at each of his two marks. If he is hitting the checks properly, his spikes will pick up the objects.

The jumper should reach his top speed before he comes to the board as he must be able to coast for several strides without a loss of momentum. This easing-up process usually takes place in the final three strides. This may shorten to a slight degree his last step and perhaps also his next to last stride, but there is no perceptible decrease in speed.

It is in these final steps that the runner gathers himself for the spring. They are the most important part of the approach as they give him one last instant in which to relax. Pliable, limber muscles are absolutely essential to the development of good spring.

When the jumper reaches the take-off board, the head and chest should be held up. Like the high jumper, the broad jumper must have his body directly over his take-off foot when he drives himself into the air.

On leaving the board the jumper must combine height with his momentum and spring. Consequently he must have no forward lean since such an angle would prevent him from lifting his body very high into the air.

On the other hand, if the body leans backward to any extent, it will lose much of the momentum of the run and spring. A backward lean causes the athlete to be far off balance when in the air. Old-style jumpers, whose limit was around 20 or 21 feet, used to think it necessary to hit the board with a backward lean. Using this style of jumping they could do little in the air but stick out their legs and sail. It was impossible for them to get the helpful hip swing that we stress today.

The jumper aims for a pronounced upward drive at the moment of leaping. At this point it is a common fault to overemphasize a foot stamp on the board. Naturally with the body gathered for the jump in the closing approach strides and with all the weight carried over the take-off leg there is a tremendous strain on the jumping foot. It comes down firmly on the board but if athletes concentrate on the main elements, which are speed and lift, they won't need to be bothered with stressing a stamp of the foot.

The left leg is normally the take-off leg of a right-handed person. He falls into the habit of using his left leg for spring because it is natural for him to reach out with the right leg which starts the upward drive at the take-off.

At the jump, presuming that the athlete takes off with his left foot, the right leg goes up and forward as though continuing the run. The upward drive comes from the spring off the board. Whereas the high jumper makes all his drive upward, the broad jumper makes his drive forward and upward.

Some jumpers fall into the habit of swinging their arms up above their head to aid in the upward drive. It is best not to worry about the arms which will naturally reach out forward at the top of the jump. When the legs swing out from the hips, the arms are automatically thrust forward.

The torso goes through the air almost in an erect position although there is a slight forward lean. At this point an inclination of the body that is too far forward will force the jumper's feet to come down too quickly and will shorten the leap. If there is not a little forward angle, the jumper will have eliminated his chance of getting a hip swing. Also he may fall back in the pit when he lands.

All successful broad jumpers attain good height. Al Olson, who had a best mark of 25 feet 8⅞ inches, regularly cleared a height of 5 feet in making his leaps. Jesse Hill hit 5 feet on his best jumps, and Dick Barber reached about 4½ feet in height, which was exceptionally good for his 180 pounds.

It appears to be relatively easy for Negro athletes to attain altitude in broad jumping and all the great colored stars in this event sailed high in the air. Jesse Owens, the record holder and

1936 Olympic champion, had so much bounce along with his spring and momentum that he soared well over 5 feet in the air during some of his most spectacular jumps.

After the take-off, some jumpers use running strides in the air. The principal aid of this motion, which is sometimes called a "hitch kick," is in maintaining balance. It gives the athlete who uses it the appearance of throwing his body forward to greater distances. Actually it cannot add to the momentum, but it may aid him to keep his feet in the air the longest possible time and thus get the maximum distance from his jumping effort.

It is not wise to talk too much about the hitch kick to beginners. If they can use it to advantage, it will come easily with experience. If they think too much about it at first, it will only add another complication to jumping and will probably do more harm than good.

Athletes vary this mid-air kick to suit their own needs and natural style. Al Olson's kick was something of a high-hurdle motion as though midway in his leap he had to clear a barrier about 5 feet in height.

If an athlete's jumping balance is uniformly good, the hitch kick is not advised. There have been many arguments over its merits and one can find examples to prove both the pro and con of the case. Jesse Owens, for example, jumped both with and without the hitch kick. If he took off from the board with perfect balance, he simply brought his legs together and sailed through the air. If he was out of balance in his take-off, he used the kick to right himself. During his last year of competition at Ohio State, he used the hitch kick sparingly as his balance was usually perfect without it.

In considering the form of our three 25-foot broad jumpers at Southern California, we find that Olson always used the hitch kick, Hill tried it about half the time, and Barber never used it.

The generally accepted method of landing is to bend the knees and fall forward. There is still enough momentum left after a jump at high speed to drive the body over the feet in the landing pit.

If a side swing of the body is made upon arriving in the pit, it is usually done by driving hard upon the jumping foot when landing, forcing the body to be swung away from that leg. If the take-off has been from the left leg, the landing is made on both feet but the push on the left foot causes the body to be twisted or thrown to the right side. The feet should be kept close together when the jumper comes down whether the landing is made with bent knees or the body is swung to the side.

To avoid losing distance on landing by having the hands or buttocks break the dirt behind the feet, the jumper should spend much time on practice landings. This should be done with a half run at about half or three-quarters speed and the landings should be practiced in places filled with shavings, such as a high-jump pit.

In discussing the hip swing that gives so much lift to our present-day jumpers, it is well first to consider its relation to the three styles of jumping.

The first and most primitive style of leaping finds the athlete hitting the board and bringing the knees up to the chest, maintaining this position in the air until the landing is reached. There is no hip swing to this method. This style is the simplest and first method used by a broad jumper, just as a boy in high jumping for the first time follows the natural scissors style. However, when a young athlete decides to go in for broad jumping in a serious way, he usually adopts one of two other methods, each of which makes use of a hip swing in mid-air.

In the second style, the athlete takes off from the board and quickly brings up his take-off leg beyond his lead leg. Then he moves the lead leg ahead again in a running motion, quickly following this action by bringing the take-off leg up even with the lead leg. This isn't as complicated as it sounds. It is simply the extra running step in the air known as the hitch kick.

The final motion of the hitch kick in bringing the feet together and throwing them forward, at the same time thrusting the arms forward, brings about the hip swing. When this motion is completed at the highest point in the leap, the jumper seems to be sitting on air in the same position he would be in if he were sitting on the ground. His feet, extending well forward and close together, are approximately the same height from the ground as his hips. The legs are flexed at the knees. This knee bend is a slight one, however, as the jumper is reaching out with his feet for every possible inch of distance.

232

In the third style of jumping, when the athlete takes off from the board, he makes no effort at first to bring his thighs or knees up to his chest. His arms go well above his head and his position in the air is usually that of a man suspending himself from a horizontal bar. When he reaches his greatest height in the air, the jumper then swings his hips. This throws his legs out ahead and at the same time his arms are thrust out in front, putting him in the sitting position already described.

In all three types of jump the object is the same—to make sure that the feet are thrust far forward when the athlete strikes the pit. In the first type of jump the legs are thrust forward right after the take-off. In the two more advanced jumping methods, the hip swing at the top of the jump throws the legs out ahead. Sometimes a perfect hip swing will throw the feet up higher off the ground than the buttocks, but beginners are not advised to try this.

It is not important which type of landing is used as long as the jumper does not let his legs drop from his hips. Any jump will be finished with enough momentum to throw the athlete's weight forward whether his body goes straight over his feet or swings to one side. At Southern California for a long time we have favored the side swing in the landing and all our best jumpers have used this method. It is more difficult to learn than the natural landing in which the body is carried over the feet, but we have found that most candidates add a few inches when they perfect this method.

However, the body-over-feet landing seems splendidly adapted to athletes who are perfectly relaxed. Jesse Owens and practically all great Negro jumpers have used this type of landing. Upon hitting the dirt they would roll over as relaxed as a kitten and rarely had the problem of falling back and losing distance by breaking the ground behind the feet with the hand or buttocks. For those who cannot drop into the pit with such relaxation, the swing landing seems better.

If a jumper decides to adopt the swing, he should frequently check the distance between the point where his feet are hitting the pit and where his body comes down. Naturally to get everything possible out of the jumping effort, the feet should be kept up and straight ahead as long as possible; if this is done, the body will swing to a descent barely beyond the landing point of the feet.

Keeping the feet up is the hardest point in jumping technique for most novices. Extremely strong abdominal muscles are needed for this and the new man in this event will find that after a few jumps he will be committing the disastrous fault of dropping his legs unless he has built up a strong torso.

When the abdominal muscles are strengthened to the point that the feet can be held up without difficulty, the technique of swinging the hips and holding the legs out in front can be practiced in a soft pit. The athlete should make repeated jumps from a standing position or from a half run.

In this part of his practice the jumper will not be trying to throw his body over his feet or to make a side swing in landing. In fact, he will not have the momentum for a regular landing. Consequently, he should drop into the pit sitting down with his legs extended forward in the position in which they should be carried after the hip swing.

Coaches favor much form jumping in soft pits not only to teach the proper carriage of the legs and body in the air but also to exaggerate the flat landing. When the athlete learns to come down with his feet far out in front, the momentum of his sprint to the board takes care of getting his body out beyond the point where his feet break the dirt. As in high jumping, there should be no overworking at the pits. Leaps in training should be mostly for form, saving the greatest distance efforts for competition.

In practice the jumps should be made from dirt and not from a regular board. Hitting the board is hard on the take-off foot and stone bruises can be avoided by staying away from the wood until the day of competition.

Broad-jump boards should be made of fairly soft wood, something that the spikes will dig into but not cause to splinter. At Southern California we have found redwood to be the most satisfactory material.

Although the broad jumper's run is not long and his event appears to the spectators to be a comparatively easy one, his legs have to be built up to withstand a strain probably greater than that placed on any other track and field man. During an afternoon of competition he has to put forth a violent sprinting

234

Hold Up Those Legs

Raising the feet up as high as the hips, or even higher, and holding them there after the hip swing is one of the secrets of getting good distances in the broad jump. Al Olson, former I.C.A.A.A.A. and N.C.A.A. champion, is shown at the finish of a good hip swing.

effort over and over again. Then he must climax each of these top-speed runs with an explosive muscular effort of his jumping leg. The frequent landing jars in the pit are also a strain on his leg muscles.

The broad jumper, therefore, must combine the sprinter's speed with the constitutional ability to take greater muscular shocks. When the candidate reports for the broad jump in the spring, he should have had a solid background of body building in the fall. This can be obtained by participation in various games, exercises at home and in the gym, walking, and periodical visits to the track if possible.

Golf and hiking are good conditioners for jumpers and it is helpful if he can also get into more active games such as volley-ball, tennis, handball, squash, and badminton. Pull-ups on the horizontal bar are essential. In another good exercise on the horizontal bar, the athlete while hanging from the bar should hold his legs straight and raise them from the hips as high as possible. Some jumpers get their abdominal muscles built up to the point where they can bring their toes up to the bar in this leg-raising exercise.

Lying on the back and raising the trunk or legs will also help develop the abdominal muscles. A particularly good exercise along this line is to lie on the back, raise the legs a few inches off the ground, and then swing them around in a wide circular movement.

Visits to the track about twice a week in the fall will help considerably in preseason conditioning. Workouts may be in the form of jogging one time and wind sprinting the next time out. Jogging up to $\frac{1}{2}$ or $\frac{3}{4}$ mile is good occasionally, but, like the sprinter, the jumper must not overdo distance work and risk losing his bounce. Since wind sprints develop speed and endurance at the same time, they are the jumper's best form of track work after his legs are in shape for occasional bursts of fast running.

Exercises to strengthen the feet and ankles should be taken every day. These should be unusually strong if sprains or pulled muscles or tendons are to be avoided in the violent effort of competition. Since bounding up and down helps the feet, it is well for the athlete, during his wind sprints in the fall, occasionally to stress a bounding stride, like that practiced by the high jumper.

As has been stressed in the preseason training for athletes in all events of track and field, the workouts should never be overdone. A sound body but not a tired one is the goal of the candidate as he builds a background in the fall for the competition he will have in the spring. The athlete should watch his condition and in his enthusiasm should not be a glutton for muscular development. Exercising and gym work are of much importance, but if one goes too far with them he can defeat his purpose by becoming muscle-bound and consequently a tense, tied-up athlete in competition.

From 6 to 8 weeks before the first competition, the broad jumper should swing into a daily training program, giving special attention to work on form during the first half of this period. At the height of the season it is inadvisable to do much jumping. However, in his early training days, the athlete has to jump often to perfect his take-off, mid-air form, and landing.

Presuming that the long walks, exercises, games, and other activities of the fall season have strengthened the jumping muscles, the athlete in his early spring work should do much supervised leaping. This is the time for him to correct faults and to get into good jumping habits, for, unless he receives proper help from a coach or another jumper who understands what should be done, he will be off on the wrong foot for the entire season.

Jumping for form should be combined with starts and other dash work with the sprinters. If the fall training has not included sufficient jogging and wind sprints to build up the legs, the starts and short dashes with the sprinters should be delayed until there will be no danger of muscle injury from a severe sprinting effort.

Jumping into a regular broad-jump pit should end about 2 weeks before the competitive season opens. From this point on, the jumper will have enough to do in building up his speed by starts and sprints with the dash men, perfecting his take-off, and working over low hurdles for form and uniform stride, coordination, and endurance. The athlete continues to work on his jumping style but this training should now be done with short runs and easy landings in a soft pit.

Throughout the season, work over low hurdles is one of the best possible conditioners for a broad jumper. In order not to risk injury by hitting a barrier and falling, the athlete should hurdle strings that are stretched between the tops of two hurdles placed about 4 feet apart. Work should be over just one string at first; later they can be taken in series of two and three and even up to five. In this hurdle practice the jumper will have excellent training in swinging the lead leg up and out. The take-off for the hurdle is always made from the same foot that hits the board in jumping.

When hurdles are cleared in a series, they should be placed from 16 to 20 yards apart depending upon the jumper's stride length. Broad jumpers and pole vaulters, to whom reaching the take-off in proper step is of the greatest importance, usually train so much over the low hurdles that they become very proficient in this event.

Norman Paul, who entered Southern California as a high school broad-jump champion, found in his training that he liked the low hurdles even better. This event developed into his specialty after a year on the team and he eventually became a coholder of the world's record for the 220 lows when the mark was 23 seconds flat.

Kenny Dills, a Southern California pole vaulter, found that running the low hurdles was fun when he used the barriers in training and in the 1940 season he suddenly blossomed out as our best low hurdler as well as our ace vaulter.

The height that jumpers get during their leaps for distance varies. Even though some men seem to be able to set good marks while barely getting off the ground, it is a good plan to emphasize altitude in form workouts. Good high school jumpers ordinarily clear a point about $3\frac{1}{2}$ or 4 feet above the ground at the top of their leaps; college stars, as has already been mentioned, often reach from $4\frac{1}{2}$ to 5 feet.

In order to be sure that they were getting proper elevation, jumpers formerly used to stretch a tape across practice pits at the height they believed they should attain at the peak of their leap. Jumpers do not bother with this now. In fact, deliberately endeavoring to clear an obstacle during a jump can interfere with the hip swing.

TRACK AND FIELD

During practice on form when the athlete is jumping into a soft pit, it is advisable for him to wear shoes that have heel spikes. In competition when he wishes to reach his maximum speed on the runway, he should use sprinting shoes. If he strikes his heel hard on the board at the take-off, he should protect this part of his foot by a piece of sponge rubber placed either inside or outside the shoe.

Before jumping in a meet, the athlete should warm up with short runs and sprints on the track. Pulled muscles can easily result from insufficient preliminary work because of the tremendous effort the jumper makes in his spring from the board.

Before the first jump, the athlete should measure and check his take-off, making whatever allowances are necessary for the speed of the runway and wind conditions. Sprinting into the wind on the approach can cut the stride down to the point where the run will be 1 or 2 feet shorter than usual. Running with the wind naturally will increase the stride and upset the accustomed length of the approach. When the approach run has been checked and adopted to meet the conditions of the runway, the athlete should take at least one practice jump before starting his official leaps.

In between his jumps he should not concern himself with the distances of his competitors but should rest as much as possible and keep comfortably warm. Worrying about what the other fellow is doing usually causes tenseness, and like all men in the cinder-path sport the broad jumper must be relaxed when he performs.

Perhaps this would be a good place for a word or two on relaxation in athletics, particularly in track and field. To many observers of athletes in action it seems logical to assume that the more muscular power they put into their work the better will be their performance. So far so good, but when increasing the effort results in strain and causes general body tenseness, the purpose of the hard try is defeated.

Relaxation of muscles does not mean that when the proper time comes they will not be used to their utmost power. It means allowing them to be loose and limber until the instant they are called into play. Then they go to work with a sudden explosive action that gives them real power.

238

Take the example of a batter in a baseball game. If he clutches his club in an iron grip and stands at the plate with all his muscles tense, his swing will be stiff, awkward, and lacking power in spite of all the violent effort he is putting forth. If, however, he waits at the plate with his bat ready but with his body relaxed, when he sees a pitch coming that he wants to smash he can spring his muscles into action with explosive force and swing his stick with real power.

Babe Ruth wasn't the home-run king of the big leagues for many years because he was the strongest man in baseball. As a matter of fact, Babe was always on the portly side and was usually far from being the game's prize physical specimen. But he knew how to relax until he saw something he liked coming over the plate and then he exploded at it.

Good golfers have the same ability to relax until it is time to hit the ball. The dub is the fellow with the death grip on the club and the stiff-arm poke who gets puny results when he hits the ball because all his muscles from face to feet are tied in knots.

Because success in any kind of athletics requires the performers to be free from tension in order to approach technical perfection, track coaches are continually imploring their candidates to relax and to try to be loose while they are making their maximum effort. The trick of keeping muscles pliable and rested until the very instant they flash into action and then of resting them again until the next instant of use is what we mean by relaxation.

Another point in the argument for avoiding tension comes from the fact apparent to everyone that use of the muscles causes the burning up of energy. Naturally when an athlete grows tense all over, he is consuming his body fuel at a rapid pace and wearing himself out. If he could only relax his muscles until the instant of use, his endurance would be much greater.

The relaxed athlete is the graceful one. Although grace may seem an effeminate word to use in describing he-man runners, jumpers, weight throwers, and whatnot, there never was a real champion who was not graceful in the performance of his event.

In considering the midseason training schedule for a broad jumper, the coach must meet individual needs since the general condition of the athlete, the amount of speed work and jumping for form he requires, and other matters of this kind vary a great

239

The jumper's weight is directly over his take-off foot at the instant he starts his leap. While the spring will be made from the ball of the foot in taking off, he hits the board firmly with his heel as well as toe. The head should have been carried straight ahead rather than thrown back. However, jumpers who strive for good altitude frequently tend to carry their head in this position in emphasizing "lift."

The jumper is getting a good drive off his left leg. His right leg is coming up fast as though he were making a combination sprint-high-hurdle stride. At the take-off, his arms are still being carried in the sprinting position.

The jumper is "riding" in the air. From his leg position he might still be sprinting. His arms are swinging upward to aid his lift and he is beginning to pull his take-off leg forward. This athlete is making a simple jump with no attempt at a hitch kick.

At this point the jumper's torso has reached its full altitude. From the athlete's position with his arms overhead and his legs swinging in a relaxed manner it looks as though he might be swinging from a horizontal bar. Although the head is still too far back, this position may help the action of the abdominal muscles in lifting the legs.

By pulling with his abdominal muscles and swinging his hips, the jumper is lifting his legs and throwing them forward. This action shows the necessity for exercises to build unusually strong muscles in the abdomen and thighs. The arms start forward and will go out to meet the feet.

The thighs are being lifted high by the swing of the hips. The jumper is now starting to come down and this is the time for him to make his big effort to hold up his feet. If the hip swing is started prematurely, the abdominal muscles tire and the legs drop too soon.

Excellent position has been reached by the athlete who has swung his legs forward and raised them to the point where his heels are as high above the pit as his hips. The low position of the arms will help the body swing forward beyond the feet at the landing.

In landing, the jumper continues to reach forward with his hands to prevent sitting down. He is holding his left leg firm and relaxing his right leg to create a pivot that will cause a side swing to the right. A pit of soft shavings is always advisable for practice. The athlete here is Art Laret, who doubles in the broad jump and low hurdles.

deal. Here is a typical training schedule for a broad jumper who has no particular individual problem except the usual need for increasing his speed and keeping his form correct:

Monday, a lap of jogging, work over one, two, or three hurdles, correction of errors in take-off if any have been found in the competition of the preceding Saturday, finish with a lap, on the whole a light workout; Tuesday, form jumping into a soft pit, a few short dashes with the sprinters and also more low-hurdle work over strings, jogging a lap at the start and finish of the workout; Wednesday, the heaviest workout of the week, form jumping with a little more effort put into the jumps than was used the previous day, two or more 220's depending on the amount of conditioning needed, a few starts, a lap of jogging to start and finish the day; Thursday, a lap of jogging at the start, no work in the jumping pit, work on speed with starts and 35-yard sprints; Friday, light exercises only for the next day's competition. Exercises and walking, of course, are on the schedule every day but that of competition.

THE HOP, STEP, AND JUMP

Closely akin to the broad jump is the hop, step, and jump, which is not regularly used in high school and college meets, although several movements have been started in recent years to have it placed on the prep and intercollegiate track and field program. Olympic games competition includes this excellent event and it is always found in national championship meets.

The hop, step, and jump is just as much fun for competitors as the broad jump, calls for the same type of training, and has the added advantage of building equal strength in both legs. As the broad jumper is inclined to have a one-sided development in favor of his take-off leg, he does not always turn out to be a good performer in the hop, step, and jump. The competitor in this event, however, is always a better than average broad jumper.

Like the broad jump, the hop, step, and jump requires the speed of a sprinter and a uniform stride to the take-off board. Whereas the broad jumper must concentrate on highly developed spring in his leaping leg, the hop, step, and jump man needs take-off power in both legs. For this reason, good candidates for the event are sometimes found among slightly undersized partic-

242

ipants in the low hurdles. The low hurdler who isn't quite long-legged enough to take the customary seven strides between the barriers and who has to use eight, thus alternating his take-off, is an excellent prospect because he has developed good spring from both legs.

In the early days of the hop, step, and jump, when a good broad jumper could double in the event and turn in acceptable marks without any special preparation, the United States did well enough in international competition. For many years, how-ever, Americans have had little success in the Olympics in this event because it has been rare for school and college athletes to specialize in it.

After J. B. Connolly won the championship in the 1896 games and Prinstein took it in the 1900 and 1904 Olympiads, American athletes earned no more first places. Athletes from Ireland, Great Britain, Sweden, Finland, and Australia followed as Olympic champions until 1928 when Japanese domination of the event started with Mikio Oda, followed in 1932 by Chuhei Nambu, and in 1936 by Naoto Tajima. Tajima set the present world's record of 52 feet 5⅞ inches in his victory in the 1936 games.

The event has not been developed anywhere near its possi-bilities as yet, having lacked outstanding competition except in international meets. If athletes take it up with the seriousness that they have shown in broad jumping, the record is certain to go many feet beyond its present mark.

The record in this event has been broken less often than any other, again owing to lack of competition. M. W. Ford of New York had the best amateur mark on record in 1884 with a distance of 44 feet 1¾ inches. Two years later he also became the record holder in the broad jump at 23 feet 3 inches. He was succeeded as the hop, step, and jump record holder in 1893 by E. B. Bloss of Harvard, who took the mark up to 48 feet 6 inches. Again the record had fallen to a broad jumper, as Bloss was I.C.A.A.A.A. champion in this event in 1892 and 1893 and was national broad-jump champ in 1895, 1896, and 1897.

Prinstein, who twice held the broad-jump record for a year at a time, was the outstanding hop, step, and jumper at the start of the century but did not break into the record-smashing class despite his two Olympic victories. P. O'Connor of Ireland, who set a world's broad-jump record in 1901 of 24 feet 11¾ inches, doubled in the hop, step, and jump and won the Olympic championship in 1906.

In 1910 the hop, step, and jump record fell to a specialist in this event for the first time when D. F. Ahearn of the Irish-American Athletic Club of New York cleared 49 feet 7⅜ inches. A year later he raised the record to 50 feet 11 inches. Ahearn had a long reign in this event as national champion, winning in 1910 and 1911 as a member of the Irish-American Club. After dropping the title in 1912 to broad jumper Platt Adams of the New York Athletic Club, he won six straight championships as a member of the Illinois Athletic Club team.

In winning the Olympic championship in 1924, A. W. Winter of Australia barely nipped Ahearn's record, raising it ¼ inch to 50 feet 11¼ inches.

Oda of Japan followed as Olympic champion and then Nambu set the record at 51 feet 7 inches in winning the 1932 Olympics. It may be recalled that Nambu had preceeded Jesse Owens as broad-jump record holder, having set the mark of 26 feet 2⅛ inches in 1931 that Owens broke four years later. Tajima followed Nambu as Olympic winner and record breaker in the hop, step, and jump in 1936.

It is interesting to note that the event is the only one in Olympic games track and field competition that has been won three times in succession by Japanese athletes. It also may be noted that world's records have been set in three of the last four Olympic meets. This indicates that there is not enough participation in the event since only the international competition of the Olympic games brings out record breaking.

Oda, Nambu, and Tajima were all fast men with exceptional power in their legs. Although slightly above the average in height for their race, they would be classed among the average run of athletes as men of medium build. They had bulging calves and thighs in contrast to the smooth, long muscles of most of the American champions and record holders in the broad jump.

In preparing for the hop, step, and jump, the athlete establishes his check marks on the runway just as he does in the broad jump. He concentrates on speed and height, but in this event he must remember to think about getting well off the ground three times.

After the take-off, he swings his lead leg out and then brings it back, thrusting the take-off leg ahead of it. The first landing is made on the take-off foot and the triple jumper must be in position for the second phase which is the step. The athlete should not attempt to get too great a distance with his opening hop. He cannot throw his feet out as in the broad jump as he must have his weight over the take-off leg when he lands. He also must have the opposite leg behind the take-off leg in order to have it ready to swing out for the step. During the hop the jumper must maintain his speed and body balance.

Following the hop, a definite effort is made to get as great a distance as possible out of the step. This is the part of the event in which champions attain winning distances and beginners make their most serious mistakes. To make a long step, the jumper gives a vigorous forward swing with his lead leg, driving it up as he seeks good height. He reaches out with it as far as possible while in the air, bringing it down just in time to have the weight of the body over it for the jump.

Enough momentum must be retained after this phase to permit a long jump. The leap is made just as in the regular broad jump with the lead leg going forward and up as in a running step and with the feet and arms then being thrust ahead with a strong hip swing. A few hop, step, and jump men sometimes use the hitch kick in this final leap. It can be employed if found helpful in maintaining balance, but the beginner shouldn't bother with it, letting it come naturally later if it seems to be needed.

As in the broad jump, a right-handed person usually makes his take-off from his left foot. Then he makes the first landing on the left foot and takes a second spring from it in executing the step. His broad jump is then made from a right-footed take-off.

However, some left-footed jumpers believe that they should concentrate on the last phase of the hop, step, and jump to the extent that they should hop and step from their right foot in order to have the jump made from the leg that is accustomed to giving the greatest spring. It is up to each individual performer to make his decision in this regard. Ordinarily it is best for left-footed jumpers to start the event with the left foot since two of the three take-offs are made from it.

The landing in the hop, step, and jump is made exactly as in

245

the broad jump and the athlete has the choice of using the side swing of the body or of bending his knees and falling forward. The side swing is even more difficult to put into this event than in the broad jump, but if the athlete can develop it he may be able to add a few inches. The record-breaking Japanese hop, step, and jumpers all used the old method of falling forward over the feet and this is standard.

When Tajima won the triple jump in the 1936 Olympics with the world's record of 52 feet 5⅞ inches, the spacing of his leaps was reported to have been as follows: hop, 20 feet; step, 15 feet 4 inches; jump, 17 feet 2 inches.

Because of the extreme sturdiness of their legs, Japanese athletes can start off with an unusually long hop without fear of knee injuries. American athletes can turn in their best performances by not trying to go too far on the hop, and gaining back what they might have lost here by putting forth an especially strong effort in the step.

In Tajima's figures it will be observed that, although as a broad jumper he was good enough to do 25 feet 4⅞ inches to win third in the 1936 Olympics, his broad jump at the end of his record-breaking triple leap was 8 feet less. It is characteristic of the iron-tendoned Japanese hop, step, and jump men to give the greatest effort to the hop. American athletes hold back in this first phase, strive for a long step, and then try to finish up with a 20-foot jump.

The triple jumper should use sponge rubber in the heel of each shoe as a protection against stone bruises since the take-off from the board and the first two landings on the hard ground give considerable punishment to the feet. Shoes with heel spikes are advisable for both practice and competition. Sprinting shoes should be tried only in championship meets where the athlete may be willing to risk a sore foot to win a high award.

The beginner in this event should do much jumping from either foot before attempting to put the three parts of the leap together. Low-hurdle work is good and the candidate should practice taking off for the barriers from one foot one day and from the opposite foot the next. After take-offs from either foot have been perfected the athlete can then place the hurdles so that he will spring over the obstacles from alternating legs. Hurdles should be placed in series of four for this type of practice.

246

The landings after the hop and step are flat-footed, but the spring for each leap always comes off the toes as in the broad jump.

In both the broad jump and the hop, step, and jump, the athlete should not take any more leaps in competition than are necessary. Because of the violent strain put on the leg muscles at the take-off, if the athlete can get off an exceptional leap early in the competition, he should start passing when his name is called for later tries. If someone exceeds his mark, he can always get back into the competition. If his mark holds up, he is at once doing away with the risk of injury and saving his pep for future meets.

The training requirements for the hop, step, and jump are practically the same as those for the single leap. The man in the triple event needs a little more strenuous conditioning program and of course should strive to develop a spring of equal power from each leg. Although the broad jumper needs no training distances of more than 220 yards, the hop, step, and jump men can run 330's occasionally. He needs greater stamina than the broad jumper since he must maintain his speed and power through three leaps.

America has had few specialists in the hop, step, and jump and there seems to be a good opportunity for young men to excel if they are willing to train hard for the event. Roland Romero, who was about the only specialist Uncle Sam had in the event in 1936, finished fifth in the Berlin Olympic games with a mark of 49 feet $5^{11}\!/_{16}$ inches.

The best mark ever made by an American is many years old. It is 50 feet 11 inches and was set by Daniel F. Ahearn in 1911. Leading hop, step, and jumper of recent seasons has been Billy Brown of Louisiana State University, who was 1940 national champion both in his event and in the broad jump.

In view of the many great sprinters and broad jumpers that America has produced, it is clear that our athletes have the speed and leg power for exceptional marks in the triple leap if the event were only taken up in a serious way. One of these days young America is going to see the possibilities of the hop, step, and jump and we shall witness at least a half-dozen men leaping beyond 50 feet each year and establishing a new series of American if not world's records.

247

XIII

THE SHOT-PUT AND HAMMER THROW

THE SHOT-PUT

Good shot-putting requires unusual strength, but a giant can heave-ho with all the power at his command and get only ludicrous results if he does not direct his muscular force with the correct form. A skillful stylist in this event can give away many pounds and win from a novice through timing that puts the full weight and speed of the body behind the shot with explosive force at just the right instant. Size, of course, is a big advantage, and when it is combined with proper technique a champion thrower is the result.

Jack Torrance, who set the present 16-pound shot record of 57 feet 1 inch, in 1934, was 6 feet 5 inches in height and at the time he set the mark he weighed around 275 pounds. Later, when his weight went considerably beyond what was normal for him, going above 300, the excess interfered with his technique, and in the 1936 Olympics he tossed the ball $6\frac{1}{2}$ feet below his best mark and finished fifth.

Playing football is no particular help to shot-putting, but we find the same athletes participating in both sports because the physical requirements are the same. The football coach needs powerful boys for his forward wall and for line-plunging fullbacks; the track mentor requires the same type to handle the weights. In university competition the champion putters are usually the biggest men to be found in athletics and few of the outstanding stars weigh less than 200 pounds.

Occasionally a lighter man will rank among the topnotchers through a combination of perfect form and unusual competitive ability. Every close follower of track and field can recall some instance where a relatively small man stood out among the giants of the event. When Clarence (Bud) Houser of the University of

248

Southern California won both the shot-put and the discus throw in the Olympic games of 1924, he tipped the beam at 180 pounds and was outweighed by as much as 100 pounds by many of his foreign rivals. Another "midget" for the event at Southern California was Owen Hansen, a 180-pounder who hit the 50-foot mark in the 16-pound shot-put several times. However, it is rare for anyone of 180 pounds or less to be able to compete on equal terms with the present-day run of jumbo throwers.

Weight men of the early days had more shove than technique, and shot-putting marks were slow to come up to presentable figures until Ralph Rose, a rotund husky from Healdsburg, Calif., combined a powerful build with good throwing form. Rose reached stardom in the 1900's, breaking the world's record for the first time in 1904 and later setting a 51-foot mark that stood for 19 years.

In the first national championship meet in 1876, H. E. Buermeyer of the New York Athletic Club won with a toss of 32 feet 5 inches. In the first I.C.A.A.A.A. championshps the same year, the shot-put winner was J. M. Mann of Princeton, whose distance was 30 feet 11½ inches.

Shot-put marks improved steadily but far from phenomenally and in 1888 G. R. Gray of the New York Athletic Club set a world's record of 43 feet 11 inches. Gray won 10 national championships during the period from 1887 to 1902. In 1893 he broke his own record with a distance of 47 feet even. As Gray began to reach the end of his long reign as America's champion shot-putter, a new star arose from Ireland in Dan Horgan. In 1899, he added an inch to Gray's record and the following year he put the mark up to 48 feet 2 inches.

The first Olympic championship was won in 1896 in Athens by Robert S. Garrett of Princeton at 36 feet 2 inches. Four years later in Paris, Richard Sheldon of Yale kept the title for America with a toss of 46 feet 3⅛ inches.

By the time of the 1904 Olympics, America was ready to defend the shot-put championship with one of the most sensational young track and field athletes of the day. Rose, the California giant, was far from our present idea of a streamlined athlete, being considerably convex around the midriff, but he knew how to use the 7-foot circle for more than a mere standing place from which to throw. He developed good speed across the ring, timed his put in such a way as to get his weight behind it, and followed through with a good reverse. The result was a new world's record of 48 feet 7 inches and a victory in the 1904 games in St. Louis.

W. W. Coe of Somerville, Mass., temporarily eclipsed the California star the next year by winning the national A.A.U. championship with a world's record toss of 49 feet 6 inches. He repeated his championship victory in 1906, but Rose continued to improve and came through with four straight national A.A.U. wins and three record-smashing shot-put efforts.

Rose raised the mark to 49 feet $7\frac{1}{4}$ inches in 1907, to 49 feet 10 inches in 1908, and to 51 feet even in 1909. Although Martin J. Sheridan won the Olympic shot-put title in the games of 1906 in Athens, Rose became a two-time winner in the games when he took the event in the 1908 Olympiad in London. Possessing tremendous strength and reasonably good, if not consistent, form, Rose was considered one of track and field's most outstanding figures for many years. His 51-foot record had shot-putters and cinder-path followers so awe-struck that many track and field experts declared flatly that the 6-foot 4-inch, 286-pound behemoth had definitely reached the limit of human possibility with the 16-pound weight. This seemed to be the case for a long time. For 16 years after Rose's performance in the A.A.U. championships of 1909, no athlete was able even to hit the 50-foot mark in the national meet.

Then came "Bud" Houser, who won the national title in 1925 with a put of 50 feet 1 inch. One of the greatest stylists that has ever been produced in the weight events, he was more than 100 pounds lighter than Rose when he was coming within a few inches of Rose's supposedly invincible record.

Along with Houser, other college stars began to approach Rose's record through steady improvement in technique. About this time Ralph G. Hills of Princeton and Glenn Hartranft of Stanford started turning in consistently good performances and a year or so later John Kuck of Kansas State Teachers College and Herman Brix of the University of Washington became consistent at better than 50 feet.

After 19 years as a world's record, Rose's mark of 51 feet fell in 1928 when Kuck heaved the iron ball 52 feet $\frac{3}{4}$ inch in winning the Olympic championship in Amsterdam. Four weeks after Kuck's accomplishment, Emil Hirschfield of Germany raised the mark to 52 feet 7½ inches.

During the Olympic year of 1932 the record fell twice more. Z. Heljasz of Poland added ⅜ inch to Hirschfield's distance, and then Leo Sexton of New York, who won the Olympic title in the Los Angeles games, took the mark up to 53 feet ½ inch. Sexton was a good-sized giant at 6 feet 3 inches in height and 240 pounds in weight, but he was 35 pounds shy of Jack Torrance, the Louisiana colossus who sent the record skyrocketing to 57 feet 1 inch two years later, in 1934. Torrance had plenty of competition in several championship meets from John Lyman of Stanford, but, although the latter had perfect technique and hit 54 feet on several occasions, he was a mere stripling of 200 pounds and had to give away too much weight to catch the Gargantuan record smasher.

Since Torrance's mighty heave, which was made in an international meet in Oslo, Norway, the most recent threats of new record making have come from Elmer Hackney, the "One Man Gang" from Kansas State College, who was N.C.A.A. champion in 1939 at 55 feet 10⅜ inches, and from Al Blozis of Georgetown University, I.C.A.A.A.A., N.C.A.A. and national A.A.U. champion in 1940. In winning the N.C.A.A. title Blozis tossed the ball 56 feet ½ inch.

In a Finnish Relief indoor meet in Madison Square Garden, New York, during the 1940 season, 6-foot 6-inch, 240-pound Blozis turned in one of the most sensational putting performances in history when he tossed the 16-pound shot 55 feet 1 inch, the 12-pound shot 65 feet even, and the 8-pound shot 78 feet ⅛ inch. The 12- and 8-pound marks were unofficial world's indoor records. The 16-pound mark was also better than the old indoor record held by Torrance but Blozis previously during the 1940 season had made an even greater distance with a heave of 55 feet 8¾ inches.

Other outstanding shot-putters of late years have been Francis Ryan of Columbia, 1938 national and I.C.A.A.A.A. champion; Lilburn Williams, tall Negro from Xavier University, who was 1939 national champion; Stan Andersen of Stanford, who hit the 55-foot distance in 1940; and Bill Watson of the University of Michigan, who had several marks of better than 54 feet in 1939.

Although Rose's 51-foot record was once considered the limit of human power, we find that it wouldn't get him very far in championship competition in the last few years. In the N.C.A.A. championships of 1939, Williams's 52 feet 9⅝ inches earned him no better than fourth place. In the national A.A.U. championships of the same year, Hackney tossed the ball 52 feet 7 inches and also wound up in a fourth place.

Despite the sensational performances of numerous American shot-putters in recent years, the United States lost the Olympic title in this event in 1936 for the first time in the history of the games. The winner was Hans Woellke of Germany with a mark of 53 feet 1¹³⁄₁₆ inches. Woellke was one of the few Europeans in this event to generate good speed in the circle and in his victory he showed that continental stars were finally beginning to adopt American technique successfully.

It has been said that fairly small athletes with proper form can beat much bigger men with poor technique. But this doesn't mean that there is much hope for the little fellow now, for the big boys in competition these days know all the tricks of the game. As they say in boxing, a good little man can't beat a good big man.

Torrance didn't account for his spectacular distances by brute power alone. He looked ponderous and sometimes found his efforts hampered by the limitations of the 7-foot ring, but his coach, Bernie Moore, had given him good technique. When his size didn't overcome his intentions, Torrance delivered his puts with correct form.

Small boys can have fun putting the shot and it is a good idea for everyone in athletics to learn something about the right technique, for tossing the ball is a good conditioner for anyone, if not overdone.

In preparing to put the shot, the athlete places it in the palm of his hand and endeavors to carry the weight as much as possible on the base of the fingers. The beginner rarely has the strength for this and usually holds the shot in the palm of his hand. However, as his strength and technique improve, he keeps getting it higher up and placing more and more of the weight on the fingers.

The best shot-putters add distance to their tosses by finishing their throws with a strong flip of the fingers. This is something that comes with long training. While the young putter aims eventually to have a finger flip, at first he must carry the shot too low in his hand to flip it.

In holding the shot, the three middle fingers are kept fairly close together. The thumb and little finger are spread out to aid in balancing the ball and holding it snug.

The rules require that the shot must not be held behind the shoulder, as such a position would make it a throw instead of a put. The pellet is usually carried in such a way that it rests against the neck during the preliminaries of the toss. In carrying the shot at the start of the put, the athlete keeps his elbow fairly high. The proper angle will come for each athlete, as it varies considerably with individuals.

John Kuck, the Kansas husky who broke Rose's long-standing record, held the shot well below his neck. He kept his elbow in close and could not understand why other putters did not use the same style. This technique was undoubtedly the best for Kuck as he had injured his wrist when a boy and this had left it stiff. It would have been extremely awkward for Kuck to have carried the shot in any other method.

Another Kansan, Elmer Hackney, was an example of the other extreme. He kept his elbow high and carried the shot so far back that his puts just missed being throws. Torrance, the record holder, also held the ball well up on his neck with the elbow high during the preliminary stage.

In lining up for the toss, the athlete stands in the back of the ring. If he is right-handed, his right foot should be just inside the circle. He starts with his feet close together, the toe of his left foot turning out somewhat toward the direction of the put. In assuming the crouch, the putter bends his right knee and carries his weight on his right leg. His body bends to the right at the waist and the right shoulder is dropped. For balance, the left arm is extended out in line with the shoulders. The arm must be kept relaxed and is bent at the elbow.

It is very important at this point for the putter to keep his head and chest up. This forces his buttocks to be kept in. The moment the shot-putter starts to protrude at the rear he will be out of

253

balance and have no chance to get the big muscles of the body behind his put.

When he is comfortably crouched, the athlete swings his left leg to aid his balance, rhythm, and sense of relaxation. The left leg should be swung out in the direction of the put. Many putters swing this leg back, but this has a tendency to break the correct body stance by forcing the buttocks out. The preliminary swings of the left leg may be continued until the putter feels that he is correctly set for the hop. He may take from one to a half-dozen swings.

The hop toward the center of the ring is made on the right foot as the left leg is swung out in the direction of the put. The purpose of this hop is to produce speed and momentum for the toss.

At the completion of the hop the putter makes his landing on both feet with the heels pointed in, toes out. The left foot comes down almost against the toeboard to take full advantage of the 7-foot diameter of the ring. Although most of the weight is still carried over the right leg, there must be enough pressure on the left leg to hold the hips in place. At this point the right hip is approximately over the right foot. This position is important as the purpose of the form is to get the big muscles of the body behind the throw. Novices don't use much more than their arms and shoulders in tossing the shot; that is why men who have learned to direct the full power of their body into the put have such a tremendous advantage.

In swinging the left leg directly away from the right, the athlete must be sure that it is directed at the center of the toeboard. The putter must make every effort to carry his body on a straight line in the direction of the throw.

The right foot may land a little to the right of an imaginary straight line and the left foot may come down a little to the left as this is the most natural position and aids in working up speed. However, if the feet land very far off a straight line, the putter cannot get full power behind his toss.

The initial drive for the put starts from the right leg and is forward and upward. The power goes quickly and smoothly from the leg to the body and the body drives the arm.

The direction of the shot is never changed. It has been carried straight across the ring in the hop and now it is delivered straight

254

out in the line of the putter's stance. The ball is released when the arm is fully extended. The wrist flip of experienced putters causes it to fly off the tips of the fingers at the instant of delivery. Those who have developed this wrist flip naturally carry the hand bent well back at the wrist during the preliminaries.

The follow-through after the shot is delivered reverses the feet. The power starts from the right leg and as the feet reverse and the body turns, the landing is made on the right foot. The foot reverse is a natural movement that should never be overly stressed. It will take care of itself following the delivery of the shot. One who concentrates on this phase of the put will likely start the movement of the feet too soon and may even be off the ground when the ball is released.

Shot-putting rules provide that the foot may touch or rest against the inside of the toeboard but hitting the top of it con- stitutes a foul. To avoid fouling from the momentum of the put, the thrower can aid in balancing himself and putting on the brakes by flexing his right leg at the knee as he comes down at the finish of the reverse. However, this is something for the expert and few athletes use it. The best way to avoid fouling is to shorten the hop and take more room for the actual put.

Although the movements of making a put are simple and few, it is no small matter to coordinate and time them. Everything about the procedure must be smooth. From a slow start, speed must be accelerated until at the finish the arm shoots out in a powerful, lightning thrust. Without hurrying or jerking, the athlete must go from the hop to the throw with a quick, continual motion in order to get full advantage of the momentum worked up by the hop.

This hop is sometimes referred to as a glide because the athlete must keep his right foot close to the ground in moving across the ring. It is a good plan to drag the spikes of the right shoe lightly on the ground to be sure that the hop isn't into the air. The athlete needs all his speed accelerated forward and a hop any distance off the ground causes a loss of straight-ahead power.

Relaxation must be stressed, as in all track and field events, so that the muscles spring into action with explosive force at the exact instant they are needed.

In training for the event the athlete works for a long period on form only, letting distance come gradually as technique is perfected. Once he has developed correct putting habits, the shot-putter can concentrate on developing greater strength and energy in his body, knowing that he now has the form that will make it possible for him to show improved results with the addition of every ounce of power.

Since the athlete cannot stand off and watch his own form to see what he is doing incorrectly, he must never be without the services of a coach or an experienced shot-putter long, especially if practice does not seem to be bringing improvement. Occasional slumps should not cause him to worry, although if they persist it is a good sign that a "bug" has crept into the technique and that an experienced teacher should be consulted.

In developing good form, one of the most important things for the shot-putter to concentrate on is holding his body in a straight line and keeping his buttocks in. To some extent he must consider himself a weight lifter. He knows that in lifting weights a man can generate little power if he is bending forward at the waist. The first principle is to get the legs and body under the weight. In shot-putting the idea is the same. The athlete must keep under the weight he is handling. To do this it is absolutely necessary to keep the tail in and make it possible for the big muscles of the hips to work smoothly with the legs and body.

In early season shot-putting drill, the athlete must be reminded often that the main driving force behind the shot comes from the legs and body. To make this point clear, no attempt should be made to have the candidate reverse his feet in early training. In fact, it is a good idea for the thrower not to move the position of his left foot when the put is made in practice.

Some coaches do not permit their shot-putters to move the left leg at all during the first 2 months of work with the weight. In this way their athletes learn that it is the leg drive and not the foot reverse that gives power to the put.

The chief fault created by too much attention to the reverse is that when the athlete concentrates on it he usually does not get into a set, driving position. His reverse is likely to be started too soon instead of coming along as a natural result of the throw. A premature movement of the legs obviously upsets the flow of power being generated behind the weight.

256

THE SHOT-PUT

The most popular fall sport for shot-putters seems to be football. Usually the weight thrower's husky build draws him to the gridiron, but unless he is lucky the athlete will find that football playing does his shot-putting more harm than good. The leg drive that football players must develop for their line charge is excellent for shot-putting, but the heavy blocking and hard tackling tend to tie up the shoulders. Football helps to some extent because it is hard work and the shot-putter is a young husky who needs plenty of strenuous exercise. However, the contact work of the gridiron game is bad for any athlete because the pounding taken by muscles and tendons lessens their spring and interferes with the relaxation that is so important in good technique.

Nevertheless, because of their powerful physiques, many of the outstanding shot-putters in recent years have also been stars on the gridiron. Torrance was a lineman for Louisiana State University and Hackney was a line-smashing fullback at Kansas State. Brix, who won four straight national A.A.U. shot-put championships, was a star tackle at the University of Washington. Jim Reynolds of Stanford, also a former national titleholder, had been a prep gridiron star although he did not play college football after his first year. Norm Anderson and Bob Hall, who won national intercollegiate championships for Southern California, were excellent tackles in varsity football, and Don McNeil, holder of the Southern California shot-put record, was a center and captained one of the Trojan championship Rose Bowl elevens. Blozis played tackle at Georgetown.

Among Stanford's star weight men, Harlow Rothert, who was N.C.A.A. champion three times and I.C.A.A.A.A. titleholder twice, was a backfield man. Stan Andersen, who reached 55 feet 3¾ inches in 1940, was a football tackle. However, there were many Stanford shot-putters who stayed away from the gridiron, among them John Lyman, who was Torrance's chief rival when the Louisianan was in his prime.

Good shot-putters usually have surprising speed for their size. Hansen, one of Southern California's best shot-putters in recent years, was a running guard in Trojan football and could outsprint any backfield man for the first 35 yards. Jack Merchant of the University of California, who used to be outstanding in the weights, once entered the 100-yard dash against Charley Paddock for a gag and finished only 3 yards back in very fast time. Merchant and Bill Watson of Michigan, like many other weight stars, developed power, speed, and spring in their legs to the point where they were also excellent competitors in the broad jump.

If the big-muscle men of shot-putting do not perform on the gridiron in the fall, they usually indulge in plenty of hard exercising that keeps them in trim. Those who play football do not need the gymnasium work that others will require, but there are a few exercises that they also should take in the morning. These training stunts will not only give better shot-putting results in the spring but will also improve their coordination and agility for football.

The following exercise is designed to stretch and strengthen the leg muscles that are used in springing up from a crouching stance. Spreading the feet far apart, the athlete first crouches down on the right side by flexing his right knee, keeping the left leg straight to the side and well stretched out. The left toe is pointed and touches the ground lightly. Then he swings over to a crouch to his left leg, straightening out and stretching the right. This should be repeated many times as it builds leg muscles that respond quickly from a crouching position. The exercise is excellent for football linemen as it helps them develop a fast charge.

To check on his hip action, the shot-putter can try an exercise that starts from a standing position. Without carrying the shot, he drops to the putting crouch that he would have at the end of a hop across the ring. Then from this position with knee flexed, he straightens the leg, throwing his right hip into the motion. As he does this, he will feel a strong forward thrust carried into his shoulder and arm.

A good way for a thrower to determine whether the right hip is reacting with the desired explosive force is to stand erect with the hands on the hips. Then dropping down to the putting crouch over the right leg, the athlete starts the leg drive that is used in putting the shot. The hands should feel the hips swinging quickly and smoothly into the driving movement that is helping to send power up to the shoulder and arm. This should be repeated in conjunction with other hip exercises to determine whether the hips are accomplishing their purpose of transferring momentum from the right leg.

Considerable pull is given by the muscles of the torso in the shot-putting movement and the bending and stretching exercises that build a strong trunk should receive much attention. The throwing of the shot necessitates a pull on the left side of the body as well as a creation of momentum on the right side and a torso that is both powerful and flexible is absolutely essential to good work in the event.

Occasional track work outside of the regular season is good for the competitor in the shot-put as well as in any other event of track and field. The weight man is usually too big to stand much distance work, and rarely needs to run more than a lap or so at a time. Wind sprints are good, however, for he can use the speed they develop.

If he plays football in the fall, the shot-putter will get all the wind sprints he will need on the gridiron. The nonfootball-playing shot-putter should walk his minimum of 2 miles a day, springing well up on the toes during these jaunts. The football-playing candidate should also put spring in his walk and use a pronounced shoulder and arm swing. Some athletes hesitate to walk in a springy manner for fear of wisecracks from onlookers as they bounce along. The shot-putter fortunately is usually sufficiently formidable in appearance to forestall any trouble on this point.

The pull-ups that are good for all track men should be done every day in the year except on days of competition. Hanging from the horizontal bar and raising the feet as high as possible in front with the legs straight is a good abdominal exercise to accompany the pull-ups.

Push-ups from the ground should be done daily, as they are exceptionally good for the hands, wrists, arms, and shoulders. When the shot-put candidate starts his push-up work, he will rest on his hands but his aim should eventually be to make his push-ups from the fingers.

Standing and walking on the hands are other exercises that aid in stretching and strengthening the hand and wrist muscles.

Punching the bag or boxing are good training exercises because they develop a quick thrust. Wrestling as a rule is not good, however, as this sport stresses the use of pulling muscles and the shot-putter needs much more push than pull.

Weight lifting is not advisable. Although it develops sinew, it tends to destroy muscular elasticity.

Sports that stress agility, such as tennis, handball, squash, badminton, basketball, and volleyball, are good for the shot-putter if he can take part in them without being run into the ground by lighter competitors. Sports of this type out of track season are especially desirable if the shot-putter leans toward the Percheron type and tends to accumulate excess weight.

Abdominal exercises, such as lying on the floor and raising the legs or trunk, or standing and bending from side to side, should be on the regular schedule. Deep knee bends will aid in developing spring and power from the crouch.

Some work should be done on the parallel and horizontal bars if the shot-putter has any gymnastic aptitude, as the swinging and stretching in this type of exercise will help to keep his big muscles loose and pliable. However, if the shot-putter is not at all adept on gymnasium equipment, no chances should be taken on his wrecking the apparatus or himself as he can get his stretching work in other ways.

Keeping in mind that along with strength it is just as important for him to have speed, agility, general muscular coordination, and relaxation, the shot-putter should plan his exercise schedule accordingly. The hurdler's stretching and bending exercises will be splendid for him and will keep his natural big muscles from getting knotty.

The aim of the shot-putter in his preseason work in the fall is not to develop physical bulk but to build a set of explosive-type muscles that will respond with sudden force when called into play. Overdevelopment to the point of being muscle-bound is just as disastrous to shot-putters as it is to participants in the events that do not require great strength.

Even though shot-putters are big men, they should be reasonable in the amount of food they eat. When weight goes beyond what is normal for an athlete, he has difficulty with his coordination and also tires easily.

As several years of training are usually required to develop the proper strength and skill for good shot-putting, young high school

OLYMPIC WINNER

Clarence (Bud) Houser caught in action as he made the winning discus throw in the 1924 Olympic Games in Paris. The explosive force at the instant of delivery is revealed in the bulging muscles of the forearm. Houser also won the shot-put in the 1924 Olympics and the discus throw in the 1928 Games.

boys should not try to force themselves to come along too fast. Fortunately it is almost impossible for a youngster with athletic inclinations to start playing with the shot too soon, but of course he should not begin with weights that are too heavy. The young beginner usually starts on the 8-pound shot. If he develops good form with this, he will be well on his way to success when he graduates to greater weights.

School competition is usually held with 8-, 10-, and 12-pound shots, with the contestants graded according to age and size. The 8-pound shot is the standard for the upper grammar school grades. The 12-pound ball is used in prep schools and the 16-pound weight is tossed only in college and A.A.U. competition.

An enjoyable feature about tossing the shot is that the athlete can put it during practically every day of training if he wants to. Jumpers and vaulters should not perform strenuously in their events during the week, but putting the shot, if done right, takes nothing out of a young athlete and he can have fun heaving it around in almost every workout.

It is well for shot-putters to work in groups. While one man puts from the circle, others toss it back to him and in this way no one is in danger of overworking. An athlete working alone might tire quickly but in group work he could play around for 2 hours or more.

There is no hard and fast rule about the number of puts that should be taken in practice. Elmer Hackney could take two or three times as many tosses as the ordinary shot-putter and would still be building up. Other powerful men of this type seemingly could put for hours and benefit from the work. The only rule is to stop just short of fatigue. If an athlete continues to throw after he is tired, he starts burning nervous energy that should be stored up for competition.

Shot-putters need a powerful wrist in the throwing arm. Bouncing the shot from one hand to another while waiting around for a turn in the ring in practice helps this part of the body. If wrist developers are available in the gymnasium, they should be worked on often.

Since shot-putting requires plenty of horsepower as well as technique, the athlete must either take a lot of exercise or engage in heavy manual labor during the time of the year he is not in

261

competition. Digging ditches, chopping down trees, and similar heavy chores that would be of no benefit to runners or jumpers are just the thing for him as he must develop unusual strength in his arms, shoulders, back, and chest.

If the shot-putter is not playing football or otherwise busily engaged in the fall, it is well for him to do some throwing then, since the sooner he can go to work on his putting form the better. If he has no chance to toss the ball in the autumn, he should figure on starting his work with the shot about two months ahead of his first competition.

The athlete's early work with the pellet should be entirely for form. Good distances will come if he will concentrate on technique and not press in an attempt to make good marks before he is in condition physically and technically for them.

One of the first elements of the put that will require much practice time is the hop across the ring. This can be practiced without the shot. In fact, the candidate can try this motion in his room during his exercise periods morning and night. In making the hop, he should drag his right toe lightly over the floor to be sure that he is gliding into position and not jumping into the air.

In the early-season work the shot-putter should start light training with the sprinters as soon as his legs feel ready for it. He should also do some low hurdling over strings. If he is right-handed, he should take off from the right foot in clearing the barriers as this is the leg from which the drive across the ring is made.

As the athlete progresses in his training, he can do more and more 30- to 40-yard dashes with the sprinters and also practice starts with them. Most good shot-putters develop real speed, and track fans who are not familiar with the training methods of weight men would be surprised to see how closely a team's star strong man can stay to the squad's ace sprinter in a short practice dash. Speed in his legs and in his general muscular reaction is just as important to the specialist in the shot-put ring as it is to the expert in the sprints.

Occasional workouts with an overweight shot may be taken. If the athlete is competing in the 16-pound weight, a 20-pound shot may be used once in a while, as the heavier the weight the more necessary proper technique becomes. High school boys of unusually strong build who toss the 12-pound shot like to use the 16-pounder in practice from time to time as their regular weight then seems much lighter when they go back to it.

To give the gripping muscles of the hand plenty of exercise, it is a good thing for a shot-putter to carry a spring grip or a tennis ball around in his right hip pocket. Then when he has nothing to do or is walking around between classes or standing and gossiping with his friends, he can put his throwing hand to work with a few squeezing exercises.

Although a weight thrower is a young husky who requires more exercise and training work than other athletes, he needs to be brought to a fine edge just as much as anyone else. That is why the putting of the shot in practice should be for form rather than for distance.

If the athlete is properly trained, the best tosses will nearly always be made in competition even though the shot-putter believes he has been trying his hardest in practice. This is because proper training will not only build strength and develop technique but will also create a fund of nervous energy that brings peak performances in the stress and excitement of competition. Because they always have something special saved up for competition, experienced shot-putters can rarely come within 1 or 2 feet of their meet marks in practice even when they are really exerting their greatest efforts.

If the athlete is to compete on Saturday, he can do considerable putting on Monday, Tuesday, and Wednesday. He may taper down to light putting on Thursday after a hard Wednesday workout.

Many weight men can profit by two days of rest from the ring and will do better on Saturday if they do no throwing on Thursday and spend most of their time on this day in working with the dash men. Friday, of course, is a good day to stay away from the track and field entirely and to keep loosened up by some exercises.

During practice and in competition the athlete should always carry the shot into the ring in his left hand, switching it to his putting hand when he takes his stance.

In making his put, the athlete should have his mind entirely off his competitors and the marks that he hopes to beat. He should concentrate on getting in perfect balance and making a

263

smooth, fast glide to the putting position. If he comes out of the glide into the correct putting stance, he can make his throw with a feeling of confidence that it will be a top effort. He can't put everything possible behind his toss unless he has that feeling of confidence in himself. The preliminary moves that send him up to his putting position are, therefore, of the greatest importance.

Should the thrower find himself going over the toeboard and fouling, he should concentrate on keeping the foot upon which he hops closer to the ground. This will help him cut the first gliding step shorter in order to have more room in the ring for the throwing movement. Many athletes foul frequently in practice and fail to spend much time correcting the fault. In their anxiety to get distance in their workout throws, they walk or fall out of the ring with little regard for the rules that will affect them in competition. Apparently they figure that when they actually compete in a meet it will be soon enough to be careful about hopping over the toeboard. This is a serious error, for bad habits of the training field follow the athlete into competition. When the man who fouls often in practice has a strike or two called on him by the officials, he is likely to choke up on his next efforts.

Sometimes we hear of sensational putting in practice by an athlete, yet when he competes in a meet his marks do not approach the distances recorded in his workouts. This is usually because he does not bother to stop at the foul line in his training. Then when he comes under the officials' scrutiny in competition, he is unable to overcome sloppy habits and finds his style cramped by the boundaries of the circle.

It is well to remember that any putter can add as much as 2 feet to his throws if he is allowed to fall over the toeboard or hop out of the ring after his toss. If he is going to use more than the 7-foot distance across the circle for his put, he can take a longer glide to begin with and can therefore throw with greater momentum than if he limits his first step in order to stay in bounds.

Don't feel sorry for the boy who has just made the greatest throw in his life but fouled. It doesn't mean a thing. Naturally it should be a better effort than an ordinary throw if he took more room than he was entitled to in order to get up speed for it. The object of the shot-put is to see how far a man can heave the ball from a 7-foot circle. If the thrower takes more than 7 feet, he is making a different event out of it.

In working with shot-putters, I find it considerably disturbing if a weight man fouls in practice. If he does it a second time, he certainly hears from me. In a meet the situation sometimes is different. The boy who never fouls in practice may come up to competition with so much pent-up pep and power that he inadvertently takes a longer hop than usual or works up so much momentum that he can't stop at the toeboard. In such a case I have no complaint; in fact, I rather like to see it. It proves that our system of preliminary training has worked out very satisfactorily if it has given the athlete so much fire that he explodes right out of the ring.

Although good height in the toss is essential, it should not be overdone. If the thrower raises the shot too high, he loses some of the drive behind it. Many of Bud Houser's longest puts were low because of the tremendous forward power he developed in his shoulder drive. When he attempted to go in for greater height, he lost distance because it checked some of his forward momentum.

Elmer Hackney's puts never went very high, but they zoomed out like a line drive to good distances because of his terrific speed across the ring and the great straight-ahead power that was developed in his shoulder. Hackney had an abnormally long hop to the putting position and consequently with his powerful line-plunging football legs he could work up excellent momentum. Like all putters with a long first step, however, he occasionally had trouble staying inside of the circle.

Although we speak of teaching athletes to put their weight behind the shot, actually, of course, what is needed behind it is speed. Big men have an advantage in the event only when they develop technique that turns their power into speed behind the shot when they release it. Bulk without well-directed motion behind it is of no more use to a shot-put coach in track than it is to a line coach in football. The weight-throwing candidate's beef must be turned into power which is expressed in terms of fast motion. For this reason the coach talks speed and more speed to his shot-putters just as much as he does to his sprinters.

On most high school and college teams the shot-putter is also a discus thrower. When this is the case, the athlete in doing his

In taking his starting position, the shot-putter seeks complete relaxation. The shot is held up on the base of the fingers and rests against the neck. The left arm is elevated to be in line with the shoulders. The left leg is taking an easy swing preparatory to the hop across the ring.

At the start of the glide, all the athlete's weight is carried over his right leg which is crouched for the forward spring. The weight falls principally upon the ball of the right foot, the heel touching the ground very lightly. The putter is about to start to hop by swinging his left leg out in the direction of the throw.

To create forward speed and keep his momentum from being dissipated upward, in his glide across the ring the athlete scrapes the dirt with his spikes. He shows an excellent crouch here with a good leg split. His right shoulder drops low and to keep it back his left arm moves across his face. The weight of the body is still carried over the right leg.

At the finish of the hop, the athlete is crouched in putting position with both feet on the ground. Note the position of the right foot, which is toed out with the knee and thigh pointing in the same direction as the toe. The left foot is braced against the toeboard. The right shoulder is well back for the put.

In starting the toss, the putter drives off his right leg. The power flows quickly from the leg to the hip and body and in an instant the athlete will develop an explosive drive with his shoulder and arm. The left leg is braced, keeping the body in balance.

At the top point of the put there is almost a straight line from the right toe to the right shoulder. The right shoulder is lifted and the hand carries the shot past the ear. The position of the shot shows that the athlete will finish the toss with a strong snap of the wrist and fingers.

Although the shot has just been released, the right foot is still on the ground. This demonstrates that the foot reverse takes place after the throw. A common fault is to concentrate on the reverse and start it too soon. The fingers are extended at the conclusion of their final flip of the shot.

With the finish of his reverse, this athlete bends his right knee to drop his weight inside the circle and prevent fouling. The arm is following straight through on the line of the throw. The athlete in this series is Owen Hansen, a remarkable shot-putter for his weight. He had several marks of more than 50 feet when he weighed less than 180 pounds.

training work should practice with the shot first. Since the discus weighs only 4 pounds 6.4 ounces, it seems much lighter to the athlete after he was worked first with the pellet. Another good reason for training with the shot first is that the action of the hip in this event is fairly slow in comparison with the fast hip motion of the discus.

In the shot put, the hip is behind the toss. In the discus throw as we shall see, the hip precedes the throwing arm all the way in order to develop the powerful whip at the finish.

Here is a typical training schedule for the average shot-putter who also spends some time during his workouts on the discus: Monday, form putting, checking against the mistakes of the previous Saturday, short dashes over one hurdle to emphasize the right leg drive, a lap of easy jogging before and after the workout; Tuesday, more form putting, making some of the throws without shifting the left leg, several short sprints of from 30 to 40 yards, a lap of jogging as a finish; Wednesday, hardest workout of the week, some trials for distance at the end of a session of putting for form, running over one or two low hurdles, a lap of jogging at the finish; Thursday, little or no putting, starts with the sprinters, no jogging; Friday, rest and tapering off on the exercises which have been an important part of the training program of the preceding days; competition on Saturday.

THE HAMMER THROW

About the only similarity between the college shot-put and the hammer throw is that a metal sphere of approximately the same weight is used in each. The ball on the end of the hammer weighs almost 16 pounds, the rules prescribing that the length of the complete implement shall be not more than 6 feet and that its weight shall be not less than 16 pounds. In the N.C.A.A. regulations for this event, the wire between the grip and the metal sphere must be best-grade spring steel not less than $\frac{1}{8}$ inch in diameter, or No. 36 piano wire, the diameter of which is $\frac{102}{1000}$ inch. The grip is of rigid construction.

Both the shot-put and hammer throw require strong men, but entirely different sets of muscles are used in each. Not often is an athlete able to combine successfully the two types of tossing.

268

Except for a last stand along the Atlantic seaboard, throwing the hammer and the heavier weights that have handles is becoming a lost art. In New England colleges and universities, excellent hammer throwers are still being developed and 56-pound weight men still huff and puff around the athletic clubs of some East Coast cities; but throughout the rest of the country the events have only scattered popularity. A recent attempt to interest the colleges in a 35-pound weight throw failed when most of the coaches of the N.C.A.A. admitted that this type of throwing event is now so rare that few of them would know how to teach it.

The hammer throw is a spectacular event, but unless all the performers are experts, it can also be dangerous. When a beginner goes into a spin with a hammer, sometimes it is hard to tell who is throwing which. Inasmuch as, when he comes out of his dizzy whirl, the novice might let the weight fly in any one of 47 or more different directions, the event can become hazardous and unpleasant for everyone in the general vicinity.

In many big meets the event is an orphan and even though it is officially included in the competition it must be held apart from the rest of the show. Few colleges have fields that are large enough or possess athletic directors with sufficient disregard for the cash customers to permit hammer throwing to go on during their regular meets. This is really unfortunate, for the whirl of an expert hammer thrower and the flight of a 16-pound ball some 170 feet through the air can furnish one of the most exciting sights in the program of track and field.

For many years four portly Irishmen of New York City, James J. Flanagan, Matthew J. McGrath, Patrick J. Ryan, and Patrick J. McDonald, dominated the whirl-and-throw events.

Flanagan, a New York policeman, broke the world's record in the hammer throw seven times, won the Olympic championship in 1900, 1904, and 1908 and took seven national A.A.U. titles between 1897 and 1907. In the 56-pound weight, he won six national championships.

The mighty McGrath won seven national championships with the hammer between 1908 and 1926 and twice cracked the world's record in the event. Flanagan's last world's mark, made in 1909, was 184 feet 4 inches, and McGrath raised this two years later to 187 feet 4 inches. He was Olympic champion in the hammer

269

throw in 1912 with a 179-foot throw that was not beaten until the 1936 games.

Competing against Ryan and McDonald in the 56-pound weight, McGrath also won seven national A.A.U. championships in this event, his first in 1913 and his last in 1925. Flanagan had cracked the world's mark in the 56-pound weight three times from 1901 to 1907, his last effort raising it to 38 feet 8 inches, and McGrath bagged this record in 1911 with a distance of 40 feet 6⅜ inches. This is still the world's record.

Between 1912 and 1921, Ryan won nine national A.A.U. hammer-throw championships and a couple of first places in the 56-pound weight. In 1913 he cut loose with his greatest throw in the hammer and set a record of 189 feet 6½ inches that still stands in the rule books.

However, the year 1939 found the muscle- and power-conscious Europeans making a series of forays on this mark. The following distances were recorded although none has as yet been accepted as a record: Lutz, Germany, 193 feet 9⅝ inches; Beirila, Finland, 192 feet 5⅞ inches; Blask, Germany, 191 feet 9½ inches; and Storch, Germany, 190 feet 11⅜ inches.

In America's heyday of heaving, McDonald was even more durable in the 56-pound weight than McGrath and Ryan had been in the hammer throw. Winning his first national championship in 1911, he accounted for ten titles by the time he earned his last one in 1933. In 1920 he won the Olympic championship in this event. The Antwerp games marked the second and last time that the 56-pound weight was on the Olympic program. In 1904 E. Desmarteau of Montreal had won the event for Canada.

It is only in comparatively recent years that college performers have figured prominently in national competition. The greatest hammer thrower that collegiate ranks ever produced was Fred D. Tootell of Bowdoin, who set the present I.C.A.A.A.A. record of 181 feet 6½ inches in 1923 and who won the Olympic championship in 1924. Tootell is now coaching at Rhode Island State, specializing in the development of outstanding hammer throwers. It is interesting to note that the second longest throw in I.C.A.A.A.A. competition was made by one of his athletes, Irving Folwartshny, who heaved the 16-pound weight 178 feet 9¾ inches in winning his third straight I.C.A.A.A.A. championship in 1938. Before Folwartshny won the national A.A.U. title in 1937 and 1938, Coach Tootell had produced two other national champions at Rhode Island State in Henry Dreyer in 1935 and William Rowe in 1936.

In the 56-pound weight, the men of might have nearly always been developed in athletic club gymnasiums. College men did not figure much in national competition until 1939 when Stanley Johnson of the University of Maine won the A.A.U. crown. Johnson followed up this victory by taking the national A.A.U. hammer championship in 1940 at 182 feet 6⁷⁄₁₆ inches. The big weight as a rule requires performers of more maturity than athletes of college age. Such old-time stars as Flanagan, Ryan, McGrath, and McDonald seemed to prove that the older they grew the better they became.

The 56-pound event is related to the hammer throw in that both are tossed by handles from a whirling position. For the most part, the only interest that college athletes have in the 56-pound weight is in training with it occasionally when they are developing strength for the hammer throw. Most hammer men prefer to use the 35-pound weight as a training implement, however.

Although the whirling weights and the shot-put are rarely combined, Pat McDonald doubled the 16-pound shot with the 56-pound weight throw successfully and won six national championships in shot putting from 1911 to 1922.

In the hammer throw the athlete has to be powerfully built and even heavier than the average shot-putter, for lightweight strong men are unable to handle the implement properly when they go into the whirl. Hammer throwing was one of my favorite pastimes in college track and field more than a few years ago, but complications arose when I tried to be heavy enough for this event and light enough for the high jump, another favorite of mine, at the same time.

The best of the hammer throwers use a triple turn in the ring, which is 7 feet in diameter, the same size as the shot-put circle. A few hammer men make the throw with only two turns and sometimes even only one, but it is difficult to generate enough speed with this method. Occasionally an athlete will use four turns, but the difficulty here is that there is hardly enough room in the circle for this number.

271

In developing hammer-throw technique, the beginner first learns to toss the weight without a turn of his body. The grip on the hammer is shaped like a spade handle. If the athlete is right-handed, he grasps this grip in his left hand and places his right hand over it. A lightweight glove with leather facing on the fingers should be worn on the left hand. Sometimes to protect their hands and also to keep them from slipping, hammer throwers wear full leather gloves on both hands.

In taking his stance the athlete faces opposite the direction he intends to throw. He plants his feet firmly in a comfortable position, not too far apart, with his heels in and toes out, and his knees flexed. The 16-pound weight is rested on the ground behind him and to the right.

The first step preliminary to the throw is made by picking up the hammer and swinging it around the head. In the swing, the ball stays low in front, almost touching the ground, and reaches its high point when it is swung up behind the head. At the low point of the swing when the hammer is out in front, the arms are extended almost straight. At the high point of the swing with the hammer behind and above the head, the thrower bends his elbows so that his hands swing across his face.

Tall men have the advantage in this event as it is easy for them to keep the ball off the ground when it is swung down in front of them. Small hammer throwers have to make a lifting effort to keep the four-foot implement from striking the ground when it comes down in this forward loop.

To accelerate the whirl of the hammer faster and faster, the athlete applies the power when the implement comes down from its high point in back. An equal pull is made by both arms with the legs and body supplying much of the force. The athlete continues to accelerate the whirling ball until he has it going as fast as he can swing it. Then with a drive of the legs and body, with the shoulders and arms supplying the final burst of power, the hammer is released over the left shoulder. The force of the throw causes the athlete's body to turn and face the toss in the follow-through.

After the hammer candidate has become adept at heaving the weight without a whirl of his body, he is ready to try one turn in the ring. To start a throw with a turn, he takes a position in the rear of the ring with his back in the direction of the throw. Then he starts the whirl of the hammer in the method already described.

When the hammer is spinning at maximum speed, the thrower starts his body turn by pivoting on his left foot. The pivot is begun as the hammer swings down in front of the body, and it is started without moving the position of the left foot. A complete turn of the body is then made ahead of the hammer. The whirl of the body is made at a speed greater than the whirl of the iron ball, thereby increasing the speed of the hammer. The pivot starts on the left foot but the force of the whirl takes both feet off the ground. As the turn is completed, the athlete lands on both feet which come down still spread apart as in the original stance. The beginner usually lands 3 or 4 feet toward the front of the circle when using one turn.

When he completes his whirl, the athlete's body is well ahead of the hammer and with a final tremendous pull he throws the weight over his shoulder. The follow-through of the toss will turn his body in the direction of the throw.

After learning to throw with one whirl, the more advanced candidate then takes up the double turn. The second turn is made exactly the same as the first. Obviously the distance covered across the ring must be cut down in each of the two turns. In the double spin, from $2\frac{1}{2}$ to 3 feet are usually used for each whirl.

Naturally the hammer thrower strives to make his tosses from the front of the ring and thus to use all the space he has available. As there is no toeboard in the hammer ring as in the shot-put circle, he has nothing to land against and must keep well balanced to avoid fouling.

After developing skill at two whirls, the candidate is ready for the triple turn. On each of the three whirls the athlete advances about 2 feet toward the front of the ring so that he has a small margin from the edge of the circle when he cuts loose with the throw.

During the time the hammer is whirled around the head, the athlete keeps his weight on both feet. At the instant he starts to pivot, his weight swings to the left but on landing on both feet the weight is distributed over both legs again. In the throw the power flows quickly from the legs, hips, and body to the left side as the hammer is released over the left shoulder.

The technique of throwing the 35- and 56-pound weights is much the same as that used in tossing the hammer. Because of the short handle used on these weights it is no problem for stubby men to keep the implements off the ground. The size of the ring— 7 feet in diameter—is the same as for the hammer-throw and shot-put circles. As the handles are wide, the grip on the heavier weights is taken with the hands placed side by side instead of one on top of the other as in the hammer throw.

The weights are whirled lower than in the hammer throw and the athlete usually takes one turn with his body to add to the centrifugal force.

In getting into condition for these Tarzan events, the athlete needs plenty of strenuous exercise to develop his muscular power. He can do weight lifting and take part in wrestling, two pastimes that are on the banned list for participants in other track and field events. Wrestling will develop his pulling muscles and weight lifting will get him accustomed to controlling heavy objects.

Tossers of the whirling weights can indulge in the same exercises and out-of-season training work as the shot-putters. Handstands and push-ups should be done in large quantities to develop the fingers, hands, wrists, and forearms. Practically every kind of apparatus work is good, with rope and pole climbing being of particular benefit.

Coordination and speed as well as unusual strength are needed for these events and when the candidate is ready to start his track training he can use plenty of starts, short dashes, and work over low hurdles. Because of the great effort that must be put forth every time an athlete in one of the whirling weights makes a throw, he needs to build up endurance, and windsprints are good for this.

Despite the heavy course of training that hammer-throw and 56-pound weight men must undergo, they must vary the work to keep their bodies as lithe as possible and to avoid becoming muscle-bound. During an afternoon of training the candidate can dabble in shot and discus tossing, jumping, hurdling, and sprinting. Such a variety will keep his training from becoming

274

monotonous and will also contribute to his general development and coordination.

During the competitive season, the hammer thrower can do considerable tossing for distance as well as for form. If he is to compete on Saturday, he should taper off the heavy work after Wednesday and start saving up energy for the hard throwing that is ahead.

The man who throws the whirling weights will help his traction in the ring if he wears jumping shoes with heel spikes. If these do not prove sturdy enough, he can try baseball shoes.

Although some weight men can stand much more work in practice than others, here is a typical training week of the average hammer thrower during the competitive season: Monday, practicing the whirl of the weight around the head to work up rhythm and high speed, some trial throws with the regular turns of the body, a few short sprints, and a lap of jogging; Tuesday, more practice of the whirl and body turns and a good workout on throwing, concentration on form more than on distance, windsprints if stamina is needed or starts and 30-yard dashes with the sprinters, a little work over low hurdles using alternate take-off legs to develop body balance; Wednesday, heavy throwing, workout for form and 8 or 10 good throws for distance, starts and either short dashes or low-hurdle work; Thursday, little or no throwing but plenty of warm-up exercises, several short sprints; Friday, rest for competition on Saturday. Each day's work on the field should be preceded by bending and stretching exercises to warm up on, and exercises should also be taken morning and evening.

XIV

THE DISCUS THROW

Discus throwing is generally considered the oldest and most popular of all field events, widely participated in during ancient days and handed down to modern track and field with scarcely a change. A world-famous statue, Myron's *Discobolus*, seems to have been responsible more than anything else for this impression. But this superb masterpiece of sculpture typifying Greek athletic perfection has misled us on the interest of the ancient Greeks in the event and on its modern revival.

Actually the javelin throw was the first of the Greek field events and undoubtedly also the leader in popularity. Whereas the spear was a highly useful implement in warfare and skill in throwing it was considered of great importance, there was little about hurling a quoit that appealed to the practical nature of the Greeks.

The event in ancient days was never standardized. The quoits varied in size and weighed anywhere from 3 to 12 pounds. The style of throwing it from either a running or standing position was also considerably different from our standard method of hurling it after a whirl.

Myron undoubtedly was struck by the unusual grace and beauty of the Greek athletes when they participated in the discus throw. His magnificent work of art has become the symbol of ancient athletic prowess, but it doesn't follow that hurling the discus was of supreme importance in bygone Olympic competition.

Even in modern times we have been slow to recognize the discus throw and to include it in the track and field program. It was not until 21 years after the first national championships that the event was added to the A.A.U. meet, and it was not until 1915 that the present size of the circle was adopted and throwers were given an opportunity to develop an efficient whirl and make sizable distances.

276

Myron may have given an exaggerated importance to the discus throw, but he at least recognized it as one of the most graceful events in the realm of sport. Rhythm, smoothness, and power are combined so well in the act of hurling the discus that there is no finer sight in athletics than a group of skilled throwers in competition.

Shot-putting, hammer throwing, and hurling the 56-pound weight were all included in the first national championships in 1876, but discus throwing was not put in the meet until 1897.

In 1896 when the first of the modern Olympic games were held in Athens, the Greeks had included the discus in the program in honor of the *diskos* of the ancient days. The event was expected to be a cinch victory for the Greek throwers as few athletes of any other nationality knew anything about the discus.

It remained for a young American to upset the dope. Back in the United States, shot-putter Robert S. Garrett of Princeton had heard of a platter throw being programed for the Olympics. Before he left for the games in company with a small group of Boston Athletic Association athletes, who comprised most of the American team, he had a disk made to what he thought were the Greek specifications. Although he had no technique from the past to go by except perhaps a few illustrations from books on Greek mythology, he figured out how to make the plate whirl and go out a respectable distance.

When Garrett arrived at the games, he found that the discus he had been using was much too large and too heavy. The Olympic discus felt light to him and he sailed it out 95 feet 7½ inches to win the championship, much to the chagrin of the Greek stars who had thought that here was at least one event that was in the bag for them.

Throwing from the 7-foot circle used at the time, C. H. Hennemann of the Chicago Athletic Association won the first national A.A.U. title at 118 feet 9 inches when American athletes took up the event the year after the first Olympiad. Hennemann's mark in the 1897 national championships was the best one on record for years.

Then came a powerful Irish-American policeman from New York City who set a series of seven world's marks and ranked as the outstanding performer from 1901 to 1911. The big star of the

277

7-foot ring was Martin J. Sheridan, Olympic champion in 1904, 1906, and 1908 and national champ in 1904, 1906, 1907, and 1911. Sheridan first raised the record to 120 feet 7¾ inches, steadily increasing it until his last mark was 141 feet 4⅜ inches. Sheridan threw from a whirl despite the confines of the small circle. He also learned how to throw well from a standing position and when the Olympic games of 1908 included a discus throw, Greek style, he won that as well as the regular hurling event. His Greek-style Olympic record was 124 feet 8 inches, and it still stands today since the games have not included the event since 1908.

About the time that Sheridan made his last world's record in 1911, discus hurlers were beginning to favor a ring that would give them enough room for a worth-while turn leading up to the throw. The new circle they adopted was 8 feet 2½ inches in diameter. This gave the lads a bit of much-needed space for foot work, and J. Duncan raised the record in 1912 to 156 feet 1⅜ inches.

The new larger ring was officially adopted for national A.A.U. championship competition in 1915. A. W. Mucks of the University of Wisconsin was the first national champ in the new circle. The colleges had been the first to adopt the bigger ring and from this time on, all the A.A.U. champions were men developed in university athletics. With the larger area in which to wind up and whirl for the toss, discus throwing grew in popularity. In 1922 it was included for the first time in the I.C.A.A.A.A. championships, Glenn Hartranft of Stanford being the first winner.

For a reason that is difficult to account for, since discus throwing for some time has been as popular in one part of the country as another, most of the national champions in the past two decades have come from the West. A. R. Pope of the University of Washington started it in 1920. Other Western champions have been Clarence (Bud) Houser and Kenneth Carpenter of the University of Southern California, Paul Jessup of Washington, and Eric Krenz, Bobby Jones, Phil Fox, and Pete Zagar of Stanford. The only interruptions in the string of Pacific Coast victories have come from Tom Lieb of Notre Dame and John Anderson of Cornell.

In I.C.A.A.A.A. competition, Western supremacy has been shown with equal consistency. In 18 meets from 1922 to 1939 in which the discus throw was included, athletes from either Stanford, Southern California, or California won the championship 15 times. In two of the three meets in which Western men did not win, none of the three California universities was entered.

If there is any particular reason for this, it may be that the absence of a severe winter in California gives the athletes there a chance to get outdoors and start throwing sooner than in the East and Middle West. Discus hurling takes much practice and the boy who wishes to succeed at it must throw over a long continuous period.

Duncan's 156-foot record stood for 13 years until a spirited rivalry that developed in the West between Hartranft of Stanford and Houser of Southern California brought new high marks. The former raised the record to 157 feet 1⅝ inches in 1925 and the latter nosed him out of it the next year by ⅛ inch.

Houser, who was the mightiest man of his size with the weights who ever lived, won both the shot and discus in the 1924 Olympic games. Four years later, after he had been graduated from college and was practicing dentistry, he made a comeback and won another Olympic championship in the discus.

Houser's record lasted until 1929 when Eric Krenz of Stanford raised it to 163 feet 8¾ inches. Pete Rasmus also broke the old record that year with a toss of 159 feet 1⅞ inches. Krenz's record fell the next season to Paul Jessup of the University of Washington who sent the mark up to 169 feet, 8⅞ inches.

Eight of eleven Olympic championships up through 1936 were won by the United States and for many years there were no threats of record breaking from abroad. European throwers had a peculiar jerky technique by which they were able to get off long throws only occasionally. During the 1930's, however, they began to insert the American smooth swing and sometimes the foot reverse into their form and their distances showed a steady climb. In 1934 the record left America when Harald Andersson of Sweden became the first man to pass the 170-mark with a throw of 171 feet 11¾ inches. This mark was broken the following year by Willie Schröder of Germany who hurled the platter 174 feet 2½ inches.

Carpenter of Southern California, winner of the 1936 Olympics,

279

and a much more consistent thrower than Schröder, tried hard to bring the record back to the United States but failed by 1 inch. He set an American record of 173 feet in winning the 1936 N.C.A.A. championship. In that meet he had five throws of more than 170 feet for the most consistent performance ever turned in by a discus man. Later in a post-Olympic meet at Prague he barely missed Schröder's record with a toss of 174 feet $1^{13}/_{16}$ inches. Phil Fox, who threw for Stanford under the name of Phil Levy, has the second-best American throw, a toss of 172 feet $4^{1}/_{2}$ inches made in winning the 1939 national A.A.U. title.

The discus is usually made of metal and wood, the metal being placed in the core and on the rim. Recent legislation has also legalized rubber or metal implements conforming to the specifications of weight, size, and shape. The platter must weigh not less than 2 kilograms, or 4 pounds 6.4 ounces; the largest dimensions must be a circle not less than $8^{5}/_{8}$ inches in diameter. The thickness through the exact center on a line perpendicular to the diameter must be not less than $1^{3}/_{4}$ inches.

In some parts of the country, a lighter discus is used in high school competition. The diameter is the same, but the thickness at the center is only $1^{5}/_{8}$ inches and the weight is 3 pounds 9 ounces. A lightweight platter is also used in competition for women. Most high schools use the standard discus as the regular size is not too heavy for beginners to throw.

Discus-throwing technique has as its object the development of centrifugal force that will whip out the arm with a fast swing at the moment the platter is released. Although this can be done from a standing position, much greater centrifugal force can be created when a whirl of the body is introduced and this is the reason for the athlete's turn in the ring.

When a candidate for this event learns technique, he makes his throws with the big muscles of the body, much of the power coming from the legs and hip. In a right-handed thrower it is essential to keep the right hip well ahead of the arm carrying the discus in whirling in the ring. Without a good fast right hip, the discus will never go far.

As in the shot-put, a giant of a man cannot get good results through strength alone. Also just as in the shot-put, the object is to develop speed. At the time the throw is made, the discus arm should be traveling at its greatest possible speed. The technique can be likened to the old game of crack-the-whip. In this game the youngster on the end of the line finds himself being propelled around at tremendous speed because of the development of centrifugal force. In discus throwing with the proper whirl, the athlete finds that the end of the arm gets the force and travels immensely faster than the body or shoulder could possibly go.

It is a big advantage for a discus thrower to be tall, for a long arm can swing in a wider arc and develop more whip than a short one. However, proper hip action, speed in the turn, and the knack of delivering the discus with a final explosion of energy are even more important.

At 6 feet even, Houser and Fox were comparatively short men for the event but proved two of the outstanding performers in discus-throwing history. Schröder and Carpenter, who have made the longest tosses on record, were both much bigger men, well over 6 feet in height. Rangy and relaxed, they showed what could be done to discus-throwing marks when the ideal tall build is combined with perfect form.

A big hand to hold the platter is also an asset. A large hand can keep the discus under good control at all times; its length is an additional advantage in the development of centrifugal power.

When a beginner takes up the discus throw, he must first learn how to make the implement sail through the air. He holds the discus in the palm of his hand usually with the fingers close together. Only a small portion of his fingers extend over the edge of the platter for the grip.

A right-handed thrower must make the plate whirl from his hand with a clockwise motion. The spin is made off the first finger with the discus taking a turn the reverse of the body turn. Beginners sometimes try to get the spinning motion off the edge of the little finger, which of course is entirely wrong. The spin starts when the discus rolls off the first finger near the first joint and this spot in a discus thrower soon becomes calloused as hard as leather from the contact with the implement. A proper spin of the discus aids it to cut through the air. If the plate is thrown with a wobble, air friction will be created and the thrower will have little chance to get good distance.

When the beginner has learned to spin the disk smoothly from

281

a stationary throw, his next objective is to start getting some momentum behind his toss. This he can do by taking a step forward to the throwing position.

In preparing for his toss, the athlete takes a position at the back of the circle with his feet together. At first it is best for him to face in the direction of the throw, although later he will start at right angles to the toss with his left shoulder pointing at his target.

He carries the discus behind his body, holding the implement with his palm down. Formerly discus throwers started with the plate in the hand, palm up. The elbow was bent so that the plate was carried with the hand almost against the middle of the back. Such a position destroyed smoothness as the arm had to be uncorked for the throw in the final movement of the turn. It also created tension in the arm, which lessened the chances for a good toss as it is necessary to keep the throwing arm relaxed. In modern discus throwing with the arm drag and fast hip being continually stressed, this position is entirely out of place. The arm must always be kept far behind the body until the final whip when the throw is made.

After the thrower has carried the discus back of his body, he makes a few preliminary swings. During these swings, the discus is held well up, almost shoulder high. The left arm is raised and kept in line with the shoulder for balance. It must be relaxed and should be bent at the elbow.

When he is ready to throw after a few swings, the athlete makes a step with his right foot toward the front of the circle. This step is made as the discus swings out in front of the body. As the discus is swung back to the rear of the body, the thrower steps to the front of the ring with his left foot. As he goes forward in this step, the right knee is bent. With his left foot forward, he is ready for the throw which he makes by swinging his arm and driving off his right leg, straightening it as he throws his hip into the effort. The discus is released at the highest point of the arm's arc. It must not be released too soon or held too long.

In this type of throw there is no reverse. The right foot may be brought up even with the left in the follow-through after the toss. This method of heaving the platter teaches the beginner the correct throwing position. The steps are extremely simple to take across the ring and they bring him into the position that he must reach later when he starts to throw with a whirl.

Because this system is almost certain to put the athlete in proper position, often when he starts to whirl it is a long time before he can get as much distance as he could from the simple stepping method. This is because it takes some time to learn the knack of arriving in the right throwing position after the whirl.

The beginner also learns from this method of practice throwing that he does not need to worry about the elevation of the discus. The straightening out of the right leg and the driving forward of the hip cause the arm to be raised to the proper throwing angle as the disk is released. The novice should not worry about the angle of his toss or the height that the discus goes into the air. His principal objective is to get the hip into the throw. When this is done properly, the correct angle for the discus will come automatically.

Later when the athlete is ready for competition, some adjustment may be made by the arm to change the angle to suit wind conditions. When the discus is thrown into the teeth of a wind, it should be kept low. With a wind or with a cross wind, it should be kept high. It is often surprising for beginning discus men to find that sometimes they can throw better into the wind than with it. A light breeze tends to hold the implement in the air; if the angle of the implement cuts through the atmosphere, the wind will not oppose the throw.

When the discus candidate is ready to take up the pivot in the circle, he can throw with either the American or the European style. Although the latter method occasionally brings good results, it is jerky and athletes using it are inconsistent in their marks.

Distances of American throwers are so much better on the average despite the record breaking of Andersson and Schröder that nearly all coaches in this country stick to the American style. This method stresses smoothness, with a slow easy start working up to a fast finish.

To throw in the American style, the athlete takes a position at the back of the circle with his right foot just inside the line. The left foot is placed to the side in the direction of the throw and slightly forward. The spread of the feet depends upon the size of

the thrower. Long-legged men must place their feet closer together than small athletes to keep from going out of the ring
when completing the whirl.

Both knees should be bent in a crouch, giving the thrower a
stance that looks slightly bowlegged. At the start, the weight of
the body is about equally distributed on the feet. The athlete
should start his swing of the discus with perfect relaxation of the
body, including the right arm which carries the platter.

In starting the arm swing, the athlete should twist his body as
far back as it will go and swing his arm well behind him. When the
disk is far back, much of the body weight naturally goes over the
right leg. The object of the backward reach is to wind up the body
like a spring. After one or more preliminary swings and when the
right arm is at its farthest point to the rear, the pivot is started
by turning the toe of the left foot to the left. The weight now
shifts to the left leg as the right leg leaves the ground with the
right knee remaining bent.

For a brief instant in the whirl of the body, the left foot leaves
the ground just before the right one lands. When the right foot
comes down, it lands somewhat to the left of an imaginary
straight line across the circle in the direction of the throw. The
position of the right foot upon landing is about 3 feet from its
original starting point at the back of the circle. When the left
foot lands, it comes down at the front of the circle in approximately a straight line with the throw.

Most of the weight of the athlete is on his right leg when he
makes the landing after the whirl. As the right knee is kept bent
throughout the spin, the thrower lands in a crouching stance.

During the entire pivot the discus must be carried far behind
the body. The implement is held on an even plane paralleling the
ground. It is important not to drop the discus to the hip at any
time during the whirl as the arm must get its longest possible
swing at the finish. The throw is made with the combined power
of the legs, hip, and body. All these are in front of the discus,
pulling it around with a great burst of power.

When the athlete makes his final effort before releasing the
discus, he straightens his right leg, driving his right hip forward.
The body swings forward in completing the whirl and the last
thing that swings is the discus. All the force of this whirl now goes

into the arm, hand, and fingers. Champions develop a flip at the end of the toss, but the beginner can forget about this and let it come with experience.

The throw may or may not be finished with a reverse of the feet. As long as he does not step over the boundaries of the ring, the athlete can let his feet take care of themselves.

The right foot may come up even with the left in the follow-through after the toss; if it seems more natural for the feet to shift to keep from going out of the ring, a reverse is all right. The reverse, which used to be tried by nearly all discus men, is not essential, and sometimes it can do more harm than good if the thrower is thinking too much about ending with it and not enough about what he should do just before releasing the platter.

Ken Carpenter is one discus thrower who will never forget that the foot shift can cause plenty of trouble. During the 1936 season at Southern California he went into a slump and his marks which had been approaching 160 feet dropped below 150. He seemed to have lost some of his knack of getting leg power behind his throws. A long practice session with him one day revealed that he was thinking so much about his finishing reverse that he was not driving hard enough off his right leg and not getting enough hip into his toss.

Carpenter had always thrown with a reverse but I told him to think only about his hip action and stop reversing for the time being even if he ended up by falling out of the ring. Concentration on getting his hip into the throw fast soon improved his distances by many feet. Within a short time he found that the reverse was no longer necessary for him and that he could stay in the ring without shifting his feet at the finish of a throw. His improvement after giving up the reverse was amazing. Within 2 or 3 months he progressed from the ranks of just another good discus thrower to N.C.A.A. champion with an American record of 173 feet and then on to the national A.A.U. and Olympic championships.

To reverse or not to reverse is one of those technical points over which there has been much argument. Like most discussions over minor details, you can find examples to prove whatever you wish. At Southern California we had a two-time Olympic champion in Bud Houser, who reversed. Also at Southern California we had an Olympic champion in Ken Carpenter who did not reverse.

We are always finding out in track and field that there is more than one proper way to do an event. The coach should never forget the basic rule of his profession: let Nature be the teacher; suit the technique to the athlete and not the athlete to the technique.

Like the shot-putter, the discus thrower must have the ability to put a sudden explosive force into his effort at the moment he delivers the implement. Speed in the ring and this concentration of power at the final moment were the chief factors in making champions out of Bud Houser and Phil Fox, who nearly always found themselves competing against much bigger men.

Often outstanding ability at the shot and discus go together. The competitor in each must be big, strong, and active, but sometimes the shot-putter does not qualify as good discus material because he is comparatively slow in the action of his hips. Discus throwing involves so much pull that fast hip action is absolutely essential. In shot-putting, comparatively slow action in the hips will suffice in transferring the momentum of the glide across the ring from the legs into the body and shoulder as they drive the arm.

Another point of difference is that shot-putting does not require such long arms. Shot-putting involves a thrust; discus throwing employs a swing.

At Southern California a few years ago a shot-putter named Phil Gaspar with fair high school marks reported for the varsity track team. In his first workouts he appeared to be only a mediocre prospect. Technically his chief fault was that he was too fast in his hip action, getting his hips in front of the weight instead of under it. His fast hip work indicated to me that he might have a much better chance for success in the discus throw if he cared to specialize in it and I suggested this to him. He took to platter heaving quickly and throughout his varsity career was consistent at 150-foot distances, winning the I.C.A.A.A.A. championship as a senior.

The only reason that discus throwers turn or do anything in the circle is to create power and speed in the swing of the throwing arm. The rules permit the discus man to work up his speed any way he can and he may do whatever he wants to inside the circle. He may walk across the ring, run around inside of it, throw from a standing position, or even take two or more whirls in it. We throw in the whirling style we do because experience has taught us that we can create the most momentum for the toss by a pivot on the left foot followed by a hop to the right.

All the action that takes place in the ring is for the purpose of generating speed and of having the throwing arm flashing out at a high rate when the discus is released. The whirl has to be practiced over and over again so that the speed is carried into the landing position, sending the power of the legs, hips, and body into the delivery of the weight.

Beginners should remember that the only difficult thing about the event is reaching the landing position properly. If the pivot and swing to the right foot have been done correctly, the thrower can be certain that a good toss will be made and he can concentrate on the final burst of muscular power that brings added distance.

If one is inclined to foul, there is a little trick in taking the starting position that will correct this. The athlete should start out by facing in the direction of the throw more than he normally does. He should keep his feet close together in the preliminary stance. In pivoting to his left foot, he should take a very short step, pointing the toe in the direction of the toss. This will throw him around with a short hop to his right foot so that on completing the whirl it will give him a wide spread for his left foot and make it impossible for him to foul.

When Bud Houser was at his peak from 1924 to 1928, his turn in the ring resembled a series of steps instead of a pivot. He went through the same type of whirl that athletes use today except that he stepped rapidly through the spin instead of pivoting on his left foot. Because of his extreme speed in the ring and his superb coordination, he could go through these steps as smoothly as present-day throwers can whirl. Houser, incidentally, could also whirl with excellent technique, but he found he could work up greater speed and power for the toss and reach a more satisfactory throwing position by a different method. The opening pivot on the left toe did not reach general use until the last 15 years.

The whirl on spikes, which must be worn to keep the athlete from slipping, tears up the ring badly, and coaches should see that the throwing area is kept in repair or new circles drawn up frequently. Discus men should wear regulation jumping shoes which have two heel spikes.

An observer seeing a European discus thrower in action is struck by the wobbliness of the arm swing and the jerkiness of the entire procedure. In the European method, the athlete in swinging the discus starts it low in back and brings it up high in front. His pivot is fast from the start in comparison with the American turn, which begins slowly and works up to a speedy climax.

In making the turn, the discus thrower, European style, carries the platter low behind him. Upon landing after the whirl, he makes the throw by driving down with his left leg and shoulder and jerking up hard with his right shoulder and arm. Because of the hard downward pull on his left side at the throw, the European tosser seems to be stamping the ground with his left foot as he releases the discus. Since there is little smoothness to this style of throwing, it is difficult for the athlete to coordinate all his movements. Consequently those who throw with this method have little consistency in the distances they reach on their tosses.

If the European-style thrower can get one life-sized toss out of three with this system of jerks he is lucky. Occasionally, however, a European discus man may uncork a terrific heave, such as the record-breaking throw of Schröder, but the smooth-working American tosser is much more consistent in his efforts and a much better bet in championship competition.

Although the discus throw usually attracts big heavy men with plenty of muscle, tall slender athletes may do well. Paul Jessup of Washington, Bobby Jones of Stanford, and Bob Hall of Southern California, who won intercollegiate championships, were men of this type.

Many discus throwers are football tackles and ends because of their ranginess, coordination, strength, and speed. Football is never recommended for track men because the pounding given the muscles often takes from them the ability to relax and then spring into action with explosive force. However, most track coaches suffer in silence during the fall as their weight men take a pounding and risk injuries on the gridiron. Unfortunately for the track coach, the big-muscle men of weight throwing make the ideal football type and usually like the rough-and-tumble game.

Football can be helpful for the leg drive it develops, the numerous wind sprints it provides, and the general all-round hard exercise it gives the weight thrower. However, after a long football season, even if the discus tosser has escaped injury, he usually has to delay starting work with the platter for a month or so to get the football kinks out of his shoulder muscles.

During the fall, whether the discus thrower plays football or not, he should also work daily with a spring grip or a soft rubber ball to strengthen the hand muscles.

The fall exercise program for the discus candidate is much the same as that prescribed for the shot-putter. For the general development of his torso, he should do plenty of pull-ups with the backs of the hands toward the face and many push-ups from the ground. When the hand strength becomes equal to it, the push-ups should be done from the fingers. Standing and walking on the hands and working on the wrist developers in the gymnasium are among the best exercises that can be taken for the type of arm strength the discus man needs. If the candidate has any gymnastic ability, handstands on the parallel bars as well as other work on this apparatus are useful.

If the discus man does any jumping or hurdling in his training program, he should take off from the right foot as this is the one that furnishes the drive in going across the ring and in starting the throw.

Because there is so much body pull in discus tossing, the candidate needs powerful abdominal and chest muscles. Lying on the back and raising the legs to a vertical position or keeping the legs on the ground and raising the trunk will help develop iron muscles in the abdomen. From a standing position, there should also be some bending at the waist forward and backward, and from side to side.

If the athlete plays football in the fall, naturally he does not need much special exercising on the side. The gridiron will give him about all the strenuous physical work he needs and his main worry will be to try to keep his heavy muscles relaxed and pliable.

For those who do not play football, the usual out-of-season games and activities that aid in the development of coordination and agility are good. By this time in our little discussion of track and field, it should go without saying that walking 2 miles a day in the proper springy manner is a "must."

In the fall, occasional visits to the discus-throwing ring to practice the form in pivoting and in getting set for the toss should be made if possible. Preliminary work of this type should be done under proper supervision for, if faults are developed and persisted in at this time, they will be hard to overcome when the regular throwing season starts.

Since good discus throwing requires precise timing and the proper technique for it takes a long time to perfect, the candidate in this event should start his regular training schedule as far ahead of the first meet as possible. If weather and time permit, he should begin his daily workouts on the field 2 months before the first competition.

Form throwing should be started at once. Throwing may be done at first from a standing position; then the candidate can go from standing to walking and finally from walking to whirling in the ring. When the athlete starts his first sessions on the whirl, he can do much of his practice footwork without the disk.

When throwing for form, the discus man may take a dozen or more tosses each day. If he is throwing his hardest, six or eight efforts may be enough. Much depends upon the constitution of the athlete as some boys can stand two or three times as much work as others. The best check on the number of throws that should be taken is for each candidate to observe his own condition and stop as soon as his arm feels the least bit tired. Too much throwing on any one day deadens the arm, and tossing with a tired arm will tear down instead of build up.

Training on the track should start the first day out with a little jogging. As the athlete gradually gets his legs in shape he should do some sprinting, starting, and low hurdling over strings. Discus throwers are often lanky, heavy men who don't care any too much about running and the coach usually has to use his best powers of persuasion to convince them that speed must be built into the legs. Those who specialize in the discus rarely run as much as shot-putters, which is all right as the platter tosser does not have to have as much straight-ahead speed as the iron ball expert.

Like shot-putting, discus technique requires several years to

290

perfect and the beginner should not expect startling distances early in his career. If he is patient and does most of his throwing for form, he will find that distances will develop along with technique.

After the competitive season has started, it is usually best for the athlete to do nearly all his hard work the first three days of each week. However, this general rule is subject to a variety of changes as numerous athletes have noticed different responses in their throwing arms.

It has been found that some men can get best results if they throw hard on Monday, skip Tuesday, and throw again on Wednesday. Others have found that they can prepare best for competition by throwing on Monday and Tuesday, skipping Wednesday, and then throwing again on Thursday. Still other discus men can get excellent results by shortening the workout period and doing some throwing every day in the week, including the day before competition. The matter of how much work can be done and when to do it is one that each candidate must determine for himself through experimentation and observation of his own condition.

Normally the best results are obtainable for Saturday competition by resting the arm two days before competition and following a schedule somewhat as follows: Monday, a jog for a lap, warm-up throws from the grass, form throwing from the circle finishing up with two or three top efforts to see if timing and coordination can be maintained in the switch from form throwing to competitive throwing, a little work over one low hurdle; Tuesday, practically the same schedule as on Monday with perhaps a few more hard throws if the arm does not tire; track work may be over one or two low hurdles, short dashes with the sprinters, or a few runs of 70 or 80 yards on the grass at fair speed; Wednesday, approximately the same as on Monday and Tuesday but more top-effort throws if the arm feels good; if a long workout is taken in the ring not much track work will be necessary; Thursday, light work on form or no throwing at all; a good day to get in some short dashes to build up the legs in the ring; Friday, light exercises only, no work in the field, rest for competition on Saturday.

Besides the daily walks and exercises that are always on the training schedule, the discus thrower should do some work with

The thrower assumes a relaxed starting position and is holding the discus steady with his left hand before beginning the backward swing. In the grip, only the tips of the fingers of the right hand reach over the edge of the platter. The toes are pointing at right angles to the direction of the throw and the right foot is almost against the back of the circle.

After a few preliminary swings for balance and relaxation, the right arm carries the discus as far back as it will reach. The arm is fully extended and remains so throughout the pivot and throw. The left arm is relaxed and across the chest to help the right shoulder go back. Preparatory to his pivot, the thrower is starting to turn his left foot to the left.

The pivot has been started on the left foot and the weight has shifted from the right leg to the left. The right arm stays far back and the discus is carried almost shoulder high. The left arm is out in front for balance. With the turn starting on the ball of the left foot, in an instant the right foot will leave the ground.

Midway in his whirl, the discus thrower is still pivoting on his left foot. The spin of the body is creating centrifugal force in the throwing arm. The right leg, which is off the ground, is well bent at the knee so that when the pivot is completed with the landing on the ball of the right foot the athlete will be in a crouch.

There has been fast action since the previous picture, and while the thrower has landed on his right foot, the body is still turning and creating tremendous speed in the right arm. The right toe is pointed to the right similar to the throwing position in the shot-put. The left arm is held fairly high. The thrower is not attempting to look in the direction of the toss and this helps him to keep his right arm back.

The left leg has reached the ground at the end of the whirl and is acting as a brace for the throw. Note the bulging muscle in the calf of the right leg as the athlete starts a final surge of power for the throw. Fast hip action is putting the hips far ahead of the discus. The right knee is still bent in a crouch as it starts the final lift.

In straightening up from the crouch the thrower not only sends leg and hip power into the toss but also develops the proper line of flight for the discus. The head and chest will be up when the discus is released, and will also aid in getting height to the toss. The hips are still swinging out fast in front of the discus.

Both feet are on the ground as the throw is made. Because of the centrifugal force that has been generated by the whirl, the arm comes up with terrific speed for the throw. The bent position of the fingers and wrist shows that the discus has been released with a final snap. This discus thrower will finish without a reverse, merely bringing his right foot up even with his left in the follow-through. The athlete is Kenneth Carpenter, 1936 Olympic champion, who holds the American record at 173 feet and who has a best mark of 174 feet $1\frac{13}{16}$ inches.

the shot even though he does not participate in this event on his team. On the days that he will throw the discus, the athlete should warm up by making a few puts with the shot. Practically the same set of muscles is used in tossing the shot and discus. Besides giving the platter tosser a good limbering up for his day's training, work with the shot will make the discus seem much lighter and easier to throw.

XV

THE JAVELIN THROW

Because Finns and Swedes have dominated the javelin throw for so many years in Olympic competition and in record breaking, it seems to be generally believed in America that they are races born to spear-throwing skill and nothing can ever be done about catching up with their prowess.

One must agree that undoubtedly they owe much to the fact that for hundreds of years these peoples used the spear in their daily life. Living amid forests, lakes, and streams, they became adept in the use of the weapon in their hunting and fishing. Also they did a great deal of wood chopping, thus adding strength to the muscles that hurl the spear.

Javelin throwing, however, is an acquired skill. No one can argue convincingly that the first time an infant Finn or Swede picks up a stick he heaves it with perfect technique just because his ancestors were spear hurlers or woodcutters. It is likely that the youngster will have a better than average chance of developing the back, shoulder, and arm strength necessary for good javelin tossing because of physical characteristics that his forefathers developed through centuries of living off the forests and streams. But if he is ever going to become a star athlete in the event, he will have to learn correct form the same as an American youth whose ancestors never hurled anything greater than an epithet.

It is my opinion that the Finns and Swedes, particularly the former, simply got the jump on Americans in developing an efficient javelin-hurling technique. When we perfect our throwing form as they have theirs and train for the event as enthusiastically as they do, there is no reason why we should not overtake them in ability.

The spear throw is a comparatively recent addition to the track and field program, having been introduced into Olympic competition in 1906 and into the national A.A.U. championships in 1909.

E. Lemming of Sweden was the earliest star of the event with three Olympic victories and several record-breaking performances, but the first really outstanding thrower was Jonni Myyra. A record smasher for the first time in 1915 and the Olympic games winner in 1920 and 1924, Myyra can well be considered the founder of the Finnish school of javelin throwing. His countrymen have not often been defeated in this event since his introduction of the throw-on-the-run style.

When I first saw Myyra in action, I was convinced that the Finns had more than heredity and racial characteristics on their side to enable them to reach long distances. They had a technique that differed considerably from that of the Americans, and I suspected that this had something to do with their prowess. After making a study of their style and experimenting with it on a number of athletes at the University of Southern California, I concluded that it was the technique of the modern Finn and not the spear throwing of his ancestors that is responsible for the record-breaking Jarvinens and Nikkanens of recent years.

The javelin throw was not included in the first three Olympic meets; when it was put on the program of the games in 1906 Lemming won for Sweden with a throw of 175 feet 6 inches. He won again in the 1908 Olympics and his winning throw of 179 feet 10½ inches went down as a world's record. Lemming improved his record in 1910 and 1911 and passed the 200-foot mark for the first time in 1912 when he hurled the stick 204 feet 5⅝ inches. In the Olympic games at Stockholm he won his third straight championship.

The Finns began to threaten Swedish supremacy in this event the same year. In addition to the regular javelin throw in the 1912 games, there was a javelin throw for the right and left hand, and J. J. Saaristo of Finland won this event with a total distance of 358 feet 11⅞ inches. During this same year Saaristo came through with the first 200-foot throw ever made by a Finn.

In the meantime American athletes became interested in the event through the stick-heaving competition of the Swedes and Finns, and eventually began throwing the wand themselves. In 1909, thirty-three years after the first national championship

296

track and field meet, the javelin throw was added to the national A.A.U. program. Possessing little knowledge of its technique, the American hurlers were somewhat less than sensational in their early championship marks. Ralph Rose, the giant shot-put champion and record holder, was the first national javelin-throw champion with a distance of 141.7 feet.

Like other American javelin throwers of his time, Rose was aware that the toss should be preceded by a run, but he didn't know exactly what to do about it. His form, and that of other American hurlers of the time, was to run up to the line, hop, stop, and throw. They used no momentum from their approach run and might just as well have thrown from a standing position.

The value of technique in throwing the javelin is well illustrated by referring to the first national championship in this event. The 286-pound shot-put champion of the world, using his big right arm without benefit of technique was the winner at a distance that a 140-pound high school boy can now equal after a few weeks of training on form.

Jonni Myyra bagged the world's record for Finland in 1915 with a throw of 212 feet 7¼ inches; 5 years later he raised the mark to 219 feet 1½ inches.

About that time the best mark ever made by an American was 202 feet 9½ inches, this distance having been reached by M. S. Angier of Chicago, who was national champion in 1920 and 1921. Americans by this time were developing a technique of their own but it was still some time before many of them reached the 200-foot class.

Myyra won the Olympic title in 1920 and repeated in 1924, but in the latter year he lost the world's record to Gunner Lindstrom of Sweden. Lindstrom's mark was 66.62 meters, or 218 feet 6⅞ inches.

Eino Penttila brought the record back to Finland in 1927 with a throw of 229 feet 3⅛ inches, but Sweden won the Olympic javelin title the following year when E. H. Lundquist finished first in the Amsterdam games. Lundquist also recaptured the record for the Swedes with a heave of 232 feet 11⅝ inches.

The Finns were not to be denied, however, and four years later Matti Jarvinen won the Olympic championship at 238 feet 7 inches, and became the world's record holder at 242 feet 10⅛

297

inches. In these games of 1932, the Finns swept the field with the first three places, Matti Seppala finishing second and Penttila, the former record holder, taking third.

Jarvinen increased the mark to 249 feet 8 inches in 1933, to 251 feet 6 inches in 1934, and to 253 feet 4½ inches in 1936. In the 1936 Olympics, however, he had injured his back and he slipped down to fifth place as Gerhard Stoeck of Germany finished first at 235 feet 8⁵⁄₁₆ inches. Jarvinen's 253-foot distance is still in the record books as a world's mark, but Yrjo Nikkanen of Finland, who was runner-up in the 1936 games, made a throw of 258 feet 3¼ inches in 1939 and this is now awaiting consideration as a new record.

American javelin throwers, getting a late start in the event and developing their own methods, steadily improved. One of the first of the outstanding American performers in the event was Jim DeMers of the University of Oregon, who was national champion in 1930 and 1931 and the first native star to pass the 220-foot mark.

The event did not get into I.C.A.A.A.A. competition until 1922. Most of the colleges now include it in their track and field program but in many states it is not yet on the high school slate. This keeps boys from developing an early interest in the sport and is one reason why we have not made greater speed in catching up with the European throwers.

A more important reason, however, is that we have been slow to recognize the superiority of the Finnish technique and to teach it to our own throwers. The best mark of a native American, a toss of 234 feet 1⅞ inches, was made in 1939 by Bob Peoples of the University of Southern California soon after he had switched from the American to the Finnish technique. When one considers that just eight years before this would have been a world's record and that it was only 1½ feet behind the winning throw in the 1936 Olympics, it can be seen that America is on its way to catch up with the foreign stars in this event.

Despite the fact that our throwers have been considerably behind the distances set by foreign record holders, recent years have brought out a number of excellent competitors in this country. Among them have been former national champions Creth B. Hines of Georgetown University, Jesse Mortensen of

298

the University of Southern California, Jim DeMers, Malcolm Metcalf of Dartmouth, Lee Bartlett of Albion College, Michigan, Ralston Legore of the University of North Carolina, Horace Odell of Manhattan, John Mottram of Stanford, Bill Reitz of the University of California at Los Angeles, Nick Vukmanic of Penn State College, and Boyd Brown of the University of Oregon. Brown approached the American record in 1940 with a throw of 232 feet 7 inches.

In the 1932 Olympics the United States showed improvement in international competition when Lee Bartlett was fifth and Kenneth Churchill of the University of California at Berkeley was sixth. America slipped a bit in the 1936 games, however, when Alton Terry of Hardin-Simmons was the only point winner with a sixth place.

Until Peoples' native American record of 234 feet, the mark was held at 231 feet 7¼ inches by Larry Bell of Miami University. Lowell Todd of San Jose State College, Ed Waterbury of California, and Hugo DeGroot of Southern California are other American throwers who have come up with excellent marks in recent years.

Although I had been making a study of Finnish javelin technique ever since I saw Myyra win in the Olympics, it was not until comparatively recent years that I decided to change all my candidates to this style. Naturally when a college coach has an athlete come to him who is already doing well in one style, he hesitates to risk upsetting him by teaching him an entirely new form. Usually our javelin candidates had a fairly good start in the American style and, as we were always able to develop a goodly number of point winners using the native technique, I was reluctant to switch entirely to teaching the Finnish method.

In the case of Bob Peoples I soon became convinced that, although he had already thrown the javelin more that 220 feet using the American style, he would never get any better unless he switched to the method used by the champion Finns. I told Bob this and after thinking it over he said he'd like to try the other method.

After he started learning the new technique, there were several weeks of worry when Bob was halfway between both methods. It seemed as though I had talked him out of one style but not into another and I began to wonder if he would ever hit 200 feet again. Suddenly he began to coordinate in the revised style and I was one of the most relieved coaches in the business when he clicked in an early season 1939 meet and sent the wand out to the 234-foot distance.

About the same time, Hugo DeGroot, a sturdy 180-pounder, reported for track and wanted to go out for the pole vault. I thought he was too heavy and not quite tall enough for this event. Because he had participated in several events successfully in prep school, I suggested to him that he seemed to have the all-round development that would make a good background for throwing the javelin. He had never thrown the javelin in his Monrovia High School track and field days, since Southern California prep schools do not have this event, but he was anxious to try it. Hugo was a conscientious worker and, starting with the Finnish form from scratch, made amazing progress. Soon after Peoples had taken the spotlight with his native American record, DeGroot proved one of the biggest surprises of the season with a throw of 227 feet 1 inch that beat his team mate in one of our meets.

On the same team was a much smaller athlete named Reed Trusel, who two years before had thrown the javelin 180 feet using the American style. I switched him to the method of the Finns and during the 1939 season he also showed remarkable progress and reached a distance of 213 feet $2\frac{1}{4}$ inches.

Perhaps all this improvement was just a bit of dumb luck that coaches have once in a while, but I believe it shows what can be done when we catch up with the foreign aces in our methods. Once I was as awe-struck as anyone else over the great distances of the European stars but now I am confident that it won't be long before we'll be competing on even terms with them in international meets.

The javelin is made of wood with a metal point and must be not less that 260 centimeters (8.53 feet) in length and not less than 800 grammes (1.765 pounds) in weight. At the center of gravity there is a grip formed by a binding of whipcord, which is 16 centimeters (6.3 inches) broad. There are a few all-metal javelins in use and they are considered legal as long as they conform to the specifications of weight, size, and shape.

The javelin must be held by the whipcord grip when it is

300

thrown. No toss is legal unless the point of the wand strikes the ground first in landing. Under the rules, throws must be measured at right angles from the point at which the javelin first strikes the ground to the scratch line or to an extension of this scratch line. Because of this, javelin men must learn how to throw the spear straight out from the board. Their tosses are not measured back to a circle as in the shot and discus.

The scratch line, which consists of a board 2¾ inches wide and 12 feet in length sunk flush with the ground, is the javelin thrower's only restraining mark. Behind it he can run as far as he wants to or do anything that he desires in getting up speed for the toss. Touching the board or going over it after the throw constitutes a foul.

In comparing the three throwing events in track and field, it can be said that putting the shot is a thrust, throwing the discus is a whip, and hurling the javelin is a pull. Although there is a throwing movement in the javelin, much of the final effort in making the toss comes from a tremendous pull on the left side of the body and it will help the beginner to understand the technique of the toss if he will think of it principally as a pull.

To learn to throw the javelin, the beginner starts from a set, standing position and first develops the ability to toss it straight. Keeping the 8½-foot stick on a straight line is not so simple a matter as it might seem. If the point is a little off line when the throw is made, on a hard toss the stick will develop a disastrous shimmy that will ruin the chances of getting good distance.

The action of throwing the javelin is much like chopping wood with an ax. The chopper swings the ax over his head and gives it a pull. The javelin man must do the same with his implement, and for this reason in the spear event we constantly emphasize "pull." The difference between a throw and a pull is this: in a throw, the hand and forearm go ahead of the elbow, as in tossing a baseball; in a pull, the elbow stays ahead of the hand.

In javelin throwing the hand swings high up over the shoulder, the head tilting slightly to the left to get out of the way, and the pull is made in a high arc. Speed for the toss comes from the run, with the legs transferring the momentum to the upper body, but one of the principal efforts in making the throw comes from the mighty pull on the left side of the body.

301

The javelin is held with the middle finger at the back of the grip. The middle finger is used because it is located in the strongest part of the hand. The thumb and first finger rest easily on the stick to aid in balancing it.

To make his first throws, the beginner, if he is right-handed, extends his right arm to the rear in such a way that the point of the javelin is against or near his face. It is a good idea to make the first tosses into a pit of shavings to get the feel of the throw. When the thrower brings his arm back preliminary to the toss, he keeps it bent slightly. The right knee is bent and all the weight falls on the right leg. The legs are spread apart in a comfortable stance and the right foot is turned at right angles to the direction of the throw.

The point of the javelin is elevated so that as the athlete gets it in position to start the toss the back end of it almost touches the ground. As the athlete starts to pull, he drives off his right leg. At this point there is a definite effort made to lift the right shoulder and to swing the arm in a wide arc as the spear comes up.

It is very important for the spear tosser to bring his throwing hand high up over his head. The pull aids in creating a whip of the arm. The arm is bent at the elbow and the spear is sent on its way with a final snap of the wrist. Should the thrower swing his arm out to the side in making the toss, he not only will fail to get the proper pull into the throwing effort but also will be in danger of injuring his elbow. The bane of all javelin men is a lame elbow and nearly all injuries to this member are the result of throwing when the arm is in an improper position out to the side.

With the left side pulling hard as the hand swings over the head, the right hip goes forward fast as in the discus throw. Not until the instant the hand is over the head is there what we may accurately call a throw. Up to that point, power has been generated by the leg drive and body pull. For a split second before the javelin is released, the pull turns into a throw as the arm flashes up and forward.

Until he has the feel of the toss, the beginner should keep on throwing from a standing position. If he is making his tosses properly, he will feel some soreness in his left side at first unless through exercise he has previously developed these muscles to a high degree.

To learn the fundamentals of the footwork used in the javelin throw, the beginner progresses from a standing position for the toss to a walk and throw. About 15 feet back of the restraining line he establishes a check mark. A few feet back of this mark he takes a preliminary step or two so that he will hit the check with his left foot. As he steps on this mark, he has his arm to the rear with the point of the javelin alongside or near his face.

In taking the step from the left foot to the right foot, he turns the right toe out, placing the right foot on the ground in a position parallel to the board. When he takes the next step to his left foot, he is in position to throw. Simultaneously with this step to the left foot he starts the drive from his right leg and the pull on his left side, whipping the spear over his head in the toss.

It helps the beginner to count "one-two-three" when he starts to throw from a walk. The count of "one" comes when he steps with his left foot on the check mark; "two" is the step to the right foot with the toe pointed out; "three" is the step to the left foot and the throw. One of the secrets of good javelin throwing is fast action between the counts "two" and "three." When the right foot is turned out and in place, there should be no delay in stepping forward to the left foot and letting the javelin fly.

The athlete may either count "one two-three" or say to himself "left right-left." In either case, the "two" and the "three" or the "right" and the "left" should be very close together.

When the thrower steps to the right foot on the count of "two," in order to keep his body in good position with his weight over his legs, it is necessary for him to cross the right leg over the left one slightly. With the right toe pointed out, the weight will be out of balance unless some effort is made to place the right heel a little off-line to the left. When the throw is made, the athlete wants all his weight and power behind the javelin.

After the javelin candidate has learned to get into proper throwing position from a walk, he then progresses to the running throw. The length of the run of champion throwers varies from 80 to 95 feet. The average is 85 feet and it is wise for the beginner to try his first running throws with this distance and then to make variations later to suit his own needs.

The check mark nearest the board, which we shall call check A, is moved two strides back of the mark that was used in the walking throw. If the mark for the walking throw was 15 feet from the foul line, check *A* is now located about 27 or 28 feet from the board, depending on the athlete's stride length. The mark farthest from the board, which may be called check *B*, is to indicate the start of the run and is located approximately 85 feet from the foul line.

Having moved check *A* two strides farther back from the board than it was in the walking throw, the athlete now has a five-count instead of a three-count to make to himself after hitting this mark on the run.

Nearly all the Finnish stars use the five-count system, although after they get in the groove it is doubtful if they have to bother any longer with much counting.

However, to get started in the running throw, the athlete will do well to count each step. The count of "one" takes place as the left foot hits check *A*. At this point the spear hurler starts to swing his throwing arm behind his body to be ready for the toss.

"Two" takes place on the step to the right foot. On this step, the right foot is toed out slightly.

The count of "three" is on the left foot, which also is turned slightly to the right. Throughout the series of steps, the feet start pointing toward the right because the body is being turned in this direction to get into the throwing crouch. However, despite the body twist, the run continues in direct line with the throw.

On the count of "four," the right foot lands pointed out practically at right angles to the line of the throw. The javelin is far back in throwing position and the body weight is carried entirely by the right leg.

When the toss is made on the count of "five," both feet are on the ground, with the left foot well out in front. The right leg is driving hard, the right hip swinging forward, the left side pulling, the right shoulder raising, the head tilting to the left, and the arm swinging high above with the elbow bent. After the toss, the athlete follows through with a short step, similar to the movement of a baseball pitcher, stopping on his right foot.

To keep from fouling, the thrower's left foot should be at least 2½ feet back of the board at the toss. Most javelin men finish the throw by hopping up and down on their right foot just inside the scratch line. It is almost impossible to make a dead stop after the throw but the hops on the right foot quickly put on the brakes.

If the athlete fouls with check A located at 27 feet, he should keep moving it back until he has room for the toss and a good margin of safety for the follow-through. Some throwers must locate this mark as far back from the board as 33 feet.

The length of the steps during the five-count after hitting the check mark and the amount of space needed for the follow-through vary considerably with different throwers.

During the run up to the throw, the javelin should be held in a relaxed manner. Peoples and DeGroot carried the spear over their shoulder parallel to the ground and pointed straight ahead, and this position seems to have the most advantages. Carrying the javelin over his shoulder, the athlete can keep his arm relaxed and also can have the wand under good control at all times. It is also helpful for him to be able to see the spear and know that it is pointed straight out in the direction of the throw.

It is sometimes best for the beginner to carry the stick with the point by the face throughout the run. By doing this he will be sure that the stick will always be in proper throwing position. Many good javelin throwers, among them former champion Malcolm Metcalf, hold the spear in throwing position throughout the run. Some throwers carry the stick with their right arm out in front and the wand pointing downward. Still others drop their right arm close to their side and turn their hand palm outward so that the javelin point is up. Jesse Mortensen of Southern California, who was national champion in 1929, used to carry the stick with his palm down.

The preliminary carry of the spear may be made in any comfortable manner as long as it creates no tension on the arm. The over-the-shoulder method is recommended because the arm is almost certain to be loose and relaxed in this style.

No matter which way the athlete carries the stick during his run, he should be certain that he does not wait too long to take the javelin back to throwing position. A common mistake made by javelin men is to hesitate too long. Many of them wait until they have landed on the right foot for the throw, which would be on the count of "four," before they draw back their arm. This delays the throw and causes a loss of momentum. It should be remembered that quick action is wanted between the counts of "four" and "five."

The javelin thrower has much to think about to get off a good throw and the coach has a nugget if he has an athlete in this event who is highly intelligent as well as well developed physically. Such a gem was Bob Peoples, who set the native American record probably because he knew more about javelin throwing than any other native American. When Bob realized the faults in the American style of throwing, he gave it up entirely, even though he had been making good marks with it, and learned everything he could about the Finnish method.

To meet his own needs, Bob made a slight variation in the use of the check mark nearest the board—check A. He hit this mark, which he placed 33 feet from the board, with his right foot instead of his left. That left him with a six-count to the throw instead of a five-count. However instead of counting from "one" to "six," he would count "one-two, one-two-three-four."

Counts "one" and "two" gave him two strides to think about relaxation and concentrate on a "gather" for the throw. Then when he began his four-count, he dropped his arm back and started his body twist on "one," stepped to his left foot on "two," pointed his right foot out and dropped into the throwing crouch on "three," and let the stick fly as his left foot came down on "four."

Bob could just as well have used the regular five-count by moving his check A to a point $27\frac{1}{2}$ feet from the board and hitting this with his left foot, but it seemed easier for him to do it his way. Also in his system he carried the spear over his shoulder one stride longer than the Finns before taking it back to the throwing position. By doing this he found that he got a recoil in his arm which was not possible when he took the spear back a stride sooner.

Peoples's second mark—check B—was located 84 feet from the board. He started his run 2 feet back of this check in order to step on it with his right foot and ran with a uniform stride to check A. He increased his speed very gradually. Thus he could use the same length stride throughout the run as he did not need to shorten his steps and dig in for a fast pickup.

Because he was running at not over two-thirds speed, which

would be about equivalent to the pace of a 15-second 100-yard dash, his stride was not long, being about $5\frac{1}{2}$ feet in length when he was running his fastest at check A.

Peoples's team mate, DeGroot, used check marks at 32 feet and 78 feet from the board, starting his run 6 feet back of check B. His was the standard method of hitting both check marks with his left foot. Although he learned the five-count method after hitting check A, like the Finns he stopped counting when he caught on to the correct footwork and body position.

Like the competitors in the broad jump, pole vault, and high jump in which there is a preliminary run, each athlete must work out his own check mark distances to suit his own way of running. There seems to be a greater variety of systems among javelin throwers than among men in other events in this matter.

Some throwers find that they need only one check, the one nearer the board, and can hit it without starting from a mark farther back. Others use three, putting in the third mark two strides closer to the board than check A and hitting this mark on the count of "three." It is up to the athlete to determine what is best for his own case. As a starter, he should try the double-check system, placing mark A from 27 to 33 feet from the board and B from 80 to 95 feet from it. Then as he grows in experience and javelin-throwing wisdom, he can work out his own problems from there.

The American system of javelin throwing differs from the Finnish style principally in the final footwook at the approach. The toss is made on the run in the Finnish style; in the American method there is a hop into the throwing position. In making this hop, javelin throwers, American style, lose nearly all the speed developed by their run. Most of the hop-and-throw boys could do almost as well if they eliminated the run entirely because they get little aid from the momentum the approach has given them.

About the only point in favor of the American style is that it is usually easier for the athlete to hop into good throwing position than to run into it. However, this is no real advantage when one considers that the hop into position has killed the benefits of the run. The American style of throwing also lacks much of the body pull used by the Finns. The native technique shows the influence of our great national pastime, for the form of many Americans looks as though they thought they were throwing a baseball instead of a long stick. About the best thing that can be said for the American javelin-throwing style is this: Don't use it.

The javelin thrower needs a good grip on the ground when he makes the throw. To ensure this, he should wear baseball shoes with the cleats on the ball of the foot moved back about ¾ inch so that the weight of the foot will be over the cleats. Baseball cleats are placed where they are to aid in sprinting, but the javelin thrower must move them back to make them an aid in gripping the ground. Some throwers prefer jumping shoes with two spikes in the heel. These are all right if the athlete feels that he is holding the ground snugly during the terrific leg drive and body pull of the throw.

Wind can play tricks with the javelin just as it can with the discus, and the thrower should keep the point down when tossing into a breeze and get good elevation when throwing with the wind behind him.

Runways differ in construction and before competition the thrower should check his step carefully. A dirt runway is considerably faster than one on grass, and the athlete who has been throwing on turf may overstride when he shifts to the hard ground.

Javelin throwing was considered a strong-man event when it was first tried in this country. A mighty arm was considered the essential thing, especially when Ralph Rose, the beefy world's record holder in the shot-put, became the first national javelin heaving champion. Upon learning that technique could get results when plain old-fashioned power would not, smaller men took up the event. Although javelin throwers must be strong, they do not need to be the bulky shot and discus type. The medium-sized athlete, who weighs from 170 to 190 pounds and who is fairly tall, seems to predominate among the champions. The well-built football halfback or end type is ideal for the event.

Abraham Lincoln would have made a great javelin thrower. He was tall and rawboned. Being a rail splitter, his wood chopping would have been an ideal conditioner for throwing the spear. What his ax wielding did for his "pulling" muscles is shown by the fact that he was a champion wrestler in his neck of the woods.

Bob Peoples weighed 185 pounds; his team mate, DeGroot, who was almost as good, weighed 5 pounds less. Brown, Vukmanic,

Reitz, Mottram, Odell, Legore, Bartlett, and Metcalf, all recent national champions, varied between 180 and 190 pounds. Beyond them, among national champions, however, was the powerful Jim DeMers, a burly athlete of 215 pounds.

Because the javelin thrower who develops correct technique puts almost all of his body behind the toss, he needs a splendid all-round physique. Peoples and Mortensen, who were champions at Southern California, also were strong enough to star as backfield men in Trojan football.

Throwing a football is good training for javelin tossing as many of the same muscles are used. However, the javelin is brought up over the head in the throw, and most good passers in football snap the ball up over their shoulder and alongside their ear.

Like other field-event men who grip implements—pole vaulters, shot-putters, and discus throwers—the javelin tosser should do squeezing exercises on a spring grip or soft rubber ball to strengthen his hands. His main effort in this regard is to develop a strong middle finger. Boyd Brown's thumb was missing from his throwing hand but this was no handicap. The thumb and first finger of a spear tosser are used only for balance, with the middle finger supplying the power at the grip.

The javelin thrower can use all the exercises that develop the upper body, particularly the pull-ups and push-ups. Work on the rings and horizontal and parallel bars will stretch his muscles and tendons and enable him to throw hard without the danger of straining or pulling a muscle.

Because he needs at least fair speed on the runway and plenty of power in his legs, the javelin thrower should combine considerable track work with his general conditioning. Wind sprints, starts, short dashes, and occasional longer runs up to 220 yards should be taken frequently to build up the speed. Work over low hurdles will aid the development of uniform stride for the runway and will also increase the drive in the right leg if the athlete will always take off from the right foot at the barriers.

The javelin candidate should start his throwing as early in the season as possible because he must develop his arm very gradually. For some time—a month or longer—he must throw only for form. Because of the tremendous strain he puts on his elbow, arm, and shoulder when throwing hard, his problem in developing

309

The javelin thrower carries the stick parallel to the ground in his approach run and is getting ready to drop it back to the throwing position. He is running easily at about three-quarters speed. In holding the javelin by the whipcord grip he puts on most of the pressure with his middle finger. Here as the thrower comes down on his left foot, he is taking the first of his final five steps.

In taking the second of his last five steps, the athlete carries the javelin down and back, dipping the body a little to get the stick into position. The point of the javelin is held close to the body. The left arm is carried low and kept relaxed. On this step, the thrower starts working up to his foot position by turning the right toe out to the right.

Here the athlete has landed on his left foot in the third of the series of five steps. The athlete's body and the javelin always move directly forward in the direction of the throw but, as the stick is carried back into position, the body and legs are turned to the right. The right leg is about to move in front of the left leg with a cross step.

The athlete is midway between the third and fourth steps and his right leg is crossing over. The left foot as well as the right foot is turned to the right. The javelin has been carried back almost as far as it will go. The left arm is now raised fairly high to help get the right shoulder far back for the throw.

Finishing the cross step, the thrower lands on his right foot in his fourth stride. Fast action now takes place to bring the left leg down in step number five and to coordinate the throw with this fifth and last step. The right knee is bent for the throwing crouch. Note the power in the right leg. The right foot is flat on the ground parallel to the foul line. The left arm stays high to keep the right shoulder back.

The landing of the left foot in the final step is the signal to call upon a mighty effort for the throw. The legs are spread comfortably with the left one acting as a brace. The hips swing forward fast and carry the power from the legs up through the back and shoulder. The head is turning to help in the body twist and to get out of the way of the javelin which will come up over it.

In the last split second before the stick is released it comes up high over the head as though the athlete were swinging an ax. The right shoulder has raised high and the left arm has been snapped down as a strong pull on the left side of the body takes place. The left leg acts as a brace as in the shot and discus events. The left foot points almost straight ahead, being turned a trifle to the right.

The javelin is on its way after having been given a final burst of power with a tremendous wrist snap. Note the powerful muscular action in the right arm and also the fact that both feet are on the ground at the instant the throw is made. The thrower will follow through and stop on his right foot after a short step. The athlete is Bob Peoples, former N.C.A.A. and I.C.A.A.A.A. champion and holder of the native American record at 234 feet 1⅞ inches.

gradually is considerably greater than that of the shot and discus man. Mastering the right technique before trying for good distances is especially important because hard throws made without good form are almost certain to injure the elbow.

When the spear thrower goes into a meet he should warm up with some light jogging on the track and take a number of easy preliminary tosses until his arm seems ready for a hard effort. No attempts at distance should be taken during this period, as the arm does not hold any too many big throws for one day and all of them should be saved for competition.

Every effort should be made to reach the greatest distances early in the competition. If the athlete can get a distance that looks good enough to win on one of his first throws, he can pass his next turns and rest his arm, returning to the competition only if a rival beats his mark.

On the day that Peoples made the American native record, I flagged him out of the competition after he had taken only two throws. The javelin thrower's arm undergoes a terrific strain when the athlete puts everything into a toss and there is no use taking chances on injury to the old soupbone.

Here is a typical weekly training schedule for a javelin tosser during the competitive season: Monday, a slow warm-up lap around the track to start, practice on foot work with the five-count if the step is giving any difficulty, easy throwing for form, from three to six dashes of from 25 to 40 yards; Tuesday, much the same type of workout as that staged on Monday; in warming up the arm, several throws into the ground to check the body pull and hip action, form throwing with about three-quarter power; for instance, an athlete who regularly hits 200 feet will throw about 150 or 160 feet, finish up with starts or short dashes; Wednesday, more of the same, form workout with three or four hard throws but not quite the maximum effort, training over one, two, or three low hurdles using strings between the barriers instead of regular hurdles; Thursday, some speed work on the track with the spear left in the training quarters, a final check on the step without carrying the javelin; Friday, rest for the competition on Saturday. The regular exercises may be taken at home, in the gymnasium, or on the field before the daily training period. And, of course, the walk of 2 miles a day is on every track and field man's program.

312

XVI

THE 1948 OLYMPIC GAMES

The wonderful honor of being head coach of the United States Olympic track and field team for the 1948 Olympic games at London was underscored again and again by the achievements of the athletes themselves during the 1948 international competition —the first to be held since the 1936 Olympic games at Berlin.

Although I had repeatedly expressed the conviction that the American team would prove dominant at London, I was pleasantly surprised—well-nigh amazed—by the record-breaking performances of our athletes, several of whom came through with the outstanding marks of their already brilliant careers. I am sure that the entire coaching staff feels, as I do, that it was an extreme privilege to be enabled to supervise such fine young men as these as they participated in the outstanding athletic competition of our era.

The United States men's track and field team was chosen at final Olympic tryouts held in Evanston, Ill., only a matter of days prior to embarking on the S.S. *America* for England. As for prior Olympiads, the team was determined solely by placings in these tryouts, for which the cream of the nation's athletes had qualified through a series of championship meets of semifinal status. If there has been some criticism of this method of choosing the team—and there was some conflicting opinion after several champions of world's record achievements failed to qualify on this particular occasion—it does not come from those directly concerned, the athletes themselves.

The method of selecting the team through a single tryout meet is sound. If an athlete must be at his peak on a given day in London, why also should he not be required to produce a championship performance at a specific moment in Evanston? When the athletes determine who makes the team on the basis of their own achievements on the track or in the field, there are no excuses, no politics, no wirepulling. I firmly support and recommend our present team-selection system for the Olympiads of the future.

Lessons learned during crossings of the Atlantic by former United States Olympic teams were apparent on our pleasant voyage. There was not a single incident antagonistic to the theme of team unity which prevailed from the very moment the team came into organization prior to our sailing from New York until our return weeks later. Team management and organization, based on long-range planning, were superior. The athletes themselves fully realized some of the problems involved, particularly those relating to food and living conditions in an area so recently ravaged by war, and cooperation and conduct were of the best.

Commendation for planning and organization should not be awarded solely to our American Olympic committee, but should also be directed with the fullest feeling of gratitude to the British Organization committee. The arrangements made for the American team for training were outstanding, as were the facilities at the actual scene of Olympic competition in Wembley Stadium. Although the track itself was not built until just a few weeks prior to the games, and the pits and runways likewise, they were of superior construction. The high-jump take-off area and the broad-jump and vault runways were soft, to be sure, but these impairments were directly traceable to the weather, rather than to improper planning.

The enthusiasm of the British populace for the games was infectious and no doubt contributed greatly to the phenomenal winning performances. Crowds of more than 80,000 were the rule, even on days of inclement weather, and many of these spectators were in the standing areas for hours prior to the start of competition. Their sportsmanship was fully in keeping with the international complexion of the games and proved inspirational to guests from all lands.

The first day of competition in men's track and field athletics included finals in the high jump and 10,000-meter run. For the purposes of this report on the 1948 games, the final events will be discussed in their order on the schedule, because, in several instances, athletes participated in a number of events and their competition in earlier endeavors sometimes affected their later performances.

The high jump provided probably the biggest disappointment to American hopes. All three of the United States representatives

—George Stanich, Dwight Eddleman, and Vern McGrew— previously had surpassed the winning Olympic performance of 6 feet 6 inches by John L. Winter of Australia, but were unable to do better than 6 feet 4¾ inches (by Stanich and Eddleman), while McGrew failed to clear 6 feet 2¾ inches.

As mentioned previously, the high-jump take-off area was soft from rains and soon became cut up by the repeated jumping of a field of 24 competitors. Winter was probably the least handicapped by this development because he utilized the Eastern cutaway style in which he ran straight toward the bar rather than from an angle, as did practically all the others who were adherents either to the Western roll or the barrel style.

Thus, it wasn't long after the start of competition before the take-off zones at the sides, used by the greater number of jumpers, were loose and mushy while the central area, used almost exclusively by Winter, was firm. As it was, Stanich came very close to clearing the winning height on his final try. Because of the Olympic rule governing ties, whereby the athlete with the fewer misses at lower heights gets the higher rating, both Stanich and Eddleman yielded second place to B. Paulson of Norway, a Western roll stylist, although all three cleared 6 feet 4¾ inches.

One of the world's great distance runners, Emil Zatopek of Czechoslovakia, won the 10,000-meter run in Olympic record time of 29:59.6. A junior officer in his nation's army, Zatopek displayed an erratic pace which deceived both his opponents and the spectators as to the amount of stamina he actually possessed.

Zatopek, encouraged by countrymen in the stands who chanted his name in unison as he completed lap on lap, stayed with the pack (the early pacesetter was V. A. Heino of Finland) for the first 3 miles. Then he took the lead and built up his margin by spurts and spasms until he broke the tape more than 300 yards ahead of A. Mimoun-O-Kacha of France, the runner-up.

The winning time was accomplished by a 66.6-seconds final lap by Zatopek, and broke the former Olympic record of 30:11.4., established in the 1932 games in Los Angeles by Jan Kusocinski of Poland.

Incidentally Heino, the world's record holder at 29:35.4, was forced to withdraw midway in the race or else Zatopek might have produced an even faster winning effort.

The three Americans—Ed O'Toole, Fred Wilt, and Herman Goffberg—were never factors in the race, which attracted a starting field of 27. Zatopek lapped almost all his rivals.

Five Olympic championships in men's track and field were settled the following day, and by far the most important from the United States viewpoint was the 100-meter dash final.

The story of the triumph of Harrison Dillard, the somewhat unexpected victor, will be told for years to come. By far the world's greatest hurdler, with a new world record of 13.6 seconds, Dillard had failed to make the United States team in that event when he hit a succession of hurdles in the final tryouts. He had entered the 100-meter in order to qualify for the sprint relay team, not being particularly intent on an individual title in an event in which he would oppose such illustrious sprinters as Mel Patton and Barney Ewell of the United States, Lloyd Labeach of Panama, and John Treloar of Australia.

But after failing to make the team in his specialty, Dillard really went to work in the sprint race. I worked regularly with him in perfecting his start during the practice sessions at Uxbridge. We were not permitted by the British government to import a starting gun, so I had to utilize a pair of wooden blocks—clapping them together sharply to simulate the crack of the pistol.

Patton, who had set a new world record of 9.3 seconds for 100 yards earlier in the season, was the prerace favorite. Both Dillard and he were equally impressive in the trial heats. Dillard won his three early heats in 10.4 seconds, 10.4 seconds, and 10.5 seconds, while Patton was winning in 10.6 seconds, 10.4 seconds, and 10.4 seconds.

In the final race it was the veteran Ewell—an aspirant for the United States Olympic team as a high school lad 'way back in 1936—who pushed Dillard right to the tape in the time of 10.3 seconds. In fact, Ewell thought he was the winner and put on a regular victory dance until the final result was learned. Actually Dillard won only by inches.

Patton finished but fifth—with Labeach third and Alan McCorquodale of Great Britain fourth—and was a very disappointed young man. But his big afternoon was yet to come.

If Dillard's triumph was a considerable surprise, then the re-

316

sult of the 400-meter hurdle final—with Roy Cochran of the United States the winner—was the exact opposite. If ever an athlete established himself as the complete master of an event, from standpoints of speed, technique and experience, it was Cochran as he set a new Olympic record of 51.1 seconds.

He won by almost 6 yards, and I am certain that Cochran could have beaten the world record of 50.6 seconds—held by Glenn Hardin of the United States, the former Olympic champion —had he really been pushed that afternoon.

Cochran, an oldtimer who might well have made either the 1940 or 1944 Olympic teams had the games been held on those occasions, had supreme confidence and possessed the ability to change stride for hurdling with either leg if necessary. This enabled him to modify his pace as the occasion demanded, as freely as he might have in a flat race over the same distance.

In preliminary heats, both Cochran and Runé Larsson of Sweden ran 51.9 seconds to break Hardin's former Olympic record of 52 seconds flat. But in the final, Larsson was only third, with Duncan White of Ceylon second. Richard Ault of the United States was fourth. The third American, Jeffrey Kirk, was eliminated in the semifinals although he ran faster than a qualifier in the opposite heat.

The running broad jump—the long jump, if you wish me to utilize its official European description—lacked some of the competitive luster of prior Olympics because of the absence of the nimble Japanese, but the performance of the winner, Willie Steele of the United States, was certainly up to championship standards.

Steele, who had leaped 26 feet 2 inches and had barely fouled at 26 feet 10 inches in the final tryouts, was the only jumper at London to better 25 feet. He did 25 feet 6½ inches in the trials and then came through with a winning effort of 25 feet 8 inches in the final round. He won by 10½ inches over Tom Bruce of Australia, with Herb Douglas and Lorenzo Wright of the United States third and fourth.

The field as a whole was indeed mediocre, although a soft runway may have contributed to the situation. The qualifying distance in the trials was set at 23 feet 7½ inches, but only four entrants did that well and so eight others with lesser marks advanced in the final group of twelve.

Steele is one of the very fine broad jumpers of all time, in some ways more impressive than the world's record holder, Jesse Owens, because of superior technique. Owens possessed wonderful speed and achieved his records almost solely through that medium. Steele, himself very fast, utilized an ideal form, including a lengthy run of more than 50 yards and a tremendous drive off the board with a perfect "kick" before landing. This impact at the take-off was so great on some occasions that his heel could not stand up under it for more than one or two leaps a day, then requiring a full week's rest, Steele told me.

The winner of the hammer throw, an event which is not particularly stressed in this nation except in the New England region, was Imry Nemeth of Hungary, of whom we had heard much in the weeks prior to the games. Nemeth was pictured to us as an unusually small, slight man, but one who could attain distances of 190 feet.

I scoffed at this—not at Nemeth's achievements, which speak for themselves—but at his alleged height and weight dimensions. Actually Nemeth is slightly above average proportions and he has a trunk of somewhat extraordinary length, thus providing him with a lowered center of gravity for negotiating three pivots in the circle.

Nemeth is a true champion. He led all the way and won with a mark of 183 feet 11½ inches, more than 5 feet ahead of I. Gubijan of Yugoslavia. Two Americans, Robert Bennet and Sam Felton, were third and fourth. Henry Dreyer, our other representative, qualified for the final but went unplaced.

The United States hammer throwers, although doing very well in this international competition, were of somewhat more imposing builds than some of their adversaries, notably Nemeth, but lacked the efficient style of many of the Europeans.

The 50,000-meter walk was a procession for its entire length of 31 miles, 120 yards. J. A. Ljunggren of Sweden won in 4 hours 41 minutes 52 seconds. The best American, Ernie Crosbie, was twelfth, more than a half-hour behind, while John Deni and Adolph Weinacker also finished in fifteenth and sixteenth places. Five of the 21 contestants dropped out.

We'll have more to say about walking competition in the Olympic games a little later.

318

After a day's lapse in the Olympic schedule for the observance of Sunday, the competition resumed with four final events, two to be won by Americans.

Malvin Whitfield triumphed for the United States in the 800-meter run. This achievement was almost beyond my wildest dreams, as I anticipated that for races of more than 400 meters in distance the top competitors of other lands would prove far superior.

Actually, however, the United States trio of Whitfield, Herb Barten, and Robert Chambers all managed to score in the final, with Whitfield defeating the favored Arthur Wint of Jamaica by a firm 2-yard margin.

Whitfield had the good fortune of drawing the pole lane for the final, and used his speed to gain the early lead which he maintained all the way. The first lap was slower than anticipated by some observers, being 54.2 seconds, but it suited the plan perfectly of Whitfield, whose experience and speed were best fitted to shorter distances.

The winning time of 1:49.2, a new Olympic record which beat the former mark set in 1932 by Tom Hampson of Great Britain by six-tenths of a second, indicates that Whitfield ran the second 400 meters in an even 55 seconds while other opponents, particularly Wint and the fast-closing Barten who placed fourth, had to run their second laps faster than their first 400 meters.

Whitfield possesses a very smooth style and he has good stamina. The long-striding Wint did not quite possess the essential sprint to overtake Whitfield in the stretch run. The race was run in a fine rain but the times didn't suffer. Marcel Hansenne of France was third in time, equal to the former record of 1:49.8. Barten's time was 1:50.1, while Chambers, sixth, was caught in 1:52.1.

Americans, who have long prevailed in the pole vault, almost yielded to an imposing collection of Scandinavian vaulters, but finally Guinn Smith, although handicapped by a runway made sloppy by the downpour, cleared 14 feet 1¼ inches to win the championship.

Where a possible United States sweep was anticipated, the other Americans—Robert Richards and Richmond Morcom—could only place third and sixth, respectively, with heights considerably shy of the 14 feet 8 inches they had cleared in the final tryouts. E. O. Kataja of Finland was second at 13 feet 9¼ inches.

Smith is another one of the veteran athletes of prior seasons who appeared to have lost Olympic hopes because of the war. But he kept in training, although bothered in the early season of 1948 by a bad knee, and retained his peak when maximum performances would mean the very most. He is tall and has good speed and could hold the pole somewhat higher than his less rangy Olympic rivals. This asset no doubt helped him considerably in the face of the adverse weather conditions.

Two Italians, Adolfo Consolini and Giuseppe Tosi, placed one-two in the discus throw, an event which had customarily been considered a sure thing for the Americans. Indeed, prior to the games, I felt that our outstanding United States champion, Fortune Gordien, who had marks very close to the world record of 180 feet 2¾ inches, set by Robert Fitch in 1946, would win.

In pre-meet practices, however, both of the Italians showed more consistent ability than the Americans—Gordien, Victor Frank, and William Burton.

Consolini, a tall athlete from northern Italy who had also competed in the 1936 Olympic games, won with an effort of 173 feet 2 inches while Tosi was close behind at 169 feet 10½ inches. Gordien's best was 166 feet 7 inches while the other Americans failed to meet the qualifying standard in the trials.

Neither of the Italians possessed as great speed or as perfect a pivot as Gordien, but both had tremendous arm whip. Consolini has since broken the world's record of Fitch with a mark of 181 feet 6⅜ inches, and I can see no reason why the record won't be advanced to more than 190 feet, probably to 200 feet. We are still learning in this event, and soon the records of today in the discus will be regarded only as ordinary performances.

Zatopek, the rambling Czech who had won the 10,000-meter run only three days before, lost no prestige although he placed second in the 5,000-meter run final to Gaston Reiff of Belgium.

Only one man ever has won both these events in the same games. Hannes Kolehmainen of Finland did so in the 1912 Olympics at Stockholm. Paavo Nurmi of Finland won the 5,000 in 1924 and the 10,000 in 1920 and again in 1928—but never both

320

in the same year. But Zatopek missed out on duplicating Koleh-mainen's feat by only two-tenths of a second.

Reiff is a very fine runner and deserves every praise for his championship race in new Olympic record time of 14:17.6, for the distance of 188 yards more than 3 miles. But I am very certain that Zatopek was actually the better man, even though he was beaten by less than a stride. Somewhere along the way the eccentric Czech runner misjudged his early pace in relation to Reiff's own leading margin.

With three laps to go, he suddenly showed this realization with a tremendous rally, although Reiff himself had advanced his own rate substantially. Zatopek was a trailing third with less than a mile to go and, with 300 yards remaining, was still perhaps 40 yards behind. He literally sprinted the rest of the way, with the crowd as excited as at any time during the entire games, but he just missed at the tape.

The old record of 14:22.2, set by Gunnar Hockert of Finland in 1936, was beaten by more than 9 seconds.

I wish to compliment Curtis Stone, the leading American who placed sixth, for his fine race in the face of the outstanding competition he encountered. He just missed fifth place. Stone's time of 14:39.4 was better than he had done in the final tryouts and he upheld my pre-Olympic prediction that either he or Jerry Thompson would place. Unfortunately neither Thompson nor Clarence Robinson, the third American entrant, qualified for the final. If the Americans could have had the advantage of some earlier races against competitors of the Europeans' ability, I am certain they would have made far better showings in the Olympics.

I cannot help but note that the next day of the 1948 Olympic games proved to be the happiest of my coaching career, as two of the champions I had coached at the University of Southern California won first places.

The first of the day was Wilbur Thompson in the shot-put. Thompson is nicknamed "Moose" rather for his lack of imposing proportions than for any tremendous height or girth.

But Thompson takes rank in my memory with another great Southern California Olympic champion, Clarence (Bud) Houser, who won this selfsame event in the 1924 games at Paris, as being one of the outstanding "clutch" performers in Olympic annals.

As an undergraduate, Thompson had a career somewhat in reverse to his Olympic achievements. He somehow just missed winning the vital championship events. Even during the early season of 1948, he lost to many another competitor.

But as the games themselves neared, he figuratively caught fire. In the final tryouts, although placing second, he came up with the best mark of his career, 54 feet 11⅞ inches, and his concentration created such tension that he actually vomited after walking from the ring. I have seen many runners do this following a race in which all their physical resources were concentrated in their efforts for maximum speed at the tape, but never before had seen a weightman overcome by such strain.

A mark of approximately 55 feet for Thompson, who weighed no more than 195 pounds and stood just 6 feet, is great enough, but in the Olympic games he produced a new record of 56 feet 2 inches and on a foul throw had one 6 inches farther. His other four efforts were all beyond 54 feet. The old record for the games was set in 1936 at Berlin by Hans Woellke of Germany at 53 feet 1¾ inches.

James Delaney and James Fuchs, the other two Americans, completed a sweep for the United States in the shot-put, and each likewise broke the former Olympic record. Delaney is similar to Thompson in being a man of ordinary build with tremendous speed and explosiveness across the ring. Fuchs is a large man who takes advantage of the higher angle of elevation in propelling the weight.

The absence of the new world's record holder, Charles Fonville, from the American team, was commented on considerably by the press. Fonville set a mark of 58 feet ¼ inch in the 1948 Kansas Relays. But in the final tryouts he placed only fourth, being handicapped by a back injury, and failed to make the team. Like all the other tryout finalists who failed, Fonville accepted the result in a true spirit of sportsmanship and fair play. I scarcely feel that, in the face of the circumstances, he would have beaten Thompson at London on Tuesday, Aug. 3, 1948.

I believe deeply that the championship performance by Thompson contributed directly to the victory in the 200-meter dash by Mel Patton, the thoroughly beaten sprinter in the 100-meter three days earlier.

322

Patton had been a team mate of Thompson on the Southern California team of 1946 and they were fast friends. A tremendous will for victory welled within Patton after his loss in the 100, and when the final of the 200 came, and he drew the pole lane, I anticipated the great race he produced.

Barney Ewell and Cliff Bourland of the American team, Herb McKenley and L. Laing of Jamaica, and Lloyd Labeach of Panama were the other finalists—as fine a single field as ever started an Olympic sprint race. Patton was off with the gun in a perfect start and set such a meteoric pace that he had 2 yards on Ewell as they came off the curve. Ewell, fated to be the runner-up in both 1948 Olympic sprints, rallied but couldn't catch Patton in 21.1 seconds, although both were timed in that identical figure. Labeach, McKenley, Bourland, and Laing trailed in that order.

Of all the champion sprinters I have ever coached—Charles Paddock, Charles Borah, Frank Wykoff, and Foy Draper, to recall a few—Patton was the greatest at the distance of 200 meters or 220 yards. Three times he ran the 220 in 20.4 seconds—only one-tenth of a second behind Jesse Owens's world record—and was timed twice in 20.7 seconds for the metric distance around a curve, which is equal to the fastest of all time under that condition.

He had a smooth stride and the greatest sustained speed over a distance of any of the fine sprint champions. His ability to rally from defeat in the earlier Olympic race marks Patton as a real champion to an even greater extent.

The achievements of both Ewell and Bourland in attaining the finals and placing so high were heartening. I have already mentioned that Ewell had been running since 1936. Bourland, likewise, could have made either the 1940 or 1944 teams had the Olympic games of those years been possible.

Bourland had been concentrating upon the 400-meter during the 1948 campaign—which followed by five years his graduation from the University—but just prior to the semifinal tryouts in Milwaukee, he realized that he possessed a real opportunity to make the Olympic team in the 200-meter.

He did so with relative ease and in the preliminary heats at London was unbeaten in times of 21.3 seconds, 21.3 seconds and

323

21.5 seconds. The fact that he placed but fifth in the final field of six takes nothing away from his remarkable comeback.

In the hop, step, and jump event, which was similar to the broad jump in lacking the remarkable Japanese performers of prior Olympics, the winner was Arne Ahman of Sweden at 50 feet 6¼ inches, which was almost 2 feet less than the 1936 winning achievement. Gordon Avery of Australia was second at 50 feet 4¾ inches.

Of the three Americans, only William Albans was able to qualify for the final and he went unplaced. Robert Beckus and Erik Koutonen were the other United States entrants. None of the three was able to do as well as in the final tryouts, but here again runway conditions at London were not of the best.

The second big United States sweep occurred in the 110-meter hurdles, when William Porter, Clyde Scott, and Craig Dixon finished one-two-three in Olympic record time of 13.9 seconds.

If ever a nation showed itself superior in a given event, this was the case, because in none of the many preliminary heats was an American beaten excepting by a team mate. Porter won successively in 14.3 seconds, 14.1 seconds and 13.9 seconds. Dixon won twice in 14.2 seconds and Scott coasted a heat in 14.8 seconds before twice running on Porter's heels.

Even without the presence of the great Harrison Dillard, whose failure in the tryouts has already been related, the Americans put on a great show. Porter is a wonderful hurdler, and Scott, who ran 13.7 seconds in the 1948 National Collegiates when aided by a slight wind, and Dixon are almost as brilliant.

In the final, both Scott in second and Dixon in third were timed identically in 14.1 seconds, which was equal to the former Olympic record set in 1936 by Forrest Towns of the United States.

Hurdling speed has now developed so tremendously that only great sprinters can approach the record-breakers. Dillard, the world's record holder, was able to win the Olympic 100 title. Scott and Dixon majored in the sprints as well as hurdles in their college dual meets in times well under even figures, while Porter, although never being actually timed in championship races on the flat, could regularly beat Scott and Dixon in the hurdles and finally defeated Dillard in the national A.A.U. championships.

324

The javelin throw was an unusual event in that an American placed second, the highest such place gained by a United States athlete in Olympic annals, while another American actually exceeded this second-place effort but gained a lesser place because of a rule technicality.

As has become almost a tradition, a Finn won the event when Kaj Tautavaara came through with a throw of 228 feet 10½ inches. Dr. Steve Seymour, who had set a new American record of 248 feet 10 inches in 1947, was second at 221 feet 7½ inches. Martin Biles was sixth for the United States at 213 feet 9½ inches.

Biles was the victim of a European rule—a rule with which I do not at all agree—which fails to credit qualifying marks for the finals. In the javelin trials he had a best toss of 222 feet ½ inch, which would have given him second place, but this achievement was ignored in the final tabulation.

In this nation, qualifying marks for field events of distance objectives—all except the high jump and pole vault—are always credited for the finals as well, and rightly so. In some prior Olympic games this American method has been utilized, but in 1948, it was the European rule which prevailed.

It is not fair to have a champion risk his well-being with a trial effort—particularly in such events as the javelin and broad jump wherein initial marks are very often the best—and then not have it counted for the final result. The disappointment for Biles when he actually threw well enough for second, yet only placed sixth, is but one example.

Rautavaara, incidentally, had only one good throw in the finals, whereas Seymour was consistent at approximately his best distance. He had been bothered by an arm ailment late in the season or else might well have attained a winning achievement of beyond 230 feet. He is certainly the best American javelin thrower of all time, having developed a form similar to that of European champions.

The third American in the javelin event, Robert Likins, went unplaced after qualifying for the final round.

The distinctive aspect of the 400-meter final of the 1948 Olympic games was that the top three contenders had all appeared in previous races. Malvin Whitfield of the United States had won the

800-meter three days before. Arthur Wint of Jamaica was a very close second. Herb McKenley, also of Jamaica, had placed in the 200-meter only two days previously.

Possibly this latter effort of McKenley, who had set a new world's record of 45.9 seconds for the 400 in the national A.A.U. championships, was the more exhausting. In any event it was Wint who upset McKenley, with Whitfield a close third as they crossed the finish.

Wint, who through their early careers had always been able to triumph over McKenley, overcame the early advantage of his speedier countryman and gained the lead with 20 yards to go, and won by a stride in Olympic record-equalling time of 46.2 seconds. Whitfield was another stride back in third place. The other two Americans, David Bolen and George Guida, were fourth and sixth, respectively.

The champion had been the most impressive in the trial heats. Wint won his first round trial in 47.7 seconds, took his second round heat in 47.7 seconds and raced his semifinal in 46.3 seconds. McKenley's earlier times were 48.4 seconds, 48 seconds and 47.3 seconds.

There is a doubt in my mind that Wint would have won had McKenley stayed out of the 200. But then perhaps the result would have still been the same had Wint not competed in the 800.

The 3000-meter steeplechase final was held on the same day as the 400 and proved to be a high point for the great Swedish runners, who swept the first three positions.

The time for the winner, Tore Sjostrand, was 9:4.6, which was just shy of Volnari Iso-Hollo's mark for Finland in 1936 of 9:3.8. Eric Elmsater and G. Hagstrom were second and third behind their countryman.

H. Browning Ross of the United States was a strong seventh but Robert McMillen and William Overton failed to qualify for the final. This is an event not commonly raced in our land, and until more stress is placed on it we cannot expect to produce a representative capable of keeping up with the Scandinavian champions.

The result of the decathlon, which covered a two-day period and was made particularly difficult because of haphazard and unknowing officiating, caught the fancy of the United States

326

populace—even many who are not close followers of athletics—because of the triumph by a seventeen-year-old high-school boy, Robert Mathias.

Encountering delay after delay on the second day of competition, and finally not finishing until long after nightfall, Mathias won by a margin of 165 points over a number of experienced and far older American and European champions.

But Mathias, equipped with a remarkable ability to relax completely while not actually in competition, produced a series of top-notch records in event after event to take rank along with such other United States Olympic all-around champions as James Thorpe, Harold Osborn, James Bausch, and Glenn Morris.

Mathias was fourth in the standings after the first day of competition, but was only 56 points behind the pacemaker, Enrique Kistenmacher of Argentina. His first-day achievements were 11.2 seconds in the 100, 21 feet 8½ inches in the broad jump, 42 feet 9¼ inches in the shot-put, 6 feet 1¼ inches in the high jump and 51.7 seconds in the 400-meter run.

In the second half of the rugged grind, Bob came through with marks of 15.7 seconds in the 110-meter hurdles, 144 feet 4 inches in the discus, 11 feet 5¾ inches in the pole vault, 165 feet 1 inch in the javelin, and 5 minutes 11 seconds in the 1500-meter run.

Ignace Heinrich of France was second with 6,974 points behind Mathias' 7,139. Floyd Simmons of the United States was third at 6,950—and here, too, was another fine all-around performer—while Kistenmacher dropped to fourth at 6,929. The third American, Irving Mondschein, was eighth at 6,715. His specialty was the high jump but he failed to attain as high a score as anticipated in that event and thereby lost all chance to win.

I cannot help but be critical of the games officials for not anticipating the decathlon pole vault schedule in advance. The field of 28 competitors was so large that two flights were necessary for the event, it is true, but the split should have been based on past performances rather than on mere luck of the draw.

As it was, there were inferior vaulters mixed with superior vaulters in the early flight, as well as in the second group, and it took hours to complete the first series of vaults before the second group—which included Mathias—even commenced competition.

If the division into groups had been based on ability, the event could have been completed in almost half the time required. I respectfully recommend to the international committee that they survey the rule for future Olympic games.

After the lengthy regular pole-vault competition in 1936, which went long hours into the night, a change in rule was made whereby trials for the elimination of inferior contestants were conducted a day in advance. My suggestion regarding the decathlon pole vault will avoid the bad situation which developed in 1948.

If it had not been for Mathias' remarkable stability and championship abilities, he would have suffered from this unfair disadvantage and probably would have lost the championship which was rightfully his as the outstanding performer. Olympic rules should be written to prevent such unfortunate conditions.

A pair of swift Swedes were the first two place winners in the 1500-meter run, but it was the least prominent of the two—from the standpoint of international acclaim—who won.

Lennart Strand, coholder of the world record of 3 minutes 43 seconds for the metric mile distance (which is actually about 120 yards short of a mile), was the favorite, but lost by six-tenths of a second to his fellow national, Henry Eriksson. The time of 3:49.8 was two seconds slower than the Olympic record set by Jack Lovelock of New Zealand in Berlin in 1936.

Strand, who told me a few days before the race that he lacked a real incentive to win, indicated this attitude in the very closing strides when Eriksson gained the lead and Strand glanced back over his shoulder—apparently much more intent on holding second place than seeking to battle it out for first.

Marcel Hansenne of France set the early pace, being timed in 58.3 seconds for the first 400 and at 2:2.6 at the 800-meter point. From there the Swedes gained command. The time of Willy Slijkhuis of the Netherlands in third place was identical with that of Strand.

Don Gehrmann, America's best man in the event, qualified for the final and placed eighth. He had won the final Olympic tryouts in 3:52.2, which would have been good enough for fifth at London. Neither Roland Sink nor Clem Eischen of the United States qualified for the final field of 12, although Sink's time for a qualifying heat in which he placed fourth—with only three making the grade—was faster than the winning time of two other heats.

The American team was minus the brilliant runner, Gilbert Dodds, who had won the national A.A.U. championship but had then been injured in a pre-Olympic exhibition race in the East. It was a distinct loss to have Dodds forced to withdraw, and I would have enjoyed seeing him perform against the best in the world. One thing is certain: with his brilliant early pace, the winning time at London would have been far faster, even though Dodds himself might not have won.

The classic marathon climaxed the final day of men's track and field athletics of the 1948 Olympic games. As is almost always the case, the winner was an unknown—this time being Delfo Cabrera of Argentina. His victory brought to mind the triumph of another runner from Argentina, Juan Carlos Zabala, in the 1932 games in Los Angeles.

Cabrera overtook the closing pacesetter, Etienne Gailly of Belgium, in the very final yards of the race within Wembley Stadium itself, to win in 2 hours 34 minutes 51.6 seconds, the third fastest time in Olympic history over a course probably more severe than those in which better times were recorded in 1932 and 1936.

Gailly, so exhausted he could barely finish, also yielded second place in the final strides to Tom Richards of England, who from many standpoints appeared to me to have been the best man in the starting field of 41 for the grind of 26 miles, 385 yards.

Richards misjudged either his pace or the ability of Cabrera, who had been up near the front all the way, and actually finished much fresher than most of the early arrivals. His time was only 16 seconds slower than the winner's. I believe Richards could have speeded up with about 5 miles to go and have won.

Ted Vogel, the American collegian, was the first of the United States trio to finish, coming in at fourteenth position in 2 hours 45 minutes 27 seconds. John Kelley was twenty-first and Ollie Manninen finished twenty-fourth. Thirty finished, with eleven entrants dropping out en route.

It was an historic race, with a thrilling finish, and all London seemed to be interested, lining the entire route 10-deep.

While the marathon was thrilling, the final of the 10,000-

meter walk was anything but. Both the trial heats and the final
of this event—held for the first time since 1924—were marred by
official edicts, warnings, and disqualifications of the entrants who
assertedly were not strictly observing the heel-and-toe rules.

May I interject the thought here that walking races—as well as
such other events of extreme controversy as boxing and water
polo—should not be a part of the Olympic games program designed to advance international good will and understanding. Let
us drop these activities which cause nothing but ill will and concentrate on events which produce good feeling and sportsmanship.

The winner of the championship was J. F. Mikaelsson of
Sweden in 45:13.2 and all three Americans failed to qualify—but
neither the winners nor the losers were happy over the arguments
associated with the competition. The American entrants were
Henry Laskau, Ernest Weber, and Fred Sharaga.

Controversy likewise centered about one of the two concluding
relays—but here only good feeling prevailed at its conclusion
because of the all-decisive evidence of the motion picture camera.

I was in the midst of this string of circumstances, so let us start
from the beginning:

In the trials of the 4 × 100-meter relay the United States
quartet appeared completely dominant—far speedier than any
other nation's team. I assigned Barney Ewell, the runner-up in
both the 100-meter and 200-meter dashes, to the first leg because
of his superior start. Lorenzo Wright, the broad jumper, took
over the second leg for the original member of the team, Edward
Conwell, who was stricken with an illness and had to return home.
Harrison Dillard, the 100-meter champion, was the third man
because he is one of the greatest of all sprinters rounding a curve,
while Mel Patton, 200-meter champion, was made the anchor
man because of his blazing finish.

It was a team fully comparable to the 1932 and 1936 United
States quartets which successively set world's records of 40 seconds and 39.8 seconds, respectively.

In the trial heat, the Americans coasted to win in 41.1 seconds
and looked so superior that I then instructed them to be particularly cautious in passing the baton in the final so as not to sacrifice
an apparently sure-fire triumph.

They did so—or apparently did so—and won by yards in the

330

respectable time of 40.6 seconds. The boys were preparing to mount the victory stand when the shocking announcement was made that there was a disqualification. The Americans had made a pass beyond the zone from No. 1 to No. 2 man and were eliminated. The winner, it was declared, was second-place Great Britain.

Naturally the British populace, which had failed to witness a single triumph by home athletes, was joyous over the turn of events.

The irregular pass, had there been one, would have been from Ewell to Wright. I was positive that this pass of the baton actually had been made with a span of 12 meters, whereas a full 20 meters is provided within the change-over zone.

I asked Ewell if the pass had been within the designated area and he assured me that it had.

Other American team officials were reluctant to take up the matter with the jury of appeal, but I knew that I must do so— not in a spirit of depriving British athletes of anything they had been awarded, but rather to see that justice prevailed and that four athletes who had rightfully won a race within the rules should attain that recognition.

The appeal, properly phrased in formal international language and duly timed and dated, was based on the contention that the alleged irregular change-over actually was proper and that official motion pictures of the race would bear out this claim both of the athletes and myself.

When the motion pictures were developed and screened, there wasn't a question but that the pass of the baton had been completed within the prescribed zone. Apparently an honest error had been made by an official who mistook the midway line of the zone for the final limit. The starts of the race had been staggered, and it would have been very easy to have made this mistake.

In any event, the jury of appeal upheld the American viewpoint and reversed the result to declare the United States team the champion.

The attitude of the British athletes themselves was completely in the spirit of international accord. If the Americans had not fouled, they wanted no part of the honor. Lord David Burghley, the 1928 Olympic champion in the 400-meter hurdles and now the chairman of the British Olympic Association, expressed this viewpoint to me even before the motion pictures were available.

I have gained many friends through my Olympic associations of 1928, 1932, 1936, and now 1948, but I think no incident in these games did so much to stress in my mind that sportsmanship and fair play are universal. The spirit of Olympianism need never be endangered by difference of opinion and as long as it is capable of conscientious and judicious consideration when such differences arise.

The final relay, the 4 × 400-meter event, was marred by an unfortunate accident when Arthur Wint, the 400-meter champion, pulled up lame on the third leg of the final, and the Jamaican team was forced to drop out.

The Jamaican team was the only group capable of pushing our American quartet. It possessed Herb McKenley as anchor man, in addition to Wint, and might have won had not the accident occurred. However, I must state my firm belief that the better balanced American team would have won under any circumstances.

The United States team was composed of Arthur Harnden, Cliff Bourland, Roy Cochran, and Malvin Whitfield. Harnden was the fourth man in the final tryouts. Bourland, an experienced quarter-miler, had run in the 200-meter final. Cochran, with a vast background in this event, was the 400-meter hurdles champion. Whitfield had won the 800-meter and was third in the 400-meter and had won the final tryouts at the distance.

The composition of this team was agreed upon by the coaching staff of the American team as a whole, acting on my recommendation, and it was a unit which—if pushed—might have beaten the Olympic record of 3:8.2 set in 1932 at Los Angeles by another United States quartet.

Cochran, incidentally, was extremely excited over being a member of the team because his older brother, C. S. Cochran, had been on the 1924 Olympic championship team in this same relay event.

In the trial heat Cochran ran the first leg, with Bourland second, Harnden third, and Whitfield the anchor man, but the agreed strategy for the final was to have Cochran run whichever leg Wint undertook for the Jamaicans. Wint had been the third runner in their trial, but we had been told that he might handle the first lap in the final.

The coaches were in agreement that Cochran was the natural rival for Wint. Roy possessed an innate sense of pace and timing and also had a remarkable closing sprint. I had once observed him make up a tremendous margin in a relay in which he was timed in 45.8 seconds for a 440-yard lap. I knew he could stick with Wint if the latter ran the first lap, or would maintain any margin built up by prior runners if Wint ran at the No. 3 spot.

As it turned out, after having Cochran all set to start the race, we learned that Wint was going to stay as the third man on the Jamaican team, so we moved Harnden back to first on the United States team.

In the race, Harnden gained a slight margin over V. G. Rhoden and then Bourland, driving the last few yards in a brilliant finish, built up the edge over L. Laing to almost 10 yards as Cochran took off. Wint kept in check until the backstretch, where he began to apply the pressure—with only a slight reduction as Cochran himself built up the pace—and then suddenly fell to the ground with a cramped muscle.

From then on, naturally, it was only a parade for the American team. Italy's team, rated for third in the event, had mispassed the baton and had dropped out, so the race was all but a walkover.

Thus ended men's track and field athletics of the 1948 Olympic games. I join with all sports enthusiasts of all lands in anticipating their next glorious revival in 1952 at Helsinki, Finland.